T0316629

.

The Life and Revelations of Pema Lingpa

The Life and Revelations

of Pema Lingpa

Translated by
Sarah Harding

SNOW LION
Boulder

Snow Lion
An imprint of Shambhala Publications, Inc.
2129 13th Street
Boulder, Colorado 80302
www.shambhala.com

Printed in the United States of America

Shambhala Publications makes every effort to print on acid-free,
recycled paper.
Snow Lion is distributed worldwide by Penguin Random House,
Inc., and its subsidiaries.

Library of Congress Cataloging-in-Publication Data
Padma-gliṅ-pa, Gter-ston, 1450?– Bla ma nor bu rgya mtsho'i chos
skor. Selections. English The life and revelations of Pema Lingpa /
translated by Sarah Harding. Ithaca, NY : Snow Lion Publications,
2003.
    xii, 180 p. : col. ill. ; 23 cm.
    BQ7662.2 .P28 2003
    ISBN: 9781559391948 (alk. paper)

Contents

དཔལ་སྐྱང་སྟེང་རིག་གཞུང་བ་འདུ་གྲུ།
མོའི་སྐུ་གཤགས་གྲོ་བཤད་རབ་བ་རྒྱས་གྲིང་།
གསང་ཆེན་རྩྩྩྩྩྩྩ་མའི་རིང་ལུགས་འཛིན་པ།

RIGZHUNG SHEDRA
DONGAG-THOESAM-RABGAY-
LING NYINGMAPA INSTITUTE

GANGTENG TRULKU RINPOCHEY

Foreword by Gangteng Tulku Rinpoche

T HIS BOOK is an important introduction to Buddhism and to the teachings of Guru Padmasambhava. In particular, it includes selections from the treasures revealed by the great Bhutanese master Pema Lingpa. The history and dialogue with Princess Pemasal is the crux – that is where Guru Rinpoche gave a series of prophecies about the princess's future lives, which eventually led to Pema Lingpa's birth. This will be of benefit to anyone interested in the Dharma and those practicing in the Peling tradition.

These dialogues with female disciples offer inspiration to women practicing the Dharma today. People might think that women did not have the same opportunities or capacities for refining their beings and attaining enlightenment. These selections show that it makes absolutely no difference whether you are female or male; it is the practitioner's faith and diligence that determine spiritual progress.

I chose *Lama Jewel Ocean* to be translated first, because it contains important instructions for the spiritual path. These teachings concern Guru Padmasambhava and provide the foundation for later practices. Along with the Dzogchen and Great Compassion cycles, *Lama Jewel Ocean* is one of the most important in the Peling tradition. It is studied and practiced first because of the importance of the guru's blessing.

In order to translate these selections from *Lama Jewel Ocean*, I invited Sarah Harding, Kalu Rinpoche's student, to Bhutan for a year. It is difficult to translate the Dharma, especially Vajrayana material. If someone has not practiced Vajrayana, the translation will not go well. I specifically asked Sarah Harding because she has completed extensive Vajrayana practice in a three-year retreat.

His Majesty Jigmi Singye Wangchuck of Bhutan approved this project in order to share the Bhutanese tradition of Pema Lingpa. The translation of the history and teachings of this tradition into English will benefit not only Westerners but also the people of Bhutan and other places where knowledge of English is common. Since Pema Lingpa is so intertwined with Bhutanese culture, this book is also a way of preserving the cultural heritage of the Bhutanese people.

May these profound teachings of the Dharma contribute to peace and happiness on earth.

Translator's Preface

ORGYEN PEMA LINGPA was a Buddhist saint who lived in Bhutan in the fifteenth century. He is a well-respected, prominent figure in the history of the Vajrayana tradition that dominates the Himalayan region, but it is especially in the small kingdom of Bhutan that he is loved as a folk hero and spiritual master, a source of national pride and inspiration. The stories still abound around the innumerable holy sites where he displayed spiritual wonders, and the drama of his extraordinary life is constantly reenacted in school plays and performances by monks throughout Bhutan. The teachings and religious practices are maintained in good health through his current incarnations, such as Gangteng Tulku Rinpoche. This living tradition is the link to deep spiritual roots, to the time when the great master Padmasambhava came to Bhutan and Tibet to tame the wild forces, bring the soothing wisdom of the Buddha's teachings, and leave behind an enduring legacy. The great Guru Rinpoche is said to have visited Bhutan three times, spreading the doctrine throughout the land and bestowing blessings that are still felt today. In particular, many of these spiritually ripening teachings were hidden in special power places throughout Bhutan and Tibet, to be revealed at the optimum time to be of maximum benefit for sentient beings in the future. It was Pema Lingpa who was destined to reveal many of these treasures.

The tradition of hiding treasures (*terma*)[1] is said to have originated with Padmasambhava in the eighth century, although it certainly had precedents in the legends of early Buddhism in India. Holy objects or scrolls of spiritual instructions were hidden in caves or cliffs, or sometimes the meaning of the teachings themselves was hidden in the very mindstreams of special disciples. The places and circumstances of their discovery are recorded in the form of prophecy in ancient texts attributed to Padmasambhava. The person who was the prophesied or destined revealer of a particular treasure is called the *tertön*, the treasure-revealer. The collected literature attributed to this special class of Buddhist saints constitutes an enormous section of Tibetan scripture. It is the special domain of the Nyingma school, although not exclusively so. The terma tradition as a whole maintains the ever-important connection to the ancient teachings while at the same time ensuring that they are alive and current. In this sense, it is very much in keeping with the spirit of Buddhism, the ancient wisdom spoken by the Buddha over twenty-five hundred years ago that is constantly adapting and ultimately pragmatic.

Pema Lingpa is recognized as the fourth of Five Tertön Kings,[2] who are among the one hundred major and one thousand minor treasure-revealers. He discovered treasures throughout Bhutan and north of its current borders, but his activity mainly centered around Bumthang and the Tang Valley where he was born. His life was in many ways characteristic of a tertön. His visions and illuminations began at an early age and launched him into the strenuous career of a treasure-revealer. A crowd of onlookers always witnessed the discovery of his treasures, but he nevertheless had his detractors and the usual problems with patronage. In hindsight, however, both his family lineage and his spiritual legacy have maintained a position of prominence in Bhutan itself and in the Vajrayana tradition as a whole. The Pema Lingpa lineage is thus one of the main streams of the terma tradition still maintained and practiced today.

The texts translated here, with the exception of the biography "Flowers of Faith," are all taken from a single treasure collection discovered by Pema Lingpa called *Lama Jewel Ocean* (*Lama Norbu Gyatso*). This was discovered in Mendo Cliff in Lhodrak, southern Tibet, when Pema Lingpa was almost fifty. The story of its origins, beginning way back with the life of Padmasambhava, constitutes the last chapter, "A Strand of Jewels." The other four selections were chosen by Gangteng Tulku Rinpoche for this first collection of translations. They are all "dialogues," literally question-and-answer sessions (*zhu len*), that various practitioners had with Padmasambhava or with a disciple close to him. They convey not only the contents of the philosophy and practice, but also a sense of the people involved and their relationships to each other. The guru-disciple relationship is paramount in the practice of Vajrayana Buddhism. The real heart of the spiritual path is transmitted in the private and sacred space created within that relationship. We as readers are privy to a whiff of this atmosphere in these dialogues, and we benefit immensely from the answers that were granted so many centuries ago to questions that we might still hope to ask.

Three of these dialogues were with women, illustrious practitioners who were contemporaries of Padmasambhava. These are of special interest in being a window into the past position and attitude of women during the time of Padmasambhava and/or Pema Lingpa. The discovered treasures most often

need to be "translated" from the secret or encoded script of the *dakinis*³ into
the idiom of the time. Thus the actual language and quite possibly the views
may represent the treasure-discoverer as much as the ancient source. In this
case, seven hundred years may not even have made much difference in the
relative position of women in Himalayan society. And though the degrading
words the women in these stories use to describe themselves were certainly
attributed to them by the dominant male culture, most often—and most
unfortunately—women tended to internalize these attitudes with characteristic low self-esteem. In these stories, the women entreat Padmasambhava for
solutions to their terrible plight of womanhood. Even those of royal birth,
wealth, and great spiritual acumen bemoan their lowly status, servitude to
men, and lack of necessary qualities to practice the holy Dharma.

Padmasambhava seemingly agrees with them! The voice of timeless wisdom tells them that indeed it is a repressive situation that needs to be overcome. Not, as we might wish now, through rectifying and improving it, but by
leaving it utterly behind. Padmasambhava, like the Buddha Shakyamuni more
than a thousand years earlier, recommends the radically alternative lifestyle of
a yogin: homeless and unattached, devoted to the spiritual path and only to
those spiritual relationships that support it. We see these women struggling to
make this change against all odds, as difficult in attitude as in actuality. Each
in her own way learns to fulfill this precious human life and achieve ultimate
realization.

These texts were translated during a year of living in Bhutan under the gracious sponsorship of Gangteng Tulku Rinpoche and the kindness of His
Majesty the King of Bhutan and the Royal Government. Bhutan is now the
only independent country in the world where Vajrayana Buddhism is the state
religion and upheld by both government and people. It is difficult to describe
how important it was for me to be living and breathing in the very source of
these teachings while working on them. It is something that only gradually
dawned until, by the end, it was an entirely palpable feeling. Seeing the same
mountains, visiting the same temples and towns, and being immersed in basically the same culture as the tertön himself brought the stories alive. Bhutan
is a country of sacred places and legends that are appreciated as much now as
in the past. Working closely with Gangteng Rinpoche, an authentic represen-
tative of the Pema Lingpa tradition and a lineage holder, was a further privilege.
The first Gangteng Tulku was the grandson of Pema Lingpa. He constructed
a monastery in the Phubjikha Valley in the place predicted by his grandfather.
It was enlarged to its present size in the sixteenth century and is now the seat

of the present Gangteng Tulku, the ninth incarnation, or body emanation. Together with Sungtrul and Tukse Rinpoches, the speech and mind emanations, he is responsible for over twenty private monasteries and monastic schools. The Nyingmapa tradition, including the Pema Lingpa lineage, are thriving due to his efforts and those of other great teachers of our time.

In addition to H.E. Gangteng Tulku Rinpoche, who provided expert guidance, and Mr. Frank Yeh, who provided support, several others were instrumental in this work. I would like to take the opportunity to thank them now. Dasho Sangye Wangchuk, Secretary for the Special Commission, took time from an impossibly busy schedule to review the translation of some parts. Chris Butters, another translator of Pema Lingpa's life story,[4] also offered many great suggestions. Chris and his whole family made my time in Bhutan a delight. Jamie Zeppa, working on her own book about life in Bhutan,[5] lent me the wisdom of her creative and literary skills, as well as her friendship, in editing the English. And my dear friend Sandy Shum faithfully stayed with the process in Bhutan long after I was gone. Altogether, the opportunity to know these people and the many other friends in Thimpu, to partake in the beauty and traditions of the place, to work on this translation and practice the Dharma in the Hidden Kingdom, was most precious. I hope the benefit to myself will translate into benefit for others through this work. Who knows but that the translations of treasure texts also appear at just the right time.

Last but not least, I would like to thank my children, Shana and Sam, for tolerating and even appreciating being completely uprooted, dragged off to an unknown place on the other side of the planet, and plunked down in another century. Although they were born and raised in the compassionate glow of my root lama, Khyabje Kalu Rinpoche, for them the way has not always been easy, and certainly not "normal." Yet they assimilated and grew beautifully during that time that Sam calls "the greatest adventure." Live long and prosper.

Introduction

BY HOLLY GAYLEY

Pema Lingpa is the quintessential Bhutanese master. He is the only one who embodies the country of Bhutan so totally. He was completely home-grown. His lineage, his family, his ethnicity were all completely Bhutanese. The treasures he discovered were here in Bhutan, where he encountered Padmasambhava and Yeshe Tsogyal face to face. He did all his study and practice here in Bhutan. He did not go to study in India or Tibet; he stayed right here. And all his work for the benefit of beings happened here in Bhutan. So he is really the epitome of Bhutan, a great role model of a Bhutanese person whose activities took place within these borders. He had a great influence. There are plenty of other Buddhist traditions here, including Kagyu, Sakya, and Geluk. But they all grew out of the influence of Tibet. —Gangteng Tulku[1]

THE LEGACY of the Buddhist saint Pema Lingpa (1450–1521) in the religious life and national identity of Bhutan is undeniable. Not only did he establish monasteries and three incarnation lineages that still thrive today, but he also introduced an enormous corpus of literature. The ritual practices contained therein were disseminated throughout Tibetan and Himalayan regions and continue to serve as the primary basis of religious life for thousands of Buddhists. Moreover, Pema Lingpa fostered a regional identity that played an important role in Bhutan's unification in the seventeenth century, and the ritual dances ('cham) he composed still serve as a centerpiece for national festivals and ceremonies. His descendants acquired the status of ecclesiastic nobility and grew in political influence after the founding of Bhutan by Shabdrung Ngawang Namgyal (1594–1651). Among Pema Lingpa's descendants are the present royal family.

As we will see, the charisma of a saint can have a far-reaching impact on the religious and secular life of a region.[2] In the Tibetan and Himalayan context, Buddhist saints were seen to possess spiritual powers enabling them to conquer local demons, heal the sick, mediate disputes, and avert war. Moreover, the perpetuation of religious institutions, through tantric initiation ceremonies and temple construction, meant an ongoing involvement on the part of many lamas with direct disciples, wealthy patrons, and the local community. A highly charismatic figure who gained wide renown in his lifetime, Pema Lingpa counted among his patrons and disciples the important political and religious figures of his day. The treasures he revealed were seen to confer blessings on the land of present-day Bhutan, and the institutions and rituals he introduced became focal points of regional identity and religiosity. Moreover, Pema Lingpa's legacy helped to shape the emergence of Bhutan as an independent nation that survives today as the only Buddhist kingdom in the Himalayas.

THE TERTÖN AS BUDDHIST SAINT

Pema Lingpa acquired prominence in large part due to his status as a tertön. The tertön (*gter ston*), or treasure-revealer, is a unique category of Buddhist saint due to its prophetic dimension.[3] Tertöns are regarded as "predetermined emissaries" of Padmasambhava,[4] the eighth-century master credited with converting Tibetan and Himalayan regions to Buddhism.[5] In biographies and prophecies revealed from the eleventh century onward, Padmasambhava is depicted as a second buddha who taught widely and appointed specific individuals to reveal his teachings in future times of strife.[6] A tertön's authenticity is based on specific prophecies attributed to Padmasambhava, and each tertön is identified as a direct disciple of Padmasambhava in a previous lifetime. Among the possible categories of Buddhist saints, tertöns alone perform the role of revelation according to prophecy; they are regarded as direct conduits through which Padmasambhava conveys instructions and blessings to future generations.

Tertöns, by their association with the past, are able to introduce new ritual forms and liturgical cycles. Their literary production is simultaneously considered to address the needs of a particular time and place as well as to represent a repository of archaic knowledge. Tertöns act as innovators, founding new lineages and religious communities on the basis of the ritual cycles they introduce, while their source of legitimacy is tied to the past.[7] Narrative accounts of the revelation process link the tertön's own time with the past as well as with the timeless domain of buddhas. The treasures revealed by a tertön are thus framed as a revival of the past and an expression of timeless wisdom.

According to the tradition, the instructions and blessings of Padmasambhava are conveyed through treasures or terma (*gter ma*). In this view, treasures
are literary works derived from the time of Padmasambhava and later discovered in condensed form either in the mind of the tertön, called "mind
treasures" (*dgongs gter*), or in the physical environment, called "earth treasures" (*sa gter*).⁸ Most treasures fall into the latter classification, and Pema
Lingpa's treasures are considered to be exclusively earth terma. In this way,
terma denotes a class of scripture, regarded by those of the ancient school or
Nyingma as the actual teachings of Padmasambhava—hidden in earth, rocks,
water, or elsewhere—for future generations.⁹

The revelation of an earth treasure is anchored to a specific place, one that
is sanctified in the process. A verse from the treasure corpus of the tertön
Ratna Lingpa (1403–1479) conveys the association of treasures with the
Himalayan landscape and the blessings of Padmasambhava:

> For each important valley there is an important hidden treasure.
> These also are signs of the one from O rgyan [Padmasambhava].
> For each little place there is a minor hidden treasure.
> These, too, are signs of the one from O rgyan.¹⁰

The activities of Padmasambhava are thought to confer blessings on the
land. In this verse, such blessings are depicted as coextensive with the Tibetan
and Himalayan landscape. The discovery of treasures occurred within a landscape already inscribed by a matrix of meaning, including a host of deities
that inhabit it. Yet each act of discovery also generated new meanings by link-
ing the present with the past at a specific site. Treasures were taken to be signs
of Padmasambhava's beneficence, directed toward the people of a particular
time and place.

The treasure tradition identifies its origins in the eighth-century reign of
Tibet's king, Trisong Detsen, when the great master Padmasambhava is said
to have visited Tibet, Bhutan, Nepal, and Sikkim. Tibet's empire was at its
zenith; it dominated vast tracts of central Asia and drew visitors from the
great civilizations of the world, including Persia, China, and India.¹¹ According to indigenous histories, Trisong Detsen invited Padmasambhava to Tibet
in order to subjugate the demons obstructing the construction of Samye,
Tibet's first monastery. In these accounts, Padmasambhava symbolically
enacted the conversion of Tibetan and Himalayan regions to Buddhism
through the subjugation of local deities. These deities, thus converted to
Buddhism, became protectors of the Buddhist teachings in general and the

treasure tradition in particular. During that time, Padmasambhava is said to have gathered a group of twenty-five disciples, including the king himself. The esoteric instructions and tantric initiations he imparted to these disciples have served as the inspiration and basis of legitimacy for the treasure tradition until the present day.

The discovery of treasures began as early as the eleventh century, and several of the most famous tertöns spent considerable time in present-day Bhutan, then known as Mön Yul or the Land of the Mön.[12] Guru Chöwang (1212–1270), Longchen Rabjam (1308–1364) and Dorje Lingpa (1346–1405) spent considerable time in Mön Yul and also left behind progeny. Of the three, Dorje Lingpa was particularly active in revealing treasures in the region.[13] By Pema Lingpa's own time, terma was a well-established phenomenon throughout the Himalayan region. Two anthologies by the nineteenth-century scholar Jamgön Kongtrul indicate the extent of the treasure phenomena. The first is a compilation of short biographies for more than one hundred tertöns.[14] Of this group, five are singled out as "tertön kings" (*gter ston rgyal po*), including Pema Lingpa.[15] The second compilation is Kongtrul's ninety-one volume anthology of treasures, the *Rinchen Terdzö*, which includes more than two thousand and five hundred texts.[16] It represents a mere sampling of the prolific literary production that resulted from this religious movement.

The treasure tradition is a trans-Himalayan phenomenon, which an individual tertön links to specific local sites. The word appended to the names of so many tertöns, "lingpa" (*gling pa*), literally means "land" or "island" and suggests a connection between person and place. Nyingma lineages were often passed through the family, such that tertöns frequently married and had children; they remained an active part of a local community in which their families held a prominent place as ecclesiastic nobility. Notably, tertöns also were often peripatetic, traveling widely to disseminate their teachings. The local and trans-local aspects of the treasure tradition are important complements. It is by understanding the tertön as a local source of charismatic power, rooted in a specific region yet achieving wide renown, that we can truly understand the significance of Pema Lingpa in the religious and secular life of present-day Bhutan.

THE PROPHETIC DIMENSION

Prophecies constitute an integral part of the conception of how esoteric knowledge and ritual forms are transmitted within the treasure tradition.

Padmasambhava is thought to anticipate the needs of the people in Tibetan and Himalayan regions and prepare in advance caches of teachings to promote religious revival. In this conception, an individual is chosen specifically by Padmasambhava to reveal a particular set of texts. As such, prophecies perform an important legitimating function. They emphasize the special destiny of a tertön and function to sanctify a body of literature. Padmasambhava is thereby linked with the individual tertön as his emissary, with a body of literature as his teachings, and also to the discovery site as the locus of his activities in the royal period.

The most famous set of such prophecies were revealed in the fourteenth century by Orgyen Lingpa (b. 1323) and called simply *The Word of Padma (Padma bka' thang)*.[17] This text contains a series of verse-long prophecies, identifying over forty names of individual tertöns and locations for their discovery of treasures. In it, the prophecy for the tertön Pema Lingpa reads as follows:

> At Pagri of Gos, homes will be sheltered by the fort.
> In the high mountains, at Tagru, will be a place where they sell poison.
> Warned by these signs not to fail and bring to light
> The treasure hidden in Burning Lake [Mebartso],
> Orgyen Padma Lingpa [Pema Lingpa] will appear.[18]

The prophecies in Orgyen Lingpa's famous collection provide only general indications about each tertön's time and place. It was then up to the individual to assert a rightful claim to one of the prophecies contained therein.[19] As we will see later, one of the miraculous accounts in Pema Lingpa's life story evoked the image of the Burning Lake (Mebartso) and thereby enabled his association with the above prophecy. Shortly thereafter, he established a monastery named Pemaling and formally adopted it as his name.[20]

Prophecies also appear within the treasure corpus of individual tertöns as a specific genre of texts (*lung bstan*). They designate the figure appointed to reveal a particular treasure cycle and also portray the tertön's own era as a time of dire straits and rampant corruption. Prophecies within Pema Lingpa's collection identify one named "Padma," a reincarnation of Princess Pemasal to be born in Bumthang after a certain number of rebirths. A profusion of bad omens is typically also given. For example, one of the prophecies in *Lama Jewel Ocean* depicts "a time when lust and hate are widespread," "a time of great famine and many shortages," "a time when lamas command troops," "a time when vice and virtue get mixed up," "a time when monks cast off their vows," and so on.[21] These negative portents signal the need for spiritual revival, the means for which is provided by the very treasure containing the prophecy. In fulfillment of these prophecies, the tertön is cast as a religious reformer, carrying the original word of Padmasambhava into the present.

Within the treasure corpus of Pema Lingpa, prophetic elements can also be found in orthographic and structural components of any text, regardless of genre. For example, the hallmark of treasure literature is an orthographic device consisting of two small circles stacked with a horizontal line between them (*gter tsheg:* ࿓). This mark distinguishes treasures from ordinary compositions and informs the reader or onlooker immediately of the text's numinous origins and status as scripture.[22] Because these orthographic marks are so distinct, one need not actually read the text to understand its hallowed status. This is important to note in a cultural milieu where lay people did not have high literacy rates and may still have handled texts as objects of veneration.

Within the treasure corpus of Pema Lingpa, prophetic elements are ubiquitous. Not only do most of his treasure cycles contain a text dedicated specifically to prophecy, but the first and last lines of many texts include prophecies, in a condensed form, that create a prophetic frame around the contents of a text.[23] This is an almost formulaic yet salient feature in Pema Lingpa's treasure corpus. From the abundance of such prophecies, we can ascertain that the connection between the royal period and the tertön's own time is presented as quite literal within the tradition.

In this prophetic frame, the main body of the text is introduced and concluded in the first-person voice of Padmasambhava, emphasizing the attribution of authorship in a direct way. These introductory lines specifically invoke the benevolent intention of Padmasambhava for the people living at the time and place of the tertön. The concluding lines, or colophon, of the text have two parts: (1) an account of hiding the treasure along with a prophecy about its discovery in the voice of Padmasambhava and (2) a brief account, sometimes a single line, of the discovery in the voice of the tertön. Throughout Pema Lingpa's corpus, the features highlighted in both sections of the colophon are the tertön's name and the place of discovery.[24] Stylistically, the prophecy attributed to Padmasambhava is juxtaposed with the discovery account, creating a suggestive conjunction between layers of the framing structure. The prophecy and its realization are side by side, conveying a direct link between the time of Padmasambhava and that of the tertön.[25]

Prophecies emphasize the conjunction of the past and present. Both person and place—namely the tertön and discovery site—are depicted as mediators between the royal period and the here and now of the discovery. The tertön is situated in the past as a disciple of Padmasambhava via a previous incarnation; that incarnation is said to receive a set of teachings later revealed as a treasure by the tertön. The convergence of past and present also occurs at a particular site where a treasure is believed to be first hidden and later discovered. As a rhetorical device, the prophetic frame presents this convergence of the past and present by juxtaposing an account of the treasure's concealment with an account of its discovery.

In addition to prophetic elements, other types of narrative—including the group of texts translated by Sarah Harding in this book—provide a framework to establish the sanctity of Pema Lingpa's entire treasure corpus. The genre of history, in particular, provides a detailed account of the origins of treasures, the process of transmission, and the methods of concealment. As described in the next section, histories depict the progression of wisdom through three temporal modes, not only the past and present but also the timeless arena of buddhas.

The Trajectory of Timeless Wisdom

The authority of a treasure cycle lay not only in its attribution of authorship to Padmasambhava but also with accounts of its origin prior to him. Treasure literature employs the genre of history (*lo rgyus*) to delineate the trajectory of a particular treasure cycle from the timeless and abstract arena of buddhas into the specific here and now of the discovery.[26] These histories invariably begin in realms inhabited by buddhas and bodhisattvas who then engage the human plane through symbolic and visionary means. The eighth century is the main time frame for the unfolding narrative with Padmasambhava as the central character, first in India and then in Tibet. Once in Tibet, these narratives focus on Padmasambhava's instructions, prophecies, and concealment of treasures, shifting the scene from the royal court in central Tibet to the specific locus of concealment. The genre of history thus provides a genealogy of the process by which abstract and timeless wisdom is considered to take textual form in a particular time and place.

This progression of esoteric knowledge from abstract to physical form constructs a chain of interconnected sites and interrelated figures. The discovery site and the tertön are powerfully linked by this genre to buddha realms and their enlightened residents, to sacred places in India and famous tantric masters, as well as to the royal court in Tibet and members of the royal family. On the one hand, these references create a network of places that invest the discovery site with symbolic meaning. As a corollary, histories portray the tertön as the proximate successor of buddhas, bodhisattvas, and tantric masters of the past.

Most important, histories play a key role in shaping the conception of treasures as scripture; the ultimate authority for each treasure cycle is traced to a buddha through a series of specific stages. This allowed treasure literature to compete for scriptural status with sutras and tantras translated from Indic sources, specifically those propagated by the new schools (*gsar ma*) that began to flourish in Tibet between the tenth and twelfth centuries. For older lineages, grouped together as the ancient school or Nyingma, treasures are viewed as the teachings of a buddha, brought to Tibet by Padmasambhava in the eighth century. Since treasures carry the authority of scripture for the Nyingma and continue to be discovered still today, they provide the important function of an "open canon."[27]

Within Pema Lingpa's collection, each treasure cycle has its own unique history with up to seven phases. This indicates that each cycle is regarded as being specifically taught by a buddha and transmitted as a discrete teaching. Three stages are held in common with the broader Nyingma tradition and involve a transmission sequence via mental, symbolic, and verbal media. The treasure tradition adds several distinct phases, which detail the means by which Padmasambhava transmitted a set of teachings and concealed them as treasure, destined for a particular tertön to discover in the future. Within the histories found in Pema Lingpa's collection, we find variations in sequence and number of stages, but all are in keeping with the same basic format.[28]

Histories provide a "theological" explanation for how the atemporal wisdom of a buddha is understood to communicate itself in the mundane world of human history. The stages in the transmission of the Nyingma doctrine closely parallel three-*kaya* theory[29] and explain how a body of knowledge moves from subtle to gross levels. The first transmission, common to the Nyingma tradition, is called the "mind transmission of a buddha" (*rgyal ba dgongs pa'i brgyud*). It represents a mind-to-mind communication between a *dharmakaya* teacher and a *sambhogakaya* student enacted, for example, between Samantabhadra and Vajrasattva in Atiyoga cycles. The next phase is called the "symbolic transmission of the *vidyadharas*" (*rig 'dzin brda'i brgyud*). It is a teaching conveyed symbolically, in the Atiyoga case, from Vajrasattva to the *nirmanakaya* figure, Garab Dorje. In just two phases, the transmission progresses from the abstract arena of the dharmakaya into a human embodiment, or nirmanakaya individual, responsible for disseminating its esoteric knowledge.

This sequence of transmissions is tailored to each specific cycle by the set of the figures involved, but the basic pattern remains more or less the same. The teacher is a buddha, often but not always Samantabhadra. For example, the longevity cycles in Pema Lingpa's collection are traced to Amitabha Buddha in the pure realm of Sukhavati. The recipients of the symbolic transmission in India vary, sometimes a group called the "eight vidyadharas" or alternately a group called the "eight masters," which includes Padmasambhava. In another example from Pema Lingpa's corpus, *The Great Compassionate One, the Lamp That Illuminates the Darkness,* the transmission flows from Amitabha to Avalokiteshvara and finally to Padmasambhava. In this case the middle phase is called the "compassionate transmission of bodhisattvas" (*byang chub sems dpa'i thugs rje'i brgyud*). It emphasizes the benevolent intention behind this movement of timeless wisdom into the vicissitudes of human history.

This mystical progression culminates in teachings on the human plane, conducted in ordinary language. This last phase is called the "aural transmission of individuals" (*gang zag snyan khung gi brgyud*). Padmasambhava is the central figure in this phase. Depending on the cycle, he might be on either end (giving or receiving) of the aural transmission. For example, in *The Union of Samantabhadra's Intentions,* Padmasambhava receives the Atiyoga teachings from Garab Dorje while still in India. On the other hand, in *The Most Secret Eight Transmitted Precepts, Mirror of the Mind,* among others, the aural transmission takes place when Padmasambhava bestows the empowerment in Tibet upon disciples such as Trisong Detsen, Yeshe Tsogyal, and Namkai Nyingpo. Padmasambhava may indeed participate in various phases in the transmission process of the same set of teachings. In the history of *Lama Jewel Ocean,* translated in this book, Padmasambhava receives the transmission for the Atiyoga tantras from Samantabhadra in a blessing, from Vajrasattva symbolically, and from Garab Dorje in words.[30] These three phases show how the Nyingma teachings are understood to derive from the wellspring of a buddha's timeless wisdom, intersecting with the human plane in eighth-century India.

The next set of transmissions, special to the treasure tradition, all take place in Tibet. They involve a set of basic features, which are arranged into varying categories in the histories of Pema Lingpa's treasure cycles. First, a cycle of teachings is transmitted from Padmasambhava to his immediate disciples, including Princess Pemasal, the figure to whom Pema Lingpa traces his own previous lifetime in the royal period. Princess Pemasal plays a brief but important role in this story as the daughter of Trisong Detsen who dies at the early age of eight years old but is momentarily revived by Padmasambhava in order to give her a series of initiations. The initiation ceremony is bestowed along with a set of instructions, which Yeshe Tsogyal transcribes onto yellow scrolls (*shog ser*). Of primary importance is the moment in the empowerment when the aspiration is made and the disciple destined to reveal the teachings is chosen. In that seminal moment, the treasure is said to be sealed in the mindstream of the future tertön.[31]

Only later in the narrative is the physical treasure hidden, once the yellow scrolls are placed into a casket and sealed. In some cases within Pema Lingpa's treasure corpus, the history will specify that Padmasambhava and Yeshe Tsogyal traveled together to the site of concealment, such as Bumthang or Lhodrak, in order to hide the treasure. Protectors are appointed on location. Various types of protectors may be appointed to guard treasure: local deities (*gzhi bdag*), Dharma protectors (*chos skyong*), and/or dakinis (*mkha' 'gro*). Once the treasure is hidden, a prophecy is given about the tertön, often with hagiographic details such as name, year and place of birth, and parents. There may be an additional section in which a small number of the tertön's disciples are listed in the form of a prophecy.

In the histories found in Pema Lingpa's treasure cycles, there are often just two phases in this second series of transmission.[32] This first phase may be named simply the "transmission of the profound treasure" (*zab mo gter gyi brgyud*). It spans the empowerment ceremony, concealment of the treasure, and appointment of dakinis. In a second phase, the sole focus is prophecy. This phase is called the "transmission of prophetic entrustment" (*lung bstan gtad rgya'i brgyud*). If there is a third phase, it involves prophecies about disciples of Pema Lingpa, called the "transmission of yogic accomplishment" (*grub thob rnal 'byor gyi brgyud*). Though the stages vary in number, the same basic features are covered, but here with more emphasis on the prophetic dimension. Prophecies play an integral role in histories, emphasizing the end point of the progression of wisdom at the time and place of the tertön.

The transmission process special to the treasure tradition, in a sense, reiterates the original journey of a set of teachings through mental, symbolic, and verbal media. As mentioned previously, during the empowerment ceremony, Padmasambhava is said to implant the treasure in the mindstream of a disciple, appointed as the one destined to reveal it. According to the third Dodrupchen, Jigme Tenpe Nyima (1865–1926), the mind is the true place of the treasure's concealment, and the physical treasure is a symbolic means to spark its recollection.[33] The cycle of teachings is then converted into a symbolic medium by Yeshe Tsogyal, who is most often responsible for transcribing and concealing treasures. The physical treasure thus serves as a symbol or "mnemonic cue" to reawaken the transmission received from Padmasambhava.[34] Only the appointed tertön possesses the necessary predisposition to decipher the symbolic script and produce the teaching in textual form. The result of the trajectory of timeless wisdom into the human plane is a set of texts or treasure cycle, propagated by the tertön to disciples.

Within this process, as it is presented in the treasure tradition, there are no more than six degrees of separation between a primordial buddha and Pema Lingpa.[35] For this reason, treasures are portrayed by their adherents as superior to the teachings passed from master to disciple in an unbroken succession.[36] In the Buddhist conception, the spiritual blessings of a teaching gradually dissipate over time. Thus, from the standpoint of the treasure tradition, the teachings of a buddha, transmitted through generations of disciples in a long transmission (*ring brgyud*), are susceptible to the vagaries of time. The tertön, on the other hand, can claim more direct access to the teachings of a buddha, mediated through Padmasambhava. This is characterized as a direct lineage (*nye brgyud*), a source of fresh teachings and renewed blessings. Spiritual blessings are seen as crucial for ritual efficacy, providing an important reason for such an emphasis on the genre of history as a form of legitimation. The tertön acts as a conduit for potent blessings, since religious innovation is understood to emerge from a short series of links directly to a buddha.

Acceptance of the above genealogy for treasures was not universal in Tibetan and Himalayan regions. There were harsh critics of treasures as well as avid defenders.[37] Such divergences between schools of Buddhism over scriptural authenticity date to the early part of the first millennium, when the appearance of Mahayana literature was regarded to be spurious by adherents to the Pali Canon. Without delving into the complex issue of canonization, it is important to note that the Nyingma were forced to compile alternative collections of scripture after many early translations (*snga 'gyur*) of tantras were excluded from the Kangyur and Tengyur canons of Indic literature.[38] For the Nyingma, treasures provide an important source of scripture, regarded as teachings from India that entered Tibet with Padmasambhava. Though not universally accepted, treasures gained recognition outside the Nyingma when important religious leaders from other schools, most famously the Fifth Dalai Lama, requested initiation into treasure cycles and also discovered treasures themselves.[39]

Regional Lore and Identity

From the preceding discussion, we can identify a beginning, middle, and end point for the trajectory of timeless wisdom. A beginning is provided by the origin account, which locates the ultimate source of a set of teachings in the timeless domain of buddhas. The midpoint involves tales of Padmasambhava that emphasize his pivotal role in transmitting timeless wisdom to Himalayan regions. And the end point occurs through recourse to prophecies that highlight the destiny of the tertön as the intended heir to a cosmic scheme. Histories work in tandem with prophetic and hagiographic elements to create a narrative progression with a dénouement at the discovery site.

The genre of hagiography, or sacred biography, elaborates the middle and end points in this grand narrative through tales of Padmasambhava and the tertön's own life story. This genre of literature in the treasure tradition, as a whole, develops the lore of the royal period through its many tales of Padmasambhava and Yeshe Tsogyal, among others. Pema Lingpa's autobiography, in turn, explicitly links him to the royal period through his past-life genealogy and numerous discovery accounts. This section focuses on narratives from the royal period, and the next section examines specific features in hagiographic accounts of Pema Lingpa.

Hagiographies can serve multiple functions. As stories of "complete liberation" (*rnam thar*), hagiographies depict the life of a saint as both an exemplar and object of veneration.[40] As such, the genre of hagiography is specifically meant to engender reverence. This is significant because Padmasambhava is represented not only as the author, and often the subject, of treasure literature but also as the central figure in devotional practices, particularly guru *sadhanas*. Tertöns also serve as a focal point of devotion in ritual contexts due to their role as emissaries of Padmasambhava, founders of new religious communities, and preceptors of tantric initiations. Within treasure literature, Padmasambhava is portrayed in mythic proportions and ultimately emerges as the central figure of his own pure realm, the Glorious Copper-Colored Mountain (*Zangs mdog dpal ri*). By contributing to Padmasambhava's exalted status, hagiographies enhance the regard for the treasures themselves and also contribute to a framework of meaning essential to the rituals disseminated by tertöns.

Importantly, hagiographies of Padmasambhava may foster national pride by their focus on a golden era of Tibetan imperial strength.[41] The royal period became an important historical marker for Tibetans during the numerous Mongolian invasions from the thirteenth century onward. It thus became a touchstone in the early history of Tibet, cast as a golden age during which Buddhism was introduced at the behest of religious kings, identified in retrospect as bodhisattvas. The Buddhist traditions surviving from that early period, grouped together as the Nyingma, were naturally active in preserving and propagating this lore.

Pema Lingpa connected this pan-Himalayan lore to his specific region in narrative accounts that suggested a parallel and independent royal period for Bumthang in the heartland of present-day Bhutan.[42] The legendary visit of Padmasambhava to Bumthang, burying treasures and subjugating local deities, was elaborated in his treasure text called *The Clear Mirror*, which concerned a local king, Sindhu Raja.[43] The tale of Sindhu Raja, an exile from India who established a kingdom in Bumthang, is still recounted in Bhutan today. According to this text, Padmasambhava was invited to Bumthang under urgent circumstances. Sindhu Raja, enraged and grief-stricken at the loss of his son in battle, repudiated his ancestral deity (*pho lha*), Shelging Karpo.[44] This deity took revenge by stealing the king's life force (*bla*), and Padmasambhava was asked to intervene in order to retrieve it. Padmasambhava spent a week in retreat with a tantric consort (*gzungs ma*), chosen from among the princesses at Sindhu Raja's palace, and subjugated the deities and demons of the region. During this retreat, Padmasambhava left his body print in rock, giving this place its name: Kurje, literally, "body print" (*sku rje*).[45] Padmasambhava remained in Bumthang to counsel the king, to settle an armed struggle with an Indian foe, and to bury treasures throughout the region. In *The Clear Mirror*, we see that Pema Lingpa promoted legends concerning an independent royal period in Bumthang.

Besides recounting the lore of Sindhu Raja, *The Clear Mirror* includes prophecies and references to a hidden land (*sbas yul*) called Khenpalung.[46] The concealing of Khenpalung involves another tale of exile, this time a Tibetan prince named Kyikha Rathö.[47] Among Pema Lingpa's treasures is a guidebook to this hidden land, including a detailed account of the prince's legend.[48] The exiled Kyikha Rathö founded a kingdom in the valley called Khenpalung from which he decided to launch an attack on Tibet. Padmasambhava intervened, quickly defeated the contentious prince, and sealed Khenpalung as a hidden land, rendering it invisible and entrusting its protection to local deities until the time when it would rediscovered. Kyikha Rathö, the text reads, then settled in the Tang Valley in Bumthang.

Both the tales of Sindhu Raja and Kyikha Rathö portray Bumthang as a place of exile, past the borders of both Tibet and India, and as a hidden land, ideal for spiritual transformation. In a similar vein, Longchen Rabjam wrote a eulogy to Bumthang in 1355, characterizing it as a hidden land, ideal for spiritual practice.[49] Sindhu Raja's story is certainly one of redemption and learning about a secular ruler's place in the sacred geography, inhabited by greater powers such as local deities and, more important, tantric masters. Pema Lingpa's propagation of the lore of hidden lands and the royal period in Bumthang can be seen as a contribution to an independent regional identity distinct from Tibet and India, over a hundred years prior to the unification of Bhutan under Shabdrung Ngawang Namgyal.

According to innumerable tales, Padmasambhava's activities spanned the Himalayan region, including Bumthang and Paro in present-day Bhutan. Padmasambhava's visit to Paro in western Bhutan is well known outside of the country because of his famous hermitage at Taktsang, the so-called Tiger's Den. The monastery, built around a retreat cave, is perched on the wall of a sheer cliff. It is certainly the most famous and awe-inspiring pilgrimage site in Bhutan.[50] One cannot underestimate the significance of Padmasambhava's stay for national pride of the Bhutanese and their conception of the sanctity of their land. Because of Padmasambhava's visit, both Bumthang and Paro are considered especially sacred places in Bhutan, and temples and monasteries have clustered in these areas. According to folklore, the staff that Padmasambhava planted in Bumthang grew into a cypress tree whose seeds have spread throughout present-day Bhutan.

Though Pema Lingpa traveled as far as central Tibet, he spent most of his career in Bumthang in the heart of present-day Bhutan. Most of the discovery sites for his treasures lay within the four valleys of Bumthang; these sites include Mebartso, Kurje, Rimochen, Tharpaling, and Tselung Lhakhang, now called Könchok Sum. (See Appendix B for a list of Pema Lingpa's treasures and their discovery sites.) In the eyes of the local populations then and now, these treasures serve to sanctify the land and provide evidence of Padmasambhava's activities in the region. The activities of an enlightened master are believed to leave an indelible trace on the landscape in the form of blessings.[51] As such, the revelation of treasures provided a material expression of Padmasambhava's blessings and are considered important relics.

Pema Lingpa's discovery sites, though predominantly local, stretched from Bumthang to Samye in central Tibet, evoking the breadth of Padmasambhava's legendary activities during the royal period. Two sites in particular mark this geographic spectrum: Kurje in Bumthang, where Padmasambhava is said to have left a full body print, and Samye in central Tibet, the locus of Tibet's first monastery constructed during the reign of Trisong Detsen. Pema Lingpa also discovered a number of treasures in Lhodrak, just north of Bumthang in southeastern Tibet, reflecting his regional involvement. Indeed, if we mapped all of the discovery sites for Pema Lingpa's treasures across the Himalayan landscape, we would see the extent to which Pema Lingpa's career had local, regional and trans-Himalayan aspects. As we will see below, within Bumthang and Lhodrak, Pema Lingpa played an active role in officiating religious rites and intervening at the behest of patrons in secular affairs. Though traveling widely, Pema Lingpa spent most of his career in his homeland, Bumthang. It is for this reason that although other famous tertöns were active in the region, no other is so associated with present-day Bhutan as Pema Lingpa.

THE VISIONARY CAREER OF PEMA LINGPA

So far we have focused on the treasure tradition through reference to the conception of its origin in the timeless realm of a buddha and the pivotal role of Padmasambhava in its transmission to Tibetan and Himalayan regions during the royal period. Let us turn to the unfolding of its climax in Pema Lingpa's career as depicted in his autobiography and later summaries of it.[52] This section does not attempt to recapitulate Pema Lingpa's life story, which is recounted in the first chapter of this book.[53] Instead, it explores the visionary propensities of the tertön and the miraculous feats that brought him regional renown. Tales of these feats would have been widespread in Bumthang during Pema Lingpa's own time. While the rise of science in the West has made the modern reader suspicious of miraculous claims, this was not true of Pema Lingpa's cultural milieu. Visionary experiences and miraculous feats were seen as part and parcel of the charismatic powers ascribed to the tertön. They were taken as evidence to validate the tertön's claim to be an emissary of Padmasambhava, and as such they represent an integral component of hagiographic accounts of the tertön's life.[54]

Pema Lingpa's autobiography juxtaposes his ordinariness with visionary propensities that beckon him to a special destiny.[55] In keeping with cultural norms of humility, Pema Lingpa assumes little agency for his achievements. Even as prophetic elements are highlighted—a distinguished past-life genealogy and miraculous accounts of revealing treasures—they are consistently credited to external forces or involuntary impulses. Visions rather than individual initiative provide the catalyst for the significant turning points in his career. His religious training is credited to past lives; treasure discoveries occur during a state of trance; and authorship for his prolific literary production is attributed to Padmasambhava. In a cultural context where individual innovation and initiative were not as highly valued as the promulgation of tradition, Pema Lingpa portrays his achievements within a religious idiom of recovery and retrieval as part of a cosmic scheme traced to the timeless buddhas and the tantric master Padmasambhava.

Pema Lingpa began his life in ordinary circumstances. In 1450, he was born in the Chökor Valley of Bumthang into a family of Nyingma priests, called the Nyö clan (*Smyos rabs*). His father, Nyöton Döndrup Zangpo, married a blacksmith's daughter, Drokmo Pema Dröl. Until his mid-twenties, Pema Lingpa balanced the trades of both his family backgrounds: training as a blacksmith under his grandfather and spending short periods of time at two different temples, Mani Gompa and Rimochen. Because of these dual obligations, Pema Lingpa never received extensive religious training, though he did receive initiations into the treasure cycle of Dorje Lingpa from his father-in-law, Lama Chokden. Up until the time when Pema Lingpa records his first visions, he lived an ordinary life in which his religious vocation was one component among other family obligations.

Tertöns may receive some training during their youth in textual study and ritual practice, but this is not seen as the basis for their literary achievements.[56] Individuals, such as Pema Lingpa, lived far from the monastic institutions of learning in central Tibet, yet they could become major disseminators of religious understanding, because the prerequisite for the tertön's vocation was identified in previous lifetimes.[57] Pema Lingpa's past-life genealogy includes not only the figure of Princess Pemasal, to locate him in the royal period as a direct disciple of Padmasambhava, but also the distinguished master Longchen Rabjam who spent considerable time in present-day Bhutan. These past-life genealogies account for the innate talents and achievements of a saint through recourse to a widespread belief in the compassion-driven impulse toward reincarnation among enlightened beings.[58]

Visions provide a turning point in the narrative of a tertön's career in which an ordinary life begins to take on special status. Characterized as sudden and unexpected, visions act as a catalyst to awaken latent dispositions of the tertön's past lives.[59] They inform the tertön of his destiny and provide the necessary details for the treasure discovery. Pema Lingpa was summoned to reveal his first treasure by a vision of "a monk in ragged robes" who gave him a scroll that read: "On the night of the full moon of this month, at the bottom of your valley there is a place called Naring Drak. There lies your destined wealth. Take five friends and go there to retrieve it."[60] Here we see a common motif, an apparition who suddenly appears to deliver a prophetic message and the details for a treasure discovery. The instructions to locate a treasure are called the prophetic guide or address (*kha byang*).[61] They contain the time and place of the discovery, as well as the companions to bring and the ritual activities to perform. Senge Naring Drak, or Long-Nosed Lion Cliff, stands above a large eddy in the Tang River near Pema Lingpa's hometown, Chel. There, down the valley from his birthplace, the Bhutanese saint is said to have revealed his first treasure.

Visions of dakinis and other numinous emissaries are regular components of the discovery process, guiding Pema Lingpa in all phases. Not only do they serve as a catalyst for the discovery, providing the prophetic guide or address, but visions are also reported to occur at the discovery site itself.[62] At the eddy beneath the Long-Nosed Lion Cliff, Pema Lingpa "felt himself transported into a kind of trance, accompanied by visions of Dakinis and other signs."[63] The following account is given by the Eighth Peling Sungtrul, Kunzang Dechen Dorje (1843–1891), in the hagiography included in this book:

> When Pema Lingpa arrived at [the river's] edge, immediately an intense experience of having lost all bearings welled up in him, and he took off his clothes and jumped in the water. Beneath the water, in a place called Palgyi Phukring (Glorious Long Cave) there was a life-size figure of the Teacher. To the left side of this was a stack of many rhinoceros-skin chests. A woman with one eye, wearing maroon clothes, handed him a treasure box from among these containing the text of *The Quintessence of the Mysteries of the Luminous Space of Samantabhadri*. After somehow being propelled back onto the cliff, he returned with his friends at midnight. He blessed his mother, father, and others with the treasure.[64]

In this account, Pema Lingpa enters a trancelike state and encounters a dakini, the one-eyed woman, who hands him the treasure chest. This dakini would likely represent the treasure guardian, appointed to ensure that only the appropriate individual retrieves the treasure casket. Note the sacred status of the treasure, regarded as a powerful relic and immediately used to confer blessings on others. This would be especially true in public treasures (*khrom gter*) in which the crowd who gathered to witness the discovery afterward received blessings from the treasure casket touched to the top of their heads by the tertön.

During the next phase of process, the decoding and understanding of the treasure's content, past-life recollection is accompanied by further visions. The tertön opens the casket in private in order to decode the symbolic script (*brda yig*), written on a yellow scroll (*shog ser*) contained inside. The symbolic script is said to awaken a memory of the instructions and initiation given by Padmasambhava during the royal period when the tertön, in a previous life, was his disciple. To unlock the cryptic symbols, a tertön may be assisted by a key (*lde mig*) or other indications. Once the treasure is decoded and transcribed, the tertön often undergoes a waiting period and/or extensive retreat before going public with the treasure content. In this phase, Pema Lingpa continued to receive further guidance through visions. The contemporary Bhutanese scholar and former Director of the National Library Padma Tshewang describes the process by which Pema Lingpa received his education in these matters:

> One night at his residence of Kunzangling he was wondering how he would conduct the coming ceremonies, realising that he had no experience at all of the performance of sacred dances, nor of the chants and gestures which were to accompany them. At that point he fell asleep, and had a new dream. Yeshe Tshogyal, the Dakini consort of Guru Padmasambhava, appeared to him dressed in the clothes of a woman of the U region of Tibet. She said: "Pemalingpa, do the chants like this," and then she sang each chapter. Then she said: "Do the Invocation of Blessings for the dances like this," and she demonstrated the dances of the Five Dakinis. He awoke, with the dream vividly in his mind, and so he recorded it and demonstrated it in stages to his followers, in the manner still maintained to this day in Bhutan.[65]

Here we see how visionary experiences are depicted as part of the tertön's religious training, informing Pema Lingpa after the discovery itself in the process of preparing to disseminate the treasure. He is instructed by none other than Yeshe Tsogyal herself, explicitly affirming his direct link to figures from the royal period. Here, the tertön is characterized as someone without extraordinary aptitude or specific preparation to disseminate the treasure; what is emphasized instead is his special proximity and ongoing connection to Padmasambhava and Yeshe Tsogyal.

From accounts of Pema Lingpa's first discovery, we can see a paradigm emerge. A physical location and ritual instructions are provided in a prophetic guide, delivered by an apparition or otherwise contained in a previous treasure cache. Pema Lingpa follows the instructions in the guide and sometimes falls into a trance at the point of retrieval. More visions occur during the retrieval of the treasure casket, involving the treasure guardian, often a dakini. Past-life recollection is utilized to decipher the symbolic script, aided by a key. Finally, visionary assistance is provided to comprehend the contents of the treasure, in the above example, by Yeshe Tsogyal herself. In all of these various phases, the tertön is depicted as a seemingly ordinary individual guided by the hand of destiny.

A treasure discovery at Vajra Rock reveals the interplay of the visionary and human aspects in the self-representation of a tertön. As in other cases, this discovery is prompted by a dream and occurs in a trance. Pema Lingpa describes effortlessly scaling a cliff in a trance state after being commanded in a dream to immediately go to retrieve the treasure.[66] This portrays the visionary side of his career, beckoned to reveal treasures by the command of destiny and fulfilling this duty via miraculous feats. However, to show a more human side, with a touch of humor, Pema Lingpa shares with the reader that partway back down the cliff wall, treasure in hand, he awoke from the trance stuck on a perch. Several disciples had to catch the treasure and help him down the remaining part of the cliff. Here is a clear example of Pema Lingpa deflecting agency for a series of events, recorded in miraculous terms. The catalyst for the event is a dream, and a miraculous feat is accomplished in a trance. Waking up from the trance, he represents himself as returned to ordinary human constraints. Through juxtaposing the visionary and human, Pema Lingpa conveys a special aptitude and destiny while appearing to be a mere vehicle for a cosmic scheme.

Visionary experience is an important component within a wider miraculous framework of the treasure tradition. Pema Lingpa records numerous dreams in which he meets Padmasambhava in visionary journeys.[67] In addition, we should not lose sight of the miraculous nature of the discovery moment itself: a casket containing an ancient scroll (or alternately a statue or ritual implement) is reportedly drawn out of a sheer rock wall. Both visions and miracles suggest a particular understanding of reality in which visions provide access to a higher order of truth and the discovery moment excavates the material deposits of timeless wisdom. In both cases, a temporal juncture occurs; an individual in the present makes contact with what is timeless. This contact is dependent on the special capacities of the tertön to serve as a mediator between the transcendent and the immanent.

Ordinary people are often portrayed in treasure literature as quite skeptical of miraculous claims by individuals, requiring public spectacles to confirm those claims. Pema Lingpa had a number of detractors during his lifetime, and many were later converted to his cause by witnessing a treasure discovery. He was tested publicly on at least two occasions and he also sought confirmation from an important religious figure of the day, as we shall see later. Some of the main challenges to Pema Lingpa's legitimacy came from governors in the area, perhaps threatened by the prospect of a charismatic figure capturing popular loyalties.

The first public test of Pema Lingpa's claim to the status of tertön is also his most famous discovery. It followed closely on the heels of his first one and indeed occurred at the same location, in the eddy of the Tang River near his hometown. This site, still a place of pilgrimage, became famous as Mebartso, or Burning Lake, due to the extraordinary circumstances of the test. It is worth quoting Padma Tshewang's account in full.

> When the time came for [Pema Lingpa's next discovery], the word spread and a large crowd of people was assembled by the governor of Chokhor, Thupa, on the rock above the river. Thupa said to Pemalingpa: "If you can reveal this treasure, I shall reward you, but if not, you shall be punished for bringing this trickery to my district." So the saint found himself under great pressure from the governor and the local people to prove himself. Standing on the Naring Drak rock above the swirling waters, he called aloud to the Guru [Padmasambhava]: "If I am a genuine revealer of your treasures, then may I return with it now, with my lamp still burning; if I am some devil, then may I perish in the water!" And now with this prayer, holding the lighted resin lamp in his hand, he leaped into the Burning Lake.
>
> Some of the crowd said to themselves that he had jumped into the river in shame; others said to his father that now his son was surely drowned. His parents began weeping. Thupa too was shocked and ashamed at the role he had played. He said to Pemalingpa's parents: "It is my fault, I shall make full amends to you."
>
> But even as he said this, the figure of Pemalingpa emerged from the water below, the lamp still burning in one hand and in the other, a statue the size of a fist and a treasure casket of joined skulls and, as if borne up on wings, he was standing beside them on the rock again.
>
> After this incident the people's doubts about him were dispelled, he gained many followers and his renown began to spread far beyond Bumthang throughout Tibet.[68]

This passage describes the custom of public witnessing for many treasure discoveries and the cultural context in which miracles were seen as a validation of a tertön's power over natural phenomena, here symbolized by the flame withstanding water.[69] Pema Lingpa won over many followers based on their belief in his magical talents. His supporters included local political figures as well as important religious figures of his times.

In another test in the Lhalung district of Lhodrak, just north of Bumthang in southern Tibet, Pema Lingpa was asked to reveal a treasure without advance warning. He was shown the address or certificate (*kha byang*) by the governor, Nangso Gyalwa, and asked to retrieve the treasure on the spot. Pema Lingpa was forced to change into a pair of borrowed trousers in order to ensure that no sleight of hand could occur. He was then hoisted down a cliff wall and proceeded to extract a treasure casket containing *Iron Hair Hayagriva*, thus converting all the onlookers to his cause. Nangso Gyalwa became his most faithful patron, and later incarnations of Pema Lingpa maintained a seat at Lhalung in Lhodrak into the present century.

When political figures were won over by Pema Lingpa, they became important patrons, which not only facilitated Pema Lingpa's religious activity and contributed to his prestige but also demanded his intervention on their behalf. Pema Lingpa was requested on numerous occasions to intervene in secular affairs and also to perform rituals to protect neighboring regions from political domination by successive powers in central Tibet. He acted as a mediator for a number of local chiefs and patrons in secular disputes and at least one regional conflict involving the western part of present-day Bhutan.[70] Moreover, successive governors of the Lhalung district requested him to avert military threats from central Tibetan forces by various means including tantric dispelling rituals.[71]

Among the many of Pema Lingpa's day who sought out his teachings and initiations, one meeting in particular stands out. This is the only case in his autobiography in which Pema Lingpa himself requested confirmation for his status as tertön. In 1503, Pema Lingpa was invited to stay with the most important lama of his day, the Seventh Karmapa, Chödrak Gyatso (1450– 1506), who was not only the head of the Karma Kagyu school of Tibetan Buddhism but also allied with the powerful Rinpung ministers controlling central Tibet at the time. During their first meeting, Pema Lingpa asked the Karmapa to judge whether he was a fraud or a genuine tertön, as follows: "Some say that I'm a charlatan, and others say that I'm an emanation of a demon. In my own mind, I believe that I accomplish the activities of Guru Rinpoche. Now, Precious Lord, since you are an omniscient buddha, you must state clearly which of these I am."[72] The Karmapa remained silent. However, in the days that followed, Chödrak Gyatso requested initiation into the full cycle of Pema Lingpa's treasures and later suggested that they travel together to Lhasa. When Pema Lingpa declined because of duties at home, the Karmapa sent him away laden with gifts.[73]

Much has been made of this exchange: what did the Karmapa's silence mean? For our purposes, it is enough to note that Pema Lingpa gained wide renown during his own lifetime such that Chödrak Gyatso invited him to meet together and later received initiation into his treasure cycles. Thus, while Pema Lingpa's activities were primarily regional, his reputation exceeded the confines of Bumthang and Lhodrak and warranted the interest of major religious figures from central Tibet. Within a century of his death, the head of the Geluk school, the Fifth Dalai Lama, Ngawang Losang Gyatso (1617–1682), assumed political power and likewise requested initiation into Pema Lingpa's treasure cycles. This might say as much about the importance of the rituals and instructions found in Pema Lingpa's treasure corpus as it does about the tertön as a focal point of regional identification who may be courted in person or through later successive incarnations by political figures of the day.

PEMA LINGPA'S LEGACY IN BHUTAN

Pema Lingpa's contribution to the religious and cultural heritage of Bumthang enriched an independent, regional identity. Pema Lingpa cultivated Bumthang's heritage in the revival of legends and the constant reminder of Padmasambhava's activities on Bhutanese soil through the numerous treasures he revealed. Pema Lingpa's roots in his birthplace were only deepened by his command over local deities and reputation for discovering treasures throughout the valleys of Bumthang. With generous donations from his many patrons, Pema Lingpa invested in restoration projects of local decaying temples and constructed new monasteries, including Tamshing and Kunzang-drak.[74] This work was continued by his lineage successors, and today Gangteng Gompa, the seat of Pema Lingpa in Bhutan, has over twenty subsidiary institutions.[75]

During his lifetime, the ceremonies Pema Lingpa conducted drew thousands of people from the surrounding region, and the total number of his followers was reckoned at twelve thousand in the biography by the Eighth Peling Sungtrul. By the end of his life, the annual festival at his temple, Tamshing, had grown to "the scale and function of a regional gathering."[76] Given the sparse population in Himalayan areas, it is likely that individuals and groups traveled far to attend religious gatherings of such magnitude, situating Bumthang as a nexus of religious life. As such, community formation is a significant feature in the regional impact of Pema Lingpa's religious activities.

Pema Lingpa's religious tradition has been propagated up to the present by three incarnation lines, representing his mind, speech, and body.[77] The mind emanations (*thugs sras*) originated with his son, Dawa Gyaltsen, also known as Tukse Dawa. It is said that on his deathbed Pema Lingpa sat up and uttered the mantric syllable *ah* three times. At that moment, "the relic of his heart, a turquoise girl, melted into his heart son Dawa" and the Bhutanese saint left this world in 1521 after an extensive teaching career.[78] According to prophecy, Dawa Gyaltsen discovered Pema Lingpa's direct reincarnation, the Peling Sungtrul named Tendzin Drakpa, in a valley in western Bhutan, where Gangteng Gompa now stands. Ganteng Tulku tells the story of his own predecessor, the body emanation:

> The mother of Pema Trinle, the first Gangteng Tulku, was the wife of Pema Lingpa's son, Tukse Dawa. While she was pregnant, Tukse Dawa—because he was old and about to die—entrusted her care to Tendzin Drakpa. Tukse Dawa knew that his wife was pregnant, and the child was born just before he died. But Tendzin Drakpa did not know [and raised the child as his own]. So that is why it is said that Pema Trinle is the son of both Tukse Dawa and Tendzin Drakpa. When the boy was born, he was not considered the body emanation of Pema Lingpa. He was called the skillful activity emanation of both Padmasambhava and Pema Lingpa and therefore named Pema Trinle [Activity of Padma]. They became known as the body, speech, and mind incarnations based on a prophecy by Padmasambhava.[79]

These three incarnation lines have been propagated until the present with the titles of Tukse (*thugs sras*), Sungtrul (*gsung sprul*), and Gangteng (*sgang steng*). (See Appendix A for a chronological list of these three incarnation lines.) The Sungtrul is regarded to be Pema Lingpa's direct incarnation, whereas the Tukse and Gangteng lines serve as emanations.

Pema Lingpa's successors, both religious and hereditary, have had a significant and enduring impact on the emerging Bhutanese nation. The incarnation lines deriving from Pema Lingpa were soon courted by new powers emerging in Lhasa and Thimpu. The founder of what is today known as Bhutan, Shabdrung Ngawang Namgyal, was an exiled Drukpa Kagyu lama from Tibet who established himself politically in Thimpu, based on a vision of a raven flying south to safety. He named his new home Druk Yul, "Land of the Thunder Dragon," and sought to unify the western and eastern halves of present-day Bhutan. During this time, the newly instated government of the Fifth Dalai Lama in Lhasa invaded the inchoate state of Druk Yul numerous times, mostly focusing on Shabdrung's stronghold in the west. During this period, Lhasa and Thimpu competed for influence in Bumthang.[80]

In order to unify the nation, Shabdrung's newly instated theocracy made every attempt to secure loyalties east of the Black Mountains. The First Gangteng Tulku was warmly received by Shabdrung himself, and his successor Tendzin Lekpai Döndrup (1645–1726) gained enough influence for the Drukpa government to include Pema Lingpa's teachings in the state monastic curriculum.[81] No doubt the new government saw it as advantageous to promote the legacy of an indigenous saint. The many lama dances composed by Pema Lingpa, grouped as the *Peling Tercham*, became integral to the major state-sponsored festivals at Punakha and Thimpu. Moreover, in a highly symbolic gesture of joining east and west, the Drukpa government relocated Pema Lingpa's body relics (*sku gdung*) to Punakha Dzong, then the capital, where they now remain, side by side with the relics of the nation's founder, Shabdrung, "still today the objects of greatest veneration."[82]

The descendants of Pema Lingpa in the Nyö clan emerged as a new aristocracy, playing a key role in the process of Bhutan's unification.[83] They supplanted many of the older families, who traced their lines to Tibetan royalty and sympathized with invading Tibetan armies. The new aristocracy quickly gained government positions at the local and national levels.[84] The ongoing tension between the eastern and western parts of Bhutan shaped the fortunes of Pema Lingpa's descendants. As the Drukpa government's control over Bhutan waned in the nineteenth century, regional governors or *pönlops* (*dpon slob*) grew in power and became the de facto rulers. Power bases were divided on an east-west axis between the pönlops of Paro and Trongsa. The Trongsa pönlop was a hereditary position, held by a single family descending from Pema Lingpa. The Paro pönlop, on the other hand, had the advantage of lucrative trade routes between India and Tibet and the disadvantage of families competing for power.[85] In the balance of power between east and west, the scales tipped after the Trongsa pönlop, Ugyen Wangchuck, assisted the Younghusband Expedition and brokered an Anglo-Tibetan treaty in 1905.[86] The present monarchy was founded by Ugyen Wangchuck in 1907 and remains a crowning legacy of Pema Lingpa in Bhutan.

The Lama Jewel Ocean

Most of the texts translated in this book are drawn from Pema Lingpa's most heterogeneous treasure cycle, *Lama Jewel Ocean*.[87] This cycle occupies the first two volumes in Pema Lingpa's sizable collection of literature, *The Precious Collection of Profound Treasure Teachings of the Great Master Pema Lingpa*.[88] The entire collection represents a multifaceted body of literature in twenty-one volumes, including fourteen major treasure cycles[89] as well as "ordinary" compositions by the tertön and later masters.[90] The content of *Lama Jewel Ocean* reflects a basic arrangement common to the entire collection. It begins with the three narrative genres discussed so far: prophecy, hagiography, and history. This is followed by a series of instructional texts, and the rest of the cycle is dedicated to rituals.

The individual texts of *Lama Jewel Ocean* are grouped more or less according to genre, and their order appears to reflect a hierarchy of values.[91] Narrative genres come first, followed by a series of instructions on various topics, in the form of dialogues set in the royal period. This reflects the reverence for texts in which Padmasambhava is specifically a protagonist. A series of tantric initiations (*dbang bskur*) and practice manuals (*sgrub thabs*) occupy a central place in the cycle, including the root text of the cycle, an Atiyoga empowerment.[92] An interesting array of mundane rites are found at the end of this cycle, including smoke offerings (*lha bsangs*), consecration ceremonies (*rab gnas*), funeral services (*bsreg chog*), and rain making instructions (*char 'bebs*).[93] These rites would most likely be performed by a lama on behalf of the laity. They are placed toward of the end of the treasure cycle, reflecting a hierarchy of values in which mundane rites form an integral part of religious life but are not as highly esteemed as tantric initiations and practice manuals intended to cultivate the goal of enlightenment.

Lama Jewel Ocean contains a series of dialogues between master and disciple set in the royal period, four of which are translated in this book. The figures tutored by Padmasambhava include members of the royal family, such as Prince Mutik and Princess Pemasal. In Tibetan and Himalayan forms of Buddhist literature, instructional texts often take the form of dialogues, following the Indian model inherited from Buddhist sutras. A disciple's questions prompt the pedagogical discourses of the learned master. In three of the dialogues to follow, Padmasambhava acts as the teacher, and his famous disciple, Namkhai Nyingpo, acts as the teacher in another. These dialogic instructions, whenever studied, read aloud, or used as the basis of oral instructions, would reinforce the prophetic character of their identification as treasures. Padmasambhava's direct instructions to his principal students are reenacted in the dialogues, which take on a performative dimension, bringing the distant past into the present for the reader or audience.

The dialogue between Padmasambhava and Princess Pemasal in Chapter 2 specifically emphasizes prophecy, and the reader will get some taste for the depictions of dark times in which the need for religious revival by a tertön is paramount. Pemasal receives a whole range of instructions: the preliminary practices (*sngon 'gro*) of refuge and bodhichitta, mandala offering, Vajrasattva purification, and guru yoga; the mainstay tantric practices of creation (*bskyed rim*) and completion (*rdzogs rim*); and the advanced Dzogchen teachings of Cutting Through Resistance (*khregs chod*) and Direct Crossing (*thod rgal*). In the midst of this practical guidance, Pemasal expresses a keen interest in predictions about her future lives, especially her final birth as one named Padma (Pema Lingpa) in Bumthang. Unlike the general prophecies found in Orgyen Lingpa's collection, those found within Pema Lingpa's corpus tend to be quite specific, mentioning biographical details about the tertön and the specific names of numerous disciples. While other dialogues set in the royal period implicitly suggest the tertön's special access to Padmasambhava's teachings, the dialogue involving Princess Pemasal indicates a direct connection through the language of prophecy.

The cluster of female disciples represented in *Lama Jewel Ocean* is striking. As central characters of three of the dialogues translated in this book, they voice the concerns of women pursuing tantric practice, and these concerns are addressed in some detail. For example, in one dialogue found in Chapter 3, Princess Trompa Gyen appeals to Padmasambhava for instructions, citing a litany of sorrows centered around marital duties. To what extent the details of her lament reflect actual social conditions of a particular time or place is unclear. It is nonetheless significant that women's concerns, evoked poetically in the aspiration of a young princess to renounce worldly life, are taken seriously in Pema Lingpa's corpus. Padmasambhava's response acknowledges her plight in some detail, emphasizing that her precious human birth should not be wasted in backbreaking service to an ill-tempered husband. Here we find a clear encouragement for women to renounce traditional roles in favor of pursuing a spiritual path.

These dialogues within *Lama Jewel Ocean* may reflect the wider valorization of female figures in the treasure tradition.[94] Yeshe Tsogyal plays a pivotal role as the principal consort and disciple of Padmasambhava; she transcribes and conceals the treasure texts. Moreover, dakinis—a class of female deity—serve a number of important functions, acting as guardians for treasures, as guides and instructors to the tertön in visions, and as a focal point in tantric rituals contained in treasure cycles.[95] Within tantric literature more generally, women themselves are valorized as living embodiments of the dakini, and the role of consorts is also framed as such. Consorts (*gsang yum*) to great lamas are generally held in high esteem within their social milieu, and the necessity of relying on a consort is often stressed in the treasure tradition.[96] Women in this role, while they escape the confines of marriage for spiritual pursuits, still engage in heterosexual relations and rely on male authority. This paradigm can be seen in the story of Princess Dorje Tso, in Chapter 4, in which the female protagonist flees her family home in the middle of the night to accompany the master Namkhai Nyingpo into retreat. During the course of the narrative, she second-guesses her choice but ultimately perseveres and gains enlightenment.

The valorization of female figures in the treasure tradition is not without its ambiguities. The spiritual potential of women is certainly affirmed in these dialogues, in which the female disciples all attain enlightenment. However, prophetic passages sometimes depict the high status of women in society as a sign of the dark ages. Moreover, a female birth is explicitly discussed as fraught with difficulties.[97] Princess Trompa Gyen, for example, articulates the aspiration to be reborn a male, a common trope in Buddhist literature. To a certain extent, this may represent an acknowledgment of social circumstances that rendered women's access to spiritual opportunities more difficult. Resistance to marriage is a theme often found in Buddhist women's hagiographies, and obstacles such as sexual harassment of solitary female meditators are voiced in the earliest Buddhist accounts of female saints.[98] Whether depicted in mythic or historic terms, both the spiritual potential of women and the external obstacles facing them are consistent themes in Buddhist literature.

No other treasure cycle in Pema Lingpa's collection contains such a cluster of dialogues nor the diversity of genres as found in *Lama Jewel Ocean*. Indeed, there is no standard format or content for a treasure cycle; each one has a distinct combination of texts.[99] Nonetheless, the predominant content of Pema Lingpa's corpus is ritual. The majority of treasures contain empowerment and practice manuals associated with Mahayoga Tantra,[100] and there are also three substantial Atiyoga cycles in the collection.[101] The collection as a whole is framed by a coherent, prophetic message and contains an amalgamation of narratives, instructions, and rituals, mirroring to a certain extent the general structure found within many cycles.[102]

Pema Lingpa's treasure corpus represents a multifaceted body of literature that addresses a variety of religious needs for a thriving community of both monastic and lay disciples. Still today, Pema Lingpa's treasures serve as the basis for rituals and religious discourses conducted by his three incarnation lines. These rituals include the ceremonies necessary to initiate those entering the tradition, as well as manuals for an individual's meditation regime and a host of mundane rites. As such, the texts of this collection serve as the primary basis of religious practice for disciples in the Peling tradition. Today, the religious community founded by Pema Lingpa is followed by thousands of Buddhists both in and outside of Bhutan. The continued use and augmentation of Pema Lingpa's treasure corpus over the centuries is a testament to the enduring importance of the religious heritage from this Bhutanese saint.

Flowers of Faith:
A Short Clarification of the Story of the Incarnations of Pema Lingpa[1]

BY THE EIGHTH SUNGTRUL RINPOCHE
Translated by Sarah Harding

Marvelous moonbeams of compassion are the remedy
To open the thousand-petaled lotus of virtue and goodness.
With faith I prostrate to Padmakara,
Perfect in the twin qualities of relinquishing and realizing.[2]

You nurture all victorious ones and command their speech,
Transforming into the *Lake-Arisen One* and emanating enlightened
    activity
As the noble and fortunate *Princess Lotus Light*.
Drawn by the wind horse of *Karmic Connection* and aspirations,
The *Expression* of the four visions is perfected.
The *Stainless Expanse* of dharmakaya
Disperses a hundred thousand *Light Rays* of compassion
And the hundred-petaled lotus of profound treasure is opened
    in the awareness-holding *Lotus Land*.[3]

THIS IS THE FATHER-CHILD succession, the crown jewel to whom I bow, and the amazing incarnation succession, the mandala of the stainless moon of autumn that appears to the many beings to be tamed like [reflections] in the waters of the lakes. There is no end to the telling, but I tell a mere part of the story, since a few fortunate ones have requested it. Not encumbered by poetics, linguistics, or synonymics,[4] not polluted by the filthy scum of deception, from the bathing pool of three kinds of faith, this is the story of sublime realization: the most beautiful divine flower.

The Second Buddha, the Great Master of Glorious Oddiyana, the Sovereign Lake-Born Vajra,[5] conferred his blessing on the many incarnations in the succession of lives and empowered them to sustain the enlightened activity of taming beings. I will briefly tell the history of the succession of births of the indisputable incarnated great treasure-revealer, king of Dharma, awareness-holder Pema Lingpa, whose name is famous and victorious in all directions. I do so first because it has been requested by a few interested individuals, and second because in future generations the holders of the Dharma lineage will, for the most part, not be inclined to look at the extensive biography. So in order to assure them of a harmonious condition by which to easily realize the history of the lineage, I have arranged this small composition.

In the expanse of reality, the original, primordially pure expanse free of elaboration, the wisdom of innate awareness possessed of six distinctive qualities,[6] is manifestly awake as the essence of Samantabhadra.[7] In its innate expression, spiritual dimensions (*kaya*) and wisdoms free of unity and separation, without ever shifting from within that state, appear in illusory emanations to the perceptions of those to be tamed, like the moon's reflection dancing in water.

From the *Sutra of the Great Bounteousness of the Buddhas*:[8]

> Although the ocean of awakening is thoroughly attained,
> In order to thoroughly ripen the ocean of sentient beings,
> The ocean of aspiration to awaken[9] is revealed
> And the ocean of perpetual activity is forever displayed.
> Such are the emanations of the joyful ones.[10]

It was the same way with our great awareness-holder, who was, in the past era, the perfect buddha Amitabha, who is presently the buddha who came to the northern world, the victorious one Sumerudipadhvaja, and who, in the future when Maitreya comes, will truly awaken as the perfect buddha Vajragarbha in the pure realm of Padmakuta and, appearing as the conqueror, the Queen of Vajra Melody (Sarasvati), will become the object of worship of both Buddhist and non-Buddhist schools.

The agent of the radiating and gathering of all the victorious ones and their heirs is certain,[11] and though the karmically powered cycle of deluded births has been relinquished since forever, the succession of births, pure or impure, is demonstrated to whatever extent is needed to manifest to those who are to be tamed. But it is never to be conceived of as anything other than the magical play of wisdom alone. The nature of such things cannot be ascertained from our ordinary human point of view. But I shall relate briefly the way in which some of the very well known incarnations occurred here in the north, in Purgyal,[12] the Land of Nine Regions.

LHACHAM PEMASAL

Through the power of the aspiration prayers made at the stupa of Jarung Khashor,[13] during the time of the early spread of the doctrine, there occurred the incarnation of Lhacham Pemasal, the daughter of Lord Tsangpa Lhai Metok[14] and Queen Jangchub Drol. From the time she was five years old, her previous propensities were awakened. Since her faith and intelligence were exceedingly great, she connected with the Second Buddha from Oddiyana and received many sacred teachings of both inner and outer Secret Mantra (Vajrayana). In particular, she was taught the heart practices *Jewel Ocean*, *The Union of Samantabhadra's Intentions*, *The Lamp That Illuminates the Darkness*, and others, the instructions of the Guru, Completion, and Compassion,[15] and she directly realized stark innate pristine wisdom. She performed the mudra of activity[16] of great bliss wisdom for the Great Orgyen.

When Princess Pemasal was eight years old she was stricken with spasmodic dysentery from parasite disease, and she passed away in Chimphu. Orgyen and Yeshe Tsogyal placed the treasure text box of those most profound texts on her head and made the aspiration and prophecy that in a future life she would be responsible for one hundred eight mind treasures.[17]

RIKMA SANGYE KYI

In a life after that, she was the awareness woman Sangye Kyi, born in Lower Drak in Central Tibet. When her former propensities reemerged, she took ordination. The lord Nyang Nyima Özer[18] took her as a secret friend in spiritual practice. As her realization of the profound path manifested, she equaled the enlightened perspective of the lord himself.

JOMO PEMA DROL

The next pure incarnation was Jomo Pema Drol, born in the Monkey year as the daughter of Tsurpa Sangye Lama in the northeast of Layak[19] Kyidrong in a place called Chörateng. She became the secret activity mudra partner of the great treasure-revealer incarnation Guru Chökyi Wangchuk.[20] The Samdrup Dewachenpo temple of Layak and its contents were constructed under her auspices. She bore a son, Pema Wangchen, and a daughter, Sangye Kundrol. With insight into the true nature of reality just as it is, she accomplished immeasurable good for the doctrine and sentient beings.

NGAKCHANG RINCHEN DRAKPA

The great mantra adept Rinchen Drakpa was born into a lineage of mantra adepts in Trongsa in Yoru.[21] He was a student of Orgyen Lingpa[22] of Yarje. He practiced *Iron Hair Hayagriva* and *The Great Completion, Padma Innermost Essence*.[23] Meeting the yidam deity face to face seven times, he achieved the level of "warmth capacity" and became a great mighty one with magical powers.

PEMA LENDRELTSAL

Pagangpa Rinchen Tsuldor, or Tulku Pema Lendreltsal,[24] was born in the year of the female Iron Hare[25] to the Nyang clan of Rishing, near Koro Cliff on the Drin plateau in the Dvakpo region. From youth his previous propensities were reawakened, so the threshold to knowledge lay wide open. He was inspired by a prophecy of Padma, and at the age of twenty-three, on the twenty-sixth day of Tönra in the Water Ox year, he extracted from near the north side of a single-trunk juniper tree in Danglung Thramo Cliff the profound teaching with which one can attain the state of buddha in one life, called the *Dakini Innermost Essence*,[26] the ultimate experience of the enlightened intention of the Great Orgyen which is like a wish-fulfilling gem. He also discovered *The Wheel of the Union of Lamas; Vajrapani Suppressing All Fierce Ones; Three Gods of Hayagriva Practice;* and *Sealing the Mouth of Yama*.[27] In Lumo Takdongmai Towa he discovered *The Poisonous Blade of Wild Planet (Rahula)*,[28] and from the cliff of Sepulare, *The Maroon-Faced Planet (Rahula)* and *Red-Eyed Butcher*.[29] From the cliffs of Ashu in the Den country, he found the cycle of *Wrathful Singhamuka and Kilaya*[30] as well as many other profound treasures, such as *Mighty Wind Lasso, The Great Capability*,[31] and others. He became the great lord of the results of the eastern treasures.[32]

Lendreltsal traveled to Tsari, Yarlung, and Samye. At Chimphu in Samye, Vajrayogini called upon him to go to Lhasa, and he went. The Dharma lord

Karmapa Rangjung Dorje bowed to him with respect and offered the hair of his head. He received the transmissions for the profound treasures and otherwise rendered service to Pema Lendreltsal as his main guru. Lendreltsal did accomplishing practice for seven months at Kora in the Drin plateau of the Dri region and gave the complete spiritual empowerments and transmissions of the *Dakini Innermost Essence* and others to Lekpa Gyaltsen of Shoben. At Serjebumpa in Lower Nyal he made a connection with the treasure-revealer Rinchen Lingpa, and entrusted him with the key of Phabong Rubal Nakpo (Black Turtle Boulder) in China and granted the prophecy for extracting it.

When the auspices were assembled according to prophecy, Lendreltsal announced that he would go to the highlands of Karak without delay. However, due to his mistaking an obstacle-inflicting demoness for an authentic dakini, his life was cut short. At the age of twenty-nine, at the border of Nyalja, he said to his son Prince Lekpa and two others, "Keep my treasure teachings undamaged. In five years, I will take birth in Upper Dra of Central Tibet as the son of a father called Tenpa and a mother named Sönam. Through the practice of all these teachings, the benefit of sentient beings will be accomplished. I will see you all then."

After he gave this advice, his form body dissolved into the expanse of reality.

Kunkhyen Chökyi Gyalpo
Drimé Özer Palzangpo [Longchenpa]
(Omniscient Dharma King Stainless Light Rays, Sublime Glory)

In the *Talgyur Root Tantra*,[33] the words of Kunzang Dorje are:

> Holder of the essential doctrine, at the end the prophesied sequence,
> After that it will be held by the supreme Intellect (Lodrö).[34]

The name "Intellect" means that all objects of knowledge can be understood without restriction, [indicating] one who can teach with utter clarity through the medium of words and sounds.

Longchen Rabjam Drimé Özer was born in the Earth Monkey year (1308) in the village of Tödrong in the Dra Valley of Yoru, into the doctrine-upholding lineage of Ngenlam that descends from Gyalwa Chokyang.[35] His mother was Sönam Gyen of the Dro clan. As soon as he was born he was actually protected by Namdru Remati.[36] A capacity for faith, compassion, and other qualities was inborn in him, and by the time he was five he could understand the written word just by having it shown to him. He thoroughly reflected on all the Dharma that he learned from his father. When he read the Prajnaparamita Sutras of twenty-five thousand and eight thousand verses a hundred times at Tsongdu Monastery in Drachi Valley,[37] he understood the meaning of all the words. At the age of twelve he took ordination from the preceptor (*khenpo*) Samdrup Rinchen at Samye and received the name Tsultrim Lodrö (Discipline Intellect). Training in the Buddhist ethical codes (*vinaya*), he composed a new commentary on them and gained renown as a learned scholar.

At Sangphu Neutok,[38] he listened to all the classic texts and commentaries on the perfection of wisdom and valid cognition from Master Tsengönpa[39] and especially from Ladrangpa Chöpal Gyaltsen, and Zhönnu Rinchen, the second Dharmakirti. Traveling around to the monastic colleges that concentrated on all the subjects of scripture and reasoning, he found no impediment to mastering the full extent of the scriptural collections, the facility of understanding, and all the expressions of intelligent awareness. He became famous far and wide as the indisputable unequaled great scholar and was called "The One from Samye with Much Transmission."

Furthermore, Longchenpa received empowerments and explanations of both New and Old Secret Mantra from over twenty masters who were unbiased about Old or New traditions, such as Master Rinchen Tashi, Zhönnu Gyalpo, Panglo Chenpo, Zhönnu Döndrup, Tingma Sangye Drak, Karmapa Rangjung Dorje, Sakyapa Daknyi Chenpo, and so on. He studied and mastered all of the areas of knowledge: the instructions and explanation styles of many greater and lesser classics of Sutra and Mantra, as well as music, composition, medicine, astrology, and so on. Thus he achieved total omniscience in the entire outer and inner canon.

At Sangphu, Longchen Rabjam performed the practices of the deities that illuminate wisdom, such as those of Achala, Sarasvati, and Varahi, and he beheld their faces. Most remarkably, the goddess Sarasvati placed him in the palm of her hand and showed him Mount Meru and the four continents for seven days, so that he mastered the powers of unrestricted intellect.

When Longchen Rabjam became disgusted with the attachments and aversions of the clergy of Kham, he did an eight-month dark retreat[40] in the cave of the spiritual adept Chokla in Gyama in Central Tibet and achieved one-pointed absorption. When only five months had passed, there appeared to him one morning at dawn the wisdom form of a noble lady of unequaled beauty. She bestowed on him her jeweled crown and assured him of receiving continual blessing and powers.

When he was twenty-seven years old, in accordance with the prophecy of the yidam, he went to meet the great awareness-holder Kumaradza in the highlands of Yartökyam.[41] After receiving many empowerments and instructions in general, but particularly after listening to the experiential commentaries of the cycles of the Supreme Secret, he practiced them all together with the great courage that does not shrink from any hardship over food, clothing, housing, seating, and so on. He reached the consummation of the very appearance of the Great Completion, unbiased enlightened perspective.[42]

In isolated places such as Chimphu, for several years he persevered in the practice of the profound spiritual path, maintaining staunch vows that he did not transgress in body, speech, or mind. Sometimes he would go to the lama to resolve all aspects of his meditative experience. In terms of the signs of warmth in meditation and view, his understanding of the full extent of knowledge, his service and reverence, and such, the lama was exceedingly pleased, and he was installed as the regent and entrusted as the keeper of the instructions.

He beheld numerous deities: at Chimphu the Dark Red Varahi, Peaceful and Wrathful Guru, Palchen[43] with an entourage of seven hundred twenty-five, Vajrasattva, Hayagriva, Tara, and so forth. Magön and other Dharma protectors revealed their actual forms to him and pledged to help accomplish his enlightened activities. In particular, the great planetary demon Rahula promised not to harm the lineage holders and pledged to be his servant. As the sign of obedience, Rahula gave him his own seal inscribed with the Kalachakra mantra called Powerful Red Ten, and his own name and means of accomplishment, offering his life-force essence and so forth. Longchen Rabjam would have Dharma discussions with dakinis that were just like conversations with ordinary people. In Lhasa, when he made offerings to the Jowo statue, light rays emanated from the circle of hair in its forehead and dissolved into him, whereupon he clearly perceived the Vulture Peak Mountain at Rajghir and the vista of Khotan, and regained the knowledge that he had in his previous lives there as a *pandita*.

At Kani Gozhi, Machik Lapkyi Drönma[44] in her wisdom body looked after him and passed on the legacy of the close lineage of Severance (*Chöd*). Because the Goddess of Vitality[45] had made the symbolic gesture of offering a volume of scripture, and also based on the requests of embodied beings, he gave the empowerment and commentary of the *Dakini Innermost Essence* to some fortunate disciples at Rimochen Red Cliff in Chimphu, and was given the name Drimé Özer (Stainless Light) by Orgyen and Dorje Ziji (Splendor Vajra) by Yeshe Tsogyal. Many hosts of oath-bound ones, such as Glorious Mantra Protector, and especially Vajravarahi, revealed the essential points of the teachings.

When it is said that after his life as Lendreltsal he wandered through the samb-hogakaya realm for a while, it is referring to this period.

He enjoyed all the immeasurable magical illusions and wonderful visions, such as hidden prophecies, as explained in *The Net of Light*.[46] In accordance with the prophecy of the five sister goddesses of Sarasvati, he recovered some of the teachings of *The Great Completion, Union of Samantabhadra's Intentions* from beneath a pillar base at Chimphu. Inspired by Yudrönma, he went to Orgyen Dzong at Kangri Tökar (White Skull Snow Mountain). There, the texts of the *Dakini Further Essence, Wish-Fulfilling Jewel*,[47] were redacted in a very short time, along with the assurance of the awareness-holder dakinis. Furthermore, most of his compositions, such as *The Further Essence Trilogy, The Natural Freedom Trilogy, The Trilogy of Rest and Recovery, Seven Great Treasures*,[48] and so on, were done in this place. From this time on, the luminous appearances of spontaneous presence and prophetic encounters with deities occurred continuously. His body could travel without obstruction through space, mountains, and cliffs. With just the smallest part of his speech he could convince those with a discerning mind; and with the profound confidence of realization in his mind, his vajra speech proclaimed again and again the *Seven Treasures* and others, so that these teachings were actualized.

When he was doing the ceremony of the peaceful and wrathful deities at Lharing Cliff, the peaceful and wrathful mandala arose in the sky and all could see it laid out there. Longchenpa also received the prophecy to restore the Temple of Zha in Uru. In the place of Gyama he defeated many pompous scholars by scriptural authority and logical reasoning. He was invited to Drikung by Gompa Kunrinpa,[49] who facilitated the conducive conditions for restoring the temple and offered him the monastery of Drok Orgyen. Longchen Rabjam nurtured him with instructions. From behind the central temple of Zha he extracted gold and the means of accomplishment of the Tenma,[50] Vajrasadhu,[51] and so on. The miraculously emanated form of the oath-bound Vajrasadhu as a young boy with turquoise earrings assisted in the building of the temple. When the earth and stones were being dug out, bad skulls surfaced and were about to be suppressed again, but they flew up with the sound of *tukchom* [like an earthquake], and the apparition of a rain of earth and stones and gusting winds brought darkness like dusk and caused the attendants to cringe in fear. With physical stances and wrathful utterance of mantras, Longchenpa stamped his foot and all the apparitions were immediately quelled. There were two long stones that fell down and could not be raised by any method at all. But by the power of proclaiming the truth and the special hand gesture of drawing hither, Longchenpa instantly erected them. At the time of performing the consecration, Longchen Rabjam himself appeared as Samantabhadra with light rays emanating from his heart, and at the tip of each ray were buddhas and bodhisattvas, filling all the space and throwing flowers with auspicious utterances. He saw the Lord Maitreya bestowing this prophecy, "After two more lifetimes you will become the victorious one Sumerudipadhvaja in the pure realm of Padmakuta."

On the tenth day of the monkey month, Guru Padmasambhava, masculine and feminine, surrounded by the five kinds of dakinis, came and conferred their blessing. At Zhotö Tidro dakinis requested him to come to Bumthang. There, he did a fulfillment-confession ceremony and miraculously traveled to lands that had never been touched by humans, planting silk banners of Dharma. At Shuksep he saw an omen of the conflict between Sakya and Pakmodrupa,[52] and thought he had better go to Bumthang. At Lhasa, the army of Yarlung was threatening him, so he miraculously became invisible. That evening he prayed to the Jowo. As he slept in a house along the way, he saw that light rays from the form of Jowo radiated in the sky above, while innumerable buddhas and bodhisattvas bestowed blessings and many oath-bound protectors were sworn in. The twenty-one *genyen* protectors of Khari and others came out to welcome him, and the great preceptor of Mentang in Layak, Gendun Khyabdal Lhundrup, respectfully made offerings and was matured through the profound path of *The Secret Innermost Essence*[53] and other teachings.

As Longchenpa traveled to Bhutan in the south, he established what are known as the Eight Ling Temples: Tharpaling at Baprön, Dechenling at Shinkar, Orgyenling at Tang, Kunzangling at Kuretö, Drechangling at Ngenlung, Pemaling[54] at Khotang, Kunzangling at Menlok, and Samtenling at Paro. In all the primitive borderlands he gave empowerments, commentaries, teachings on engendering the thought of awakening, and so on. Thus the lamp of the Dharma for the fortunate ones illuminated the path of liberation.

As related in *The Golden Rosary Dialogue of the Innermost Essence*,[55] while Longchen Rabjam was staying mainly at Tharpaling near Bumthang, his partner in secret practice was Kyipayak. The second of their two children was an emanation of Hayagriva named Jamyang Drakpa Özer, who became a peerless scholar-practitioner. Longchenpa hid some esoteric instructions in his bedroom at Tharpaling, such as the cycle of *The Union of Samantabhadra's Intentions* [that he had previously discovered]. Again going to Lhodrak, conferring the empowerment and commentary of *The Secret Innermost Essence*, he entrusted the doctrine to the great preceptor of Lhalung in Layak and a gathering of one thousand who attended. In response to the offerings of the myriarch of Yamdrok, Dorje Gyaltsen, he bestowed *The Innermost Essence* to just fifty fortunate ones and turned the vast wheel of the Dharma for the many gathered there. Tai Situ Jangchub Gyaltsen[56] had developed faith in Long-chenpa's knowledge, realization, and enlightened activity, and at the government of Yerpo lengthy offerings were made with excellent veneration, and an assembly of two thousand was given empowerments and commentaries. Amazed at his great wisdom, they offered their devotion to "the Infinite Vast Expanse." Thus he became known as Longchen Rabjam.

In Yoru in Central Tibet, he established the three places: Fortunate Jamding, Yuding, and Peding. The glorious lama of the Sakyapa[57] and Drakzang of Sangphu had written a letter, which he answered according to the Dharma. This inspired their devotion and appreciative faith so they called him Omniscient Dharma Lord, an appropriate name that stuck with him. At Lhasa, many sangha members welcomed him in a beautiful procession. For half a month he stayed between Lhasa and Ramoche[58] upon a built-up Dharma throne, turning the Dharma wheel of many subjects, such as the aspiration for enlightenment. Many proud scholars of Sangphu, Tsurphu, and De were thoroughly defeated in scriptural authority and logical reasoning and were established in an attitude of faith. He made offerings of places and representations to the many orders of colleges and retreats, and so the accumulation of merit was vastly increased. It was all dedicated to the cause of increasing the benefit and happiness of the doctrine and beings. At Shuksep, he gave the maturing, liberating Great Completion to a gathering of one thousand fortunate people. At Khawari in upper Uru, Situ Shakya Zangpo[59] honored him. During the summer retreat, a gathering of three thousand people, including abbots, preceptors, and powerful people, turned out. He gave them the empowerments and instructions for *The Clear Light Vajra Essence.*[60] He satisfied them with material goods as well and did not adhere to the custom of accepting dues for the Dharma. He did not squander the objects of faith, but used two-thirds as offerings on the tenth day and one-third for the immediate necessities of those attending. He paid respect only to the sangha and did not try to save face before important people. No matter how many things were given to him by the patrons, he did not favor them, and when the poor and humble made offerings, he showed equal delight at the most meager of gifts and made dedication prayers. Thus in his life of freedom he never made choices based on the eight worldly concerns.

One day when the exceptional instructions of a hundred powers to benefit others and other intructions had been given in their entirety, he told the Prince Zöpaka to transcribe the last testaments. At the end of the composition of the two testaments called *Flawless Light* and *Mirror of Key Points*,[61] he said, "Now, don't linger, Pema Lendreltsal, go capture the throne of immortal great bliss." During the feast circle for the completion of the teachings, he urged his followers with this advice: "Now we, master and students, have turned the wheel of Dharma and completed the feast offerings. It is enough. All of you, please, give up attachment to this life and take up the essence of abiding bliss from the profound path."

Making offerings at the Temple of Zha, he gave a public teaching during which it rained flowers. On the road while traveling to Samye, the patrons of Gyama became his followers. At Chimphu he said, "Oh, this is just like the Cool Grove charnel ground in India. I would rather die here than be born elsewhere. I will leave this illusory spirit body of mine here." To the many gathered there, he bestowed the supreme secret empowerment and instruction and many days of commentary, until the sixteenth. Then, at the age of fifty-six, on the morning of the eighteenth day of the victory month of the Water Hare year (1363), assuming the dharmakaya position, he departed to primordial extinction.

TÖKAR

The next birth took place to the east of Tharpaling, in a place called Dömadeng where a son was born to Pema Khyab and his wife Lhakyi Zangmo, whom they called Tökar. When he was seven years old, he tried to steal peas from a neighbor's field. A stone was thrown and struck his head, and he passed away. Then for twenty-five human years he dwelt with the Guru on the Glorious Mountain in Chamara. Finally the Guru said, "Son, do not remain here. You must make the connection[62] with another rebirth in the world of Jambu and be involved in my profound treasures, performing an enormous service for beings." So in accordance with this wish, he manifested in magical emanation.

THE GREAT TREASURE-REVEALER DHARMA KING AWARENESS-HOLDER PEMA LINGPA

As it is told in many of the authentic treasures, such as in the secret prophecies of his own treasures, Pema Lingpa was born in Bhutan in the central area of Chökor of Bumthang, in Baridrang of Chel in the Iron Horse year (1450), on the full moon, the fifteenth day of the first or tiger month of spring, under the constellation of victory.[63] His father, Nyötön Döndrup Zangpo, was from the radiant Nyö clan,[64] and his mother was the Drokmo Pema Drol.[65] At the time of his birth, three suns shone in the sky, flowers fell like rain, and rainbows clustered all around. For a long time after the birth, both mother and son were surrounded by rainbows day and night. Many heroes and dakinis offered ablution water and danced, sang, and sported with him, and other unimaginable, marvelous sights such as these manifested as well. He was given the name Paljor. From the time he was small, he lived with his grandfather, the blacksmith Yönten Jangchub, and grandmother, Ani Döndrup Zangmo, at Mani Gonpa.[66] Dorling Thukse Chöying[67] once said, "Blacksmith, this boy of yours will be of great benefit to the doctrine and to beings." Even playing around in his youth, he would sit on a throne and act as if he were giving empowerments and instructions, sing incantations, perform sacred dances, gather together a following, enter into meditative absorption, and generally engage in activities beyond the scope of most children. At those times, his hands and feet would leave many imprints in hard stone as if it were mud. These can now be seen by everyone. He never listened to the advice of his mother or father or anyone else, but rather practiced the tantric deportment of immediately acting on whatever occurred to him. All the people called him "King of Farce, Accomplishing His Aims."

From the age of nine years, he naturally understood without effort the various crafts such as ironwork, carpentry, masonry, and tailoring, as well as reading and writing. The lama Chokdenpa welcomed him to his place at Rimochen,[68] and at one point he stayed there, but because of the imminent last testament of his dying grandfather he returned to Mani Gonpa. During this time he had a dream in which he was practicing tantric discipline in a charnel ground with many dakinis and heroes. Arriving at the peak of the Supreme Mountain, he distinctly perceived the world and its contents of beings. Many wondrous sights appeared to him, such as the sun and moon falling into his hands, whereupon he stuffed them into his jacket pouch.

In particular, on the tenth day of the first month of autumn in the Fire Monkey year (1476), while staying at the monastery in a deep state of melancholy, he went alone up into the woods to look for mushrooms. Not finding any, he turned back and fell asleep at the foot of the chapel room in front of the monastery. Hearing "Get up and work!" he looked around. Standing close by was a monk in ragged robes. After much questioning, the monk handed him a paper scroll and said, "Look well, and give me some food."[69] After preparing the food inside, Pema Lingpa again went outside to call the monk, but he had disappeared without a trace. Looking at the paper scroll, he read, "On the night of the full moon of this month, at the bottom of your valley there is a place called Naring Drak (Long-Nosed Cliff). There lies your destined wealth. Take five friends and go there to retrieve it." When he got home, he showed the scroll to his father and mother and Ani Deshek, explaining the situation. His father said, "It's a lie," but Ani said, "This same thing happened before to Ratna Lingpa. How do we know what it is?" Basically, they didn't believe in it.

On the night of the full moon, Pema Lingpa persuaded five friends to come with him. Unwilling, they pretended that they were first going to fetch a yak cow from Tangsibi, and they tried to confuse him by acting as if they would come to meet him. In the lower part of Chel, the Tang River twists and knots at the place called Senge Naring Drak (Long-Nosed Lion Cliff), or Mebartso (Burning Lake). When Pema Lingpa arrived at its edge, immediately an intense experience of having lost all bearings welled up in him, and he took off his clothes and jumped in the water. Beneath the water, in a place called Palgyi Phukring (Glorious Long Cave) there was a life-size figure of the Teacher.[70] To the left side of this was a stack of many rhinoceros-skin chests. A woman with one eye, wearing maroon clothes, handed him a treasure box from among these containing the text of *The Quintessence of the Mysteries of the Luminous Space of Samantabhadri.*[71] After somehow being propelled back onto the cliff, he returned with his friends at midnight. He blessed his mother, father, and others with the treasure.

Back at Mani Gonpa, when it was time to transcribe the yellow scroll, the ink ran out. Immediately a dakini appeared and offered a self-filling pot of ink and made a prophecy about the scribe and other things. At the village of Dangkhabi, when he opened the door of the empowerment and instruction of this sacred teaching for the first time, myriad good signs appeared, such as a rain of flowers and a canopy of rainbows. Every night he experienced the Great Orgyen and Tsogyal explaining the exact details of how to confer the empowerment and give the instructions, how to perform the dances, the musical notation for the ritual activity, and so on, and he would precisely implement these instructions on the following day.

One time, on the fifteenth of the month, Pema Lingpa fell asleep on the steps of a stupa. The awareness-holder Ratna Lingpa[72] appeared to him and said, "You have acted as the lama for three lifetimes. I am going to Chamara, and you must stay to benefit sentient beings." He then disappeared like a rainbow. Later Pema Lingpa found out that Ratna Lingpa had died on that very day.

On the fourteenth day of the eighth month of that year, in the midst of a large crowd who were gathered at the edge of Mebartso, Pema Lingpa held up a butter lamp in his hand and declared, "If I am a demonic emanation, then may I die in these waters. If I am a son of Orgyen, then may I find the necessary treasure and may this butter lamp not be extinguished."

Saying that, he jumped. The people had all kinds of reactions and a great clamor arose, but immediately thereupon the figure of Pema Lingpa shot glistening out of the water, holding a buddha statue and with a joined skull box filled with sacred substances held under his armpit. What is more, the butter lamp was still burning. All the skeptics were inspired then with trusting faith and were placed in a state of liberated awakening.

Not long after that, Pema Lingpa built a house on Tsen Mountain in Chel and lived there. On the full moon of the first month of spring of the Bird year (1477), Pema Lingpa and three students extracted a rhinoceros-skin box containing *The Great Compassionate One, the Lamp That Illuminates the Darkness* from Zangphuk Dorje Rawa (Copper Cave Vajra Fence) at the Tang Cliff at Rimochen in Bumthang. On the tenth day of the victory month, before a crowd of over a hundred, he took out the box containing a copied yellow scroll and a statue of Padma Guru from the Senge Drawa Cliff (Lion-like Cliff) in Lower Bumthang where the two rivers knot together. A rain of stones fell and other great violent eruptions and then the sky filled with rainbows. In the first month of winter in the Kuré Valley, a patron offered him a huge copper cauldron filled with beer. He completely downed it, a miracle that demonstrated his realization of the great equanimity in the purity of phenomenal existence. At Rimochen Cliff he extracted a vase filled with nectar and the yellow scroll of *The Supreme Intention*.[73] In Imja village he left his handprint, signifying his realization that appearances are false. On the fifteenth day of the monkey month, in Lower Bumthang where the three rivers[74] entwine and three districts meet, he took out a statue of Single Hayagriva and five hundred flesh pills of a brahmin from Senge Namdzong Drak (Lion Sky Fort Cliff).

Pema Lingpa erected a bamboo hut at Sershong above the monastery and meditated there for three months. He then perceived the whole world as if it were *kyurura*[75] in the palm of his hand. At Pemaling he gave the profound instructions of *Luminous Space*[76] for one month. During the dark moon of the month of Min he extracted *The Cycle of Longevity Practice, Applying Jewels on the Path* from the cliff at Kurje[77] that looks like nine skulls stacked up. In the outlying country of Bulé[78] the Great Orgyen arrived in the guise of a scholar (*geshe*) and gave many practices and revelatory instructions concerning the intermediate state. In the earth month of the Dog year (1478) he took a bronze statue of the Teacher from a boulder that looks like the lung of an elephant at Gyagar Khamphuk in Upper Kuré. In the upper cave where even a lance could not reach, he miraculously left his footprints in the stone. On the tenth day of the dog month, he revealed the text box of *The Wrathful Red Guru, the Fire Twister*[79] in Senge Kyichok in the lower part of Bumthang Valley. In the Pig year (1479), as prophesied by the Guru, he respectfully entreated all the patrons of Chökor[80] to refurbish the outer structure and inner contents of the Chökor Temple. As an auspicious circumstance for such a restoration, he took out a small amount of gold from the ear of the Vairochana statue. Incredibly, it expanded to cover all the costs.

At Pemaling, the five kinds of dakinis implored him, so he extracted a bronze statue of the Teacher one cubit high and the treasure box of *Single Wrathful Guru*[81] from Senge Kyichok in Lower Bumthang. At Orgyenling in the Kuré Valley he built three representations of enlightened Body, Speech, and Mind, and his accumulation of merit was vastly increased. In the Dragon year (1484), at Kuré Valley he flew like a bird vibrating with the sound of *mani*[82] from the Rimochen Cliff and extracted a crystal vase filled with long-life water, topped with peacocks intertwined at the neck. On the tenth day of the monkey month, in accordance with the exhortation by Yeshe Tsogyal in a dream, he revealed a one-cubit-high statue of Single Hayagriva from a cliff in the lower part of Bumthang.

Then he stayed in meditation in Serzhong. Within one month there dawned in him a great realization experience, such as had never occurred before, of the ways of all cyclic existence and its transcendence, and in particular the knowledge of the thoughts and activities of all beings in the six realms.

That summer he went to Tibet. In Lhodrak at the temple of Chukyer Bentsa, in the knot formed by the crossed legs of a Vairochana statue, he revealed a crystal *tsatsa*,[83] light blue in color, filled with the white and red bodhichitta of the Guru, masculine and feminine. He also extracted an image of Padmasambhava from a boulder shaped like a tortoise on the flat ledge of the neck of Khari Mountain.

Again back in Bumthang, being instructed by the dakini's prophecy and Dorje Lekpa, he revealed the text box of *The Most Secret Eight Transmitted Precepts, Mirror of the Mind*[84] from Lha Drak (Gods' Cliff) behind the Tsilung Temple. In the Iron Ox year (1481), at the age of thirty-two, while he was sleeping near the west window of Pemaling during the full moon of the snake month, he had a pure vision at dawn. Three girls leading a white horse invited him to come with them. They took him to the palace on the Copper-Colored Mountain of Lesser Chamara. On a jeweled throne in the center of an extraordinarily elegant palace of many wonderful arrangements was seated the glorious Orgyen Vajradhara in the manifestation of Maharaksha. To his right and left were many of the awareness-holding saints of India and Tibet all lined up, with inconceivable numbers of heroes and dakinis emanating clouds of offerings and praying and prostrating to them with intense devotion. They were extremely pleased, engaging in many dialogues. Continuing outside to the marvels there, he saw the entirety of wondrous lands and conditions. Most of all, in a room made out of the five kinds of precious jewels, with Tsogyal and Mutik Tsenpo as the shrine masters, he beheld the mandala of *The Compendium of the Lama's Most Secret Precepts*[85] and for seven days engaged in its practice. He received the four empowerments in their entirety with their conferral objects: the vase empowerment conferred through an external object, the secret empowerment conferred through the inner nectar, the wisdom empowerment conferred through the secret means and wisdom, and the word empowerment conferred through the most secret revelation, as well as the empowerment of abundant precepts of the vajra master. The Dharma protectors displayed each of their forms and deferred to him with strict promises of obedience. At this time he received the secret name Orgyen Pema Lingpa. After requesting the guidance of many practices, prophecies, and profound teachings, he returned with the three girls to his own country and woke up.

In the snake month, according to the urging of the treasure protector, he extracted the cycle of accomplishment and a statue of the Single Wrathful Guru made out of the sand of Lake Manasarovar[86] from the northeast of Tharpaling, from the south face of Senge Drak where it looks like an upside-down frying pan. In the Tiger year (1482), after the treasure lord Shelging Karpo[87] had twice entreated him, he brought out from underneath a cliff like an upside-down frying-pan in the left corner of the Vajra Tent cave at Kurjé *The Great Red Wrathful Guru, Necklace of Flames*[88] and the address[89] of *Jewel Ocean*. In the middle room of the chapel house of Tashi Gomang, he bestowed the empowerment and instruction of the supreme secret to many fortunate ones, did the visualizations of creation and completion, the practice of accomplishment and enlightened activity, and so on, after which the participants studied, meditated, and practiced until they had mastered them. One time when Pema Lingpa was staying in Kunzangling for a month doing the secret practice of the Guru, he vividly perceived the five families of Tötreng in the midst of a rainbow canopy. At Mani Gonpa he threw a pestle for grinding medicine at a hen and left clear handprints in it.

Because of the address key that had been found at the cliff at Kurje (Body Print) on the tenth day of the sheep month and also the dakini's entreaty, on the tenth day of the first fall month of the Earth Hare year,[90] he went to

Lhodrak in Tibet. There, amid a crowd of many monks and layfolk of Dangtro Lechung, he extracted from a lion-faced rock on the northeast side of Mendo Cliff (Medicine Rock Cliff), where it looks like three hearthstones, the text box of the mind practice [*Lama*] *Jewel Ocean*, along with a hundred flesh pills of a seven-times-born brahmin, two images of Hayagriva and Vajravarahi, two of Padma Guru, and one of Vajravarahi inside a container made of a peacock egg. He blessed all those gathered there and established them in the stages of total purification.

In response to the supplication of the prefect Gögö Gyalwa, he extracted in public the treasure of the cycle of accomplishment of *Iron Hair Hayagriva*[91] from where the treasure sign was a cover-stone blocking a hole thirteen yards up in the big cliff of Drakmotrang. The patron then bowed to him with undivided devotion and invited him to Lhalung. With offerings of resources, Pema Lingpa fostered him with the instructions that ripen and liberate.

Again at Mendo, from the right and left ears of the lion face in the cliffside, he revealed the teaching cycles of Kilaya and Hayagriva. While staying in Mentang, entreated by the command of the Guru, he took out the public treasure of *The Cycle of Wrathful Vajrapani*[92] from Mardo Drak (Red Rock Cliff). A great storm arose with gusting winds and hail, but it totally subsided when he reminded Yadüd Nakpo of his oath of obedience. According to the exhortation of Genyen Khari, he took out *The Dakini's Ocean of Shortcuts*[93] from the nostrils of the Lion-Faced Cliff and from the eyes, the cycle of the Dharma protectors, along with the tantric means of accomplishment. In the cliff above the monastery of Mentang Dzalung there was a treasure sign, and from there he took one lasé[94] amulet box. But since there was no prophecy, there was very great treasure disturbance. On the tenth day of the tiger month, after the mantra protector had twice entreated him, he found four volumes wrapped in silk on the window ledge in the room at Tharpaling where he had hidden them in his previous life as Longchenpa. As soon as his hand touched them, some of them completely disintegrated. But the texts of *The Union of the Intentions*[95] remained undamaged, and he left with these.

In Zhong he conferred the long-life empowerment on the patron Lama Khyab. While the shrine was being set up, some of the barley grains that were being scattered fell into the ritual vase. During the refuge and aspiration parts of the ceremony, these turned green and sprouted to four finger-lengths. By the time the creation phase was finished, the ears of grain had begun to form. When the invocation and request to remain were done, they produced unripened grain. And during the capturing of the life force the grain had ripened, so that the offering patrons could all eat of it.

At the village of Tegang in Kuré district, various disturbances of gods and demons arose. They were suppressed by the splendor of Pema Lingpa's fearless heroism. Traveling to Laok Yulsum,[96] he revealed a footprint of the Guru at Domtsangrong (Bear's Lair). In accordance with the dakini's prophecy and the meaning in the address, on the eighth day of the pig month, from the cover-stone in the center of the three stupas at Samye Chimphu, he extracted the secret treasure of a joined lasé amulet box wrapped in white silk stamped with seals. The treasure disturbance was very great. Going to Mani Gonpa and opening it, he found the twenty-five scrolls of *The Union of Samantabhadra's Intentions*. Also, within the fresh red joined skulls of the brahmin Pema Karpo and Princess Pemasal, he found the princess's spirit turquoise called "red house snow peak";[97] Zicho Pelma's braid; the silver mirror of long-distance clarity; the relics of Manjushrimitra inside two glazed tsatsas; the collar of Orgyen's robes decorated with patterns in gold thread; Tsogyal's seamless single-piece robe; the white and red bodhichitta of the Guru, masculine and feminine, inside a tsatsa of new turquoise; and many other marvelous sacred objects.

In the hidden land of Khenpajong, at Tong Zhong Phukmar in Tashigang there is a black boulder that looks like a nomad's tent, and three levels of caves. From the upper one, Pema Lingpa extracted the treasure box of *The Guidebook to Khenpalung*[98] and others. In the Bird year, urged to reveal it by Genyen Khari, he took a lasé amulet box decorated with six seals from a hole just big enough for a cat in a boulder with turquoise veins above Mönkhar in Layak. In the Dog year, on the eighth day of the horse month, to the east of Tharpaling in Bumthang, while experiencing a kind of trance, he took a cubit-high bronze statue of Vajrasattva, the means of accomplishment, and the profound seal of the letter *ah* from the tip of the vajra cliff that faces southwest from the place of the so-called Bird Cliff. Lama Özer of Tangsibi offered him the transcribed text of *The Small Child Tantra of the Great Completion*[99] that had been revealed previously by the treasure-revealer Sherab Mebar.[100] Pema Lingpa could see that the actual yellow paper had been carried to the treasure site of Rimochen, but, having deteriorated, it had not been able to benefit beings. In accordance with the prophetic command of Orgyen, on the tenth day of the dog month, Pema Lingpa revealed a cubit-high bronze statue of the Teacher in a lasé amulet box in the right ear of the lion-faced cliff of Copper Vajra Railing at Rimochen in Bumthang, and a treasure box with an inventory scroll in its lap. As in the prophecy that Trisong Detsen made at Samye, a treasure was revealed in the retreat center at Chimphu, but, abandoning its extraction, Pema Lingpa instead brought out from the crossed legs of the Mahabodhi statue the cycle of accomplishment of *Wrathful Blue Guru*[101] and offering-medicine of sixty pills of a seven-times-born brahmin, as well as a scroll of esoteric instructions from the right armpit of Düdtsi Kyilpa.[102]

Generally it was taught in the secret treasure prophecies that Pema Lingpa would be the master of one hundred eight treasures, but for the time being, through the force of necessity, only thirty-two were actually discovered. Most of them were public treasures.[103] Furthermore, some lesser treasures were taken from indefinite treasure sites, such as Tsaldo Traring Drak and Tsilung Gosung Ngönpo. Although these are not mentioned in the extensive biography, they can be found in the treasure colophons of miscellaneous teachings.

At the time of his discoveries, Pema Lingpa's realization had reached the stage of the exhaustion of the four visions,[104] and the expanse of his perspective was like the sky, the exhaustion of phenomena and of conceptual mind. He had made the leap into recognizing whatever appears as the play of reality itself, and so was freed of accepting or rejecting cyclic existence and its transcendence. Soaring through space like a bird, he could pass unobstructed through mountain cliffs. He left his handprints and footprints in hard stone as if it were mud.

At Kunzangling in Kuretö, four dakinis came to get him with a silken hammock. He encountered Orgyen in the form of Vajradhara, who gave him symbolic teachings. Again doing the secret empowerment of *The Union of Samantabhadra's Intentions*, in the evening the five kinds of dakinis demonstrated the symbolic teaching of the three kayas using a three-bloom, single-stemmed lotus. In the winter of the Iron Horse year (1510) at Mani Gonpa, four girls summoned him to Orgyen Khandro Ling, where the five kinds of dakinis introduced him to the ultimate meaning, and the Great Orgyen gave him instructions. When he was staying in the west wing of the monastery at Lhalung, he saw the Genyen Khari Palace, and again when he was on the blue rooftop, Khari summoned him. From the top of the palace he could see Chamara, Five-Peaked Mountain, Potala, Changlochen, and Ghanavyuha.[105] He gave the empowerment and explanation of *The Secret Union of Genyen, Wife, Sister*[106] and others. Whether in actuality or in vision, he met many great ones, such as the Great Master and Tsogyal, and had immeasurable visions of receiving precepts, prophecies, and assurances. Whenever he was giving empowerments and instructions, the nectar would boil up, flowers would rain down, rainbows would cluster around, and many other marvelous sights would occur; not just one time but continuously. Just a portion of the nectar of his speech could liberate upon hearing, such as when he would sing the "vajra melody that inspires realization." It would captivate the minds of all in attendance. His unimpeded clairvoyance would reveal whatever was hidden in the three times, causing those with doubts to be convinced and become interested. Even the kind of unfortunate ones with wrong view were near the end of cyclic existence, being taken under his protection through his aspiration prayers that in future lives they would become disciples. These infinite qualities of the great bliss of the sublime body, speech, and mind of Pema Lingpa are all beyond the capabilities of the ordinary rational mind to fathom. Guru Padma's prophecy states:

> In my heart son Pema Lingpa
> Oh, how happy are the faithful beings.
> Even the skeptical are near the end of cyclic existence.
> Even a grub has entered the path.

As he says in his own supplication prayer:

> Through the power of those to be tamed I have been to many countries,
> Made many empowerments and Dharma connections,
> Placed men and women with karma on the path of ripening and
> liberation,
> And prayed that even the skeptical become converted.

As stated here, Pema Lingpa traveled to many districts, such as the four valleys of Bumthang, upper and lower Kuré, Dungrang Lechung,[107] the eastern part of India, the three areas of Laok Yul, as well as Men, Lo, Nyal, Jar, Central Tibet, and in particular Lhoyak, which he visited twenty times.[108] He also built many temples and their contents, such as Tamzhing Lhundrup Chöling in Bumthang; Pemaling, Dechenling, and Kunzangdrak in Chel; Kunzangling in Kuretö; Dekyiling in Bamrin; Orgyenling in Tsangchu; Kyerechung Tashi Tengye in Layak; and so on. He restored the damage and reconsecrated Gyatso Lhalung and others. Thus he accomplished meaningful enlightened action of the four activities, such as establishing the auspicious conditions for turning back invading armies. The benefit and well-being of the religion and the people flourished.

His disciples included many powerful men such as the minister ruler Tashi Dargye, Karmapa Chödrak Gyatso, Gyaltse chief Rabten Pak, the Yamdrok ruler, King Dharma of India's Donga, the king of Kamata; the treasure-revealers such as Tulku Chokden Gönpo, Jangchub Lingpa, Zablung Tulku, Chögyal Wangpo, Langlung Kukye, and Drangsowa Shakya Zangpo; the spiritual adepts such as Drukpa Jadral Kunlek, Lama Hyaghriwa of China, Tsan-glungpa, Karchen Kundrak, Jetsun Dechen Zangmo. In particular, as foretold in the prophecy of the Guru, there were three heart sons who were emanations of the lords of the three families:[109] Könchok Zangpo, Dawa Gyaltsen, and Drakpa Gyalpo; the physical sons Kedrup Kunwang, Lama Kun, and Sang-dak; and seven keepers of the mandala: Tulku Natsok Rangdrol, Khenchen Tsultrim Paljor, Umdze Drubpa Kundü, Nangso Gyalwa Döndrup, and so on. Those with a karmic connection were twelve thousand. In Tibet and the regions of greater Tibet, Bhutan, all over the east and west of India, upon uncountable numbers of fortunate ones, he showered down the Dharma of empowerments, great accomplishments, explanations, transmissions, and eso-teric instructions, and maintained nonsectarian enlightened activity to ben-efit others. The lists of these can be found in the extensive biography itself. Here we have only mentioned a small portion of his activity.

Thus he dwelt within unwavering spontaneous enlightened activity of the two purposes, meaningful for all he encountered. In order to demonstrate that life is illusory to those of his disciples in this land who were clinging to the idea of permanence, in Lhundrup Chöling in Bumthang, after granting a last audience to all his heart sons, students, and subjects wherein he gave them much advice and training, on the morning of the third day of the first Hor month of the Snake year (1521) at the age of seventy-two, sitting up straight with legs in vajra position, he placed his hands on the heads of his two heart sons Dawa and Drakgyel, and said, "*ah ah ah.*" With this sound of the unborn, the magical illusion of emanation passed into inner space, the great state of primordial extinction. At that time, the whole area of Chökor was filled with an extremely sweet, continuous sound of horns and cymbals, and the fra-grance of saffron pervaded everywhere. The sky became a canopy of rainbow light of five colors, a rain of flowers fell, there was a great rumbling sound, and the earth moved again and again. These and other auspicious sights occurred for two or three months before the body passed away. After it passed, for many days continuously, the awareness-holder displayed the unmistakable appari-tions of escalating to higher and higher levels. In particular, as in the prophecy, the relic of his heart, a turquoise girl, melted into his heart son Dawa. Pema Lingpa's precious remains rest in a great tomb for the merit of sentient beings.

Refined Gold:
The Dialogue of Princess Pemasal and the Guru

FROM LAMA JEWEL OCEAN[1]

Homage to Master Padma.

PRINCESS PEMASAL filled a golden bowl with turquoise. Coming into the presence of Orgyen Rinpoche on the roof of the Golden Orphan Temple,[2] she offered it to the master and said, "Oh, Orgyen Rinpoche! I am a child in a girl's body, of lowly birth and little worth, feeble of speech, vastly discursive, and forgetful of the Dharma. I have a half human body, half human slave's body. Lord Guru, hold with compassion one such as I, who has not accumulated merit. Do not drop me in the swamp of cyclic existence. I request a method to become buddha in this life by practicing some Dharma myself."

I, Padmasambhava, replied, "Princess, listen! To you, a girl, Dharma won't come. Even more so, to a princess it won't come. Powerlessly consigned to cyclic prison by your parents, you must track your husband's moods. Dwelling your whole life in the state of ego-clinging, you must act as man's servant without wages. And after living this wasted human life, finally you will go on to a bad existence, Princess."

When she heard this, the princess's eyes filled with tears, and she laid her head on the master's lap and said, "Glorious guide of beings, Orgyen Rinpoche, hold with compassion this girl with no refuge. You know the happy and sad aims of this and future lives. I request a Dharma for attaining buddhahood in this life."

Knowing that the princess was subject to some previous karmic ripening and would not live out her full lifespan, I decided I should teach her some Dharma. I said, "Princess, the deeds of this life are like a dream, an illusion. Your work won't help you, but may harm you later. If you wish to achieve your next life's aims now, listen to me for some Dharma that is appropriate for your mind."

"Lord, knower of the three times, Padmasambhava," she said, "though dwelling in the state beyond speech, thought, or utterance—the inconceivable—at this point you have spoken your thoughts to me. Please tell me what precedes all Dharma practice."

I, Padma, replied, "As for that which precedes all Dharma practice, first there is only this before all teachings: contemplating the difficult-to-find, free, and endowed human life, and death and impermanence. These go first."

The princess then asked me to explain death and impermanence [and many other topics. These are her many questions and the answers I gave]:

"How is death and impermanence the nature of cyclic existence?"

"Princess, the free and endowed human life is hard to obtain and easy to lose. Death and impermanence are the nature of cyclic existence. The free and endowed human life is difficult to obtain because there is no chance of a human life without the accumulation of merit. It is easy to lose because your being is affected by the ripening of previous karma, so you live without knowing the specific duration of your life. Now, while still alive, while listening, contemplate this as if your heart were pained with disease. Otherwise, the chance to escape from the chains of suffering in cyclic existence will never come. Think of the suffering of each of the six realms. Other than the sacred Dharma, a great path that can liberate you from that suffering does not exist. If you do not seek it right now, death could come just today or tomorrow, for its time is uncertain.

"Think well on this, Pemasal. Many a person who is today bright-eyed and resonant will tomorrow become a dried-up black corpse. They were not planning to die on the morrow. Do not put your trust in this illusory body. Breath is just steam, warmth just a spark, life force just a horsehair about to break. Think about it: all previous lives have ended. Future ones will follow this pattern. The one that exists now is the same. As everything hangs in a state of flux, there is no young or old stage of life. Everything will certainly expire, and at that time the continuity of karma and the continuity of karmic activities, the continuity of eating food, the bedclothes and body clothes, plates, bowls, and so on are abandoned and you must go. In your wake there is no lack of bad talk about you, the dead one, but from amid it all, you alone must go forth, like a hair pulled out of butter. And when the time to depart is upon you, how terrifying! As if dying weren't enough—afterward there is no place to go. You roam through bad places of the three intermediate stages,[3] and the power of karma propels you into one of the six realms. If born in hell, you experience the suffering of boiling and burning; if born as a hungry ghost, the pain of hunger and thirst; if as an animal, the pain of being mute and dumb; if as a demigod, the pain of conflict and battle; if as a god, the pain of the change and the fall from that existence; and if born as a human, you experience the pain of toil and poverty. If you did not practice the Dharma before, this is what will happen. But with some accumulation of merit, a human life could be obtained. If you do not develop the power to practice some Dharma in this life, what happens in the next life will be uncertain. Who knows?

"Now, Pemasal, when you have the choice, like a feverish person tortured by thirst, in a state of unwavering perseverance, exert yourself in the Dharma until you attain the fruition of complete awakening."

"In giving up afflictive emotions, where does one seek refuge?"

"That which emancipates from those aforementioned sufferings is none other than the Three Jewel refuge. The lama and Three Jewels are the complete refuge and protector of beings. To go for refuge in them, think that you, leading all sentient beings, go for refuge with longing attention in order to be liberated from the ocean of suffering of cyclic existence and attain the fruition, the unborn. Visualize that in the space in front of you is a throne supported by eight lions, with a seat of sun, moon, and lotus. On it are the sacred sources of refuge: the root and lineage lamas and the yidam deities clustered like clouds, coming to take their seats. Led by yourself and your parents, all sentient beings, tormented by the yearning to just be freed from prison, go for refuge:

Namo!
Buddha, chief of bipeds,
Sacred Dharma, peaceful and free of attachment,
Sangha, field for accumulating merit:
I and all sentient beings go for refuge.

Lord Lama, possessed of three insights,[4]
Yidam deities, granting spiritual powers,
Host of dakinis, eliminating all obstacles:
I and all sentient beings go for refuge.

Dharmakaya, possessed of two purities,[5]
Sambhogakaya, possessed of five certainties,[6]
Nirmanakaya, accomplishing nonspecific purposes:
I and all sentient beings go for refuge.

From emptiness free of embellishment,
The kaya, unembellished and unconditioned,
Is beyond rational mind, without fixation: in that very state
I and all sentient beings go for refuge.

Embodiment of essence, nature, and compassion,
From the natural open expanse, equal and complete,
Thought-free innate radiance dawns nakedly:
I and all sentient beings go for refuge.

In the expanse of spheres, the innate radiance of space and awareness,
Unimpeded innate energy pervades everywhere
As beautiful chains of awareness wisdom:
I and all sentient beings go for refuge.

"Say this refuge prayer and others as well. Everything you do becomes the Dharma. The temporary obstacles are all pacified and you are given refuge from the sufferings of cyclic existence. Without straying onto the wrong path, with whatever you do being Dharma, call for refuge, Pemasal!"

"What is the aspiration for awakening [bodhichitta]?"

"Princess, the aspiration is this. Even if you were to actualize the profound meaning of reality itself, without the aspiration—the compassionate method— you would become no different from those of the Lesser Vehicle. After you arouse the compassion and this aspiration for awakening, the compassion you feel for all our parents in the six kinds of existence is unbearable, and so with the four immeasurables,[7] you think of helping them. For the sake of this love of all sentient beings of the six realms, from now until you attain full awakening you should adhere to this vow taught by the victorious ones. There are three aspects of this vow: wishing, engaging, and concluding.

"First, the taking of the wishing aspiration vow:

Victorious ones of the three times, all of you,
My only friends in the cyclic three realms,
I have no hope except for you.
Hold me with compassion and give refuge.
For the sake of sentient beings,
Without thought for my own body and life,
Thinking only of the welfare, happiness, and prosperity of others,
I aspire to full awakening in my wishes.

The vow of engaging in this aspiration:

All of the former victorious ones
Dwelt in the aspiration, and in the same way
I too aspire to enter into that supreme way
And achieve the welfare of others.

The conclusion:

Taking the six perfections as a basis,
In order to benefit sentient beings,
With the three disciplines[8] as a basis,
I will apply myself with all diligences.[9]

Say this and enter into the conduct of the supreme Secret Mantra. It is the special method of joining the ranks of the Great Vehicle. Apply yourself to this aspiration, Pemasal!"

"What is the method for gathering the two accumulations?"

"Princess, the methods for gathering the two accumulations are these: Outwardly, the accumulation of merit is gathered based on the mandala; inwardly, the accumulation is gathered based on substances; and secretly, the accumulation of wisdom, the fruition, is gathered based on the mendicant.[10]
   "Imagine that in the space in front of you, in the center of an extremely open rainbow pure realm, upon a stacked lotus, sun, and moon, are the root and lineage lamas surrounded by buddhas, bodhisattvas, dakinis, and Dharma protectors. Hold the mandala in your left hand and say om ah hung and purify with the svabhava mantra.[11] First offer the gold and turquoise mandala, second

the medicine mandala, and third the grain mandala by placing ten or eleven heaps of each substance, saying:

> In pure realms of the three-thousand-fold universe of worlds and beings
> Are the supreme mountain and four continents, decorated by the sun
>   and moon,
> Encircled by the iron mountain ring, deep and vast.
> All this I offer to the nirmanakaya lama yidam.
> Consider me with loving compassion and accept it.
> May all beings enjoy the nirmanakaya realm.

> The mandala of my body, pure channels, and elements,
> Decorated by the radiant luster of the five organs,
> With totally pure constituents and sense fields,
> I offer to the sambhogakaya lama yidam host.
> Accept it in the state of loving compassion.
> May all beings enjoy the sambhogakaya realm.

> The dharmakaya mandala of pure mind itself,
> Adorned with the decorations of five-light wisdoms and forms,
> Unembellished fundamental character, totally pure since forever,
> I offer to the dharmakaya lama yidam.
> Consider the benefit of beings with compassion and accept it.
> May all beings enjoy the dharmakaya realm.

> *Om ah hung guru dewa ratna dakini mandal la putsa megha samudra*
>   *saparana samaye hung*

Gathering the accumulations of substances:

> All my wealth, substances, objects, and articles
> Are presented as offerings up to the Lama Jewel,
> As offerings to the yidam deities,
> As feast torma to the dakinis,
> As torma feast to the Dharma protectors,
> As service to the noble sangha,
> As charity to those disabled and destitute.
> If I strive toward virtue, whatever wealth and objects I have
> Become the sacred two accumulations.

Gathering the accumulations of the mendicant:

Visualize your own body as the pure realm of the victorious ones. Perceive the aggregates, elements, and sense fields as the nature of gods and goddesses. Form, object of the eye; sound, object of the ear; smell, object of the nose; taste, object of the tongue; touch, object of the body; and thoughts, object of mind, are all generated as a vast heap of desirables. The five senses that the body enjoys and flesh, bone, heart, innards, and brains, as well as power and influence, are all offered up as 'first fruits' to the Lama Jewel and as offerings to yidam deities, buddhas, and bodhisattvas. In the middle, they are presented as offerings to the dakinis, heroes, Dharma protectors, and oath-bound ones. Lastly, they bring satisfaction to those dwelling in the six realms of being, the local deities, earth lords, spirits, and hungry ghosts.

"The benefits of doing this are that the lama is pleased, the dakinis and protectors are fulfilled, beings of the six realms and all the guests are satisfied, and all those who would obstruct your life force are contented, satisfied, and happy.

"Based on the gathering of the accumulations in this way, pray for what you wish. Seal with the dedication prayer: dedicate the virtue to the supreme awakening. By doing this you will please the Lama Jewel and yidam deities. Mothers and dakinis will be pleased, thereby repairing any infractions in the sacred pledge with them. Dharma protectors and oath-bound ones will be pleased, clearing away obstacles. Bad karma, wrongdoings, and obscurations will be purified and the two accumulations gathered.

"Apply yourself in such a gathering of the accumulations, Pemasal!"

"What is the method for purifying obscurations?"

"Princess, this is the method for purifying obscurations. For someone who has reached the ultimate profound meaning of emptiness, the discipline to be kept and the keeping of it are not two. Purity and purification are not two. But those who do not have such realization, who are obscured by the neurotic emotions and even the five acts of immediate consequence,[12] should purify obscurations in this way:

"In the space one cubit above one's crown, on a sun, moon, and lotus is Lama Vajrasattva. He is white, with one face and two hands, the right one holding a golden vajra and the left one a silver bell facing his hip. He wears a jeweled crown on his head and jeweled ornaments on his body, and he sits with crossed legs. Create this in such a way that you cannot get enough of looking at him, like the sun rising on snow mountains. On a sun and moon in his heart, visualize a white *hung* encircled by the hundred syllable mantra. Light radiating from this syllable invokes the lamas, yidams, dakinis, buddhas, and bodhisattvas of the ten directions. They dissolve into the letters and become nectar. Imagine that this fills up the inside of his body and falls from his right big toe like milky nectar into the crown of your head. The entire inside of your body is filled like a milk bag. Your infractions, wrongdoings, and obscurations are expelled through the soles of your feet like used washing water, black and flowing out. Then recite the hundred syllables:

> *Om benzra satto samaya manu palaya benzra satto tenopa tikta dridho*
> *mebhawa suto kayo mebhawa anu rakto mebhawa supo kayo mebhawa*
> *sarwa siddhi metrayatsa sarwa karma sutsame tsittam shriyam kuru*
> *hung ha ha ha ha ho bhagawan sarwa tathagata benzra mamemuntsa*
> *benzri bhawa maha samaya sato ah*[13]

After hundreds and thousands of recitations, the world and its contents all dissolve into Vajrasattva. Vajrasattva dissolves into the letter *hung*. The letter dissolves into your head and arrives at the heart. That dissolves from the edges into the center and into the *hung*. The *hung* melts into red-tinged white nectar. It completely diffuses into the channels and elements of the body, filling it with the nectar of stainless pristine wisdom. Your own body, speech, and mind mix inseparably with Vajrasattva's. With that thought, rest in an uncontrived state free of embellishment. Then recite the usual confessions, and give rise to the knowledge that all infractions and obscurations are purified.

"This is the special amendment of infractions of the inner supreme way.[14] If you do this, the karmic obscurations of a thousand eons will be purified; all the infractions and breaks in the sacred pledge and even the five acts of immediate consequence will be purified. If a yogin strives at this, then the fruition of buddhahood will be attained in this lifetime."

"What is the method of prayer?"

"Princess, although the seed of buddha exists primordially in you, without the lama there is no one to show it to you. Therefore, the lama is better than the buddhas of the three times. Visualize that facing you in the space in front of the top of your head, upon a throne supported by eight lions, on a seat of a thousand-petaled lotus, sun, and moon, is the brilliant form of your root lama. In the lama's heart, light radiates from the letter *hung* and there appear to the lama's right the Jewel of the Buddha, to the left the Jewel of the Sangha, in front the host of yidam deities, and in the back the dakinis and protectors all around. Pray to the lama with immeasurable devotion, purified by tears of longing and with the hairs on your body standing up, thinking, 'I have nowhere to put my hope, nowhere to look, other than you.'

"As for the supplication, either do the prayers to all the root and lineage lamas or the prayer of needs and wishes in *Lama Jewel Ocean:*

> *Hri.* Amitabha, unborn dharmakaya,
> In the pure realm of Sukhavati in the west,
> I, a child without refuge, supplicate you:
> Bless me to attain primordially pure dharmakaya.
>
> Mahakaruna, sambhogakaya,
> In the pure realm of Riwotala in the east,
> I, a child without refuge, supplicate you:
> Bless me to attain the radiant sambhogakaya.
>
> Padmasambhava, great awareness-holder,
> In the palace of Lotus Light on the Glorious Mountain,
> I, a child without refuge, supplicate you:
> Bless me to attain nonfixated nirmanakaya.
>
> Yeshe Tsogyal, single mother dakini,
> In the pure realm of assembled awareness-holders in the Sky Realm,
> I, a child without refuge, supplicate you:
> Bless me with the increase of experience and realization.
>
> Mutik Tsenpo, great prince
> In the snows of deep valleys of Shang,
> I, a child without refuge, supplicate you:
> Bless me to empty cyclic existence in the great snow range.
>
> Gracious Root Lama
> On the sun-moon-lotus seat above my head,
> I, a child without refuge, supplicate you:
> Bless me to realize the original true nature.

Jewel Ocean, quintessence of the lama's mind,
In the Mendo treasure site of many profundities in Lhodrak,
I, a child without refuge, supplicate you:
Bless me to recognize myself, mind itself.

Powerful yidams, Hayagriva and Varahi in union,
In the citadel of channels, totally pure innate appearance,
I, a child without refuge, supplicate you:
Bless me to attain supreme and ordinary spiritual power.

I supplicate the heroes, dakinis, and Dharma protectors
In the citadel of subjugation of powerful evil:
Bless me with the pacifying of conditions and obstacles.
Hold the destitute refugee child with compassion,
Hold the bewildered neurotic one with compassion,
Hold me, the spirit of ego-clinging, with compassion,
Hold this lazy, indolent person with compassion.
Confer fully the four empowerments.
Bless me right now.

After praying in this way, think that the lamas, yidams, dakinis, and protectors on the right, left, front, and back are gathered into the lama's heart. The lama becomes Vajradhara in union. From the union of the lama, masculine and feminine, white and red bodhichitta falls into the crown of your head and is absorbed. Physical obscurations are purified and the vase empowerment is obtained. As it falls to the throat, verbal obscurations are purified and the secret empowerment is obtained. Again, it falls to the heart and mental obscurations are purified and the insight wisdom empowerment is obtained. Then it falls to the navel and the obscuration of neurotic emotion is purified and the word empowerment is obtained. After you have meditated in that way, the lama, masculine and feminine, dissolves into your head and falls downward, coming to rest in the center of the heart. Melting into light, the lama becomes inseparable from you. Practicing in this way, you will meet the nonconceptual, absolute lama. In that state, remain in the uncontrived completion phase.

"If you practice like that in four sessions, attaining the full chalice of the lama's blessing, you will attain the citadel of Vajradhara in this life. Pray for this realization, Pemasal!"

"What is the procedure for conduct when practicing Dharma?"

"If you want to practice the profound instructions of Secret Mantra, here is the procedure for conduct: first, act like a prisoner condemned for murder; second, act like a bee; third, act like a householder; fourth, act like a wounded antelope; fifth, act like a madman; sixth, act like a lion; seventh, act like a dog or a pig; eighth, act like a king; ninth, act with the understanding of secret methods; tenth, act in natural freedom without attachment.

"The conduct of a prisoner: Seeing impermanence, the suffering of cyclic existence, leaves no other thought than the Dharma. It is like a prisoner who thinks, 'When will I ever be free from the depths of this prison? What method will help me right now? If I am ever freed of this, I must make sure it will never happen again.' Thinking in this way, you then ask, 'Now, when will we people be freed from this place of cyclic existence?' You feel that you must do something about escaping from cyclic existence.

"The conduct of a bee: The bee does not investigate the pros and cons of big or small flowers but, regarding all as perfectly fine, takes the vital essence of the pith and leaves the dregs. Similarly, those who desire the Dharma should seek a lama and instructions, listen openly without prejudice, and show interest and respect to all Dharma practitioners no matter what their instructions are. By doing so, you will gain familiarity with the instructions, eliminate doubts, and gain confidence, Pemasal.

"The conduct of a householder: Householders find many means through which to accumulate desired wealth and property. In this way, practitioners of Dharma should, in the beginning, do prostrations; make offerings; formulate aspiration prayers; offer mandalas; do recitation; do confession and purification of obscurations; and strive to accumulate merit through many means.

"The conduct of an antelope: Antelopes, having once been wounded, have no desire for mates. If without a companion, they do not go in search of one but rather stay alone in an isolated area or mountain valley where no one will see them. So too, Dharma practitioners, until the practice of the lama's instructions has been internalized, should stay alone in an isolated place in order to practice. These are places where one needn't worry about getting along with anybody, and one may contemplate death. Living with undivided attention to practice, not straying off in any other direction, you will attain the signs and spiritual powers.

"The conduct of a madman: A madman does not have to act according to conventions toward friends or strangers, nobility or peasants, but acts without any regard or attachment, just living without having a destination. So too, Dharma practitioners, when exerting themselves in practice, until they attain the signs and spiritual powers, should not give over to the desire to be with a nice person, the bias of a pleasant facade, their own desire to save face, or any kind of dualistic clinging. After the experiences and signs have arisen, there will be an equal appreciation of everything.

"The conduct of a lion: The lion, sovereign of beasts, is perfect in the three strengths of body, fears nothing and shrinks from nobody, for nothing can harm it. With that freedom from all fear, the lion attains independence and captures the stronghold. So too, Dharma practitioners reach the ultimate accomplishment and manifest realization. They realize that cyclic existence has no intrinsic nature. They arrive at the total confidence of irreversibility. Knowing your own mind, you are free from fear. Realizing your own mind as dharmakaya, you capture the stronghold.

"The conduct of a dog or pig: Dogs and pigs don't think about cleanliness or filth in the act of eating or sensual enjoyment. When desire is aroused in their private parts, they take whatever comes, even their own mothers and daughters. In the same way, at the time of empowerment and practice, yogins who practice Dharma properly indulge with equanimity, without fixed opinions, in whatever food and enjoyment they use. When relying on the authentic mudra, such as during the secret empowerment, you must engage whether it is your mother or daughter, wife or sister. Despite whatever vows you may have concerning pure and impure, you should refrain from conceptuality and consider everything as the nature of the heruka. But do not recklessly engage at the wrong time. Appropriate conduct is most important.

"The conduct of a king: Since a great Dharma king is the master of all lawmakers, he must ensure the happiness of all his administrators, attendants, and subjects in an impartial manner, without regard to good or bad, great or small. In short, without any prejudice whatsoever, not differentiating, he establishes them all in happiness. It is the same if you act in accordance with the ways of Dharma. Manifesting the realizations, when the energy of emptiness and compassion arises, without tiring of altruism, give the gift of Dharma and of material possessions for the sake of all beings without exception. Through skillful methods and auspicious connections, maintaining great concern for beings, engage in the path of happiness in harmony with the conduct of bodhisattvas.

"The conduct of the knowledge of the secret method: Those who practice the Secret Mantra should befriend the *karmamudra* of the secret conduct and, in retreat in an isolated place, should secretly integrate bliss into the path. The experiential realization of bliss-emptiness will arise.

"The conduct of natural liberation without attachment: In a state without conceptions of how to act, concepts are free upon arising and free of attachment. Rest alert and at ease, without contrivance, innately purified of the fixation on meditation or postmeditation. This is the equal appreciation of joy and pain, transparent openness without bearing, free of action or something to act on.

"In this way, summon the ten approaches to action, Pemasal."

"What is the instruction on the creation phase?"[15]

"In creation phase, at first you create yourself as the sacred pledge being[16] from the seed syllable in the heart. There are two ways to create this visualization: creation by the rite of three procedures and creation that is complete the instant you think it.

"First, creation from the rite. When visualizing the three parts—the mandala, the vase, and the torma—you are the sacred pledge being, and from your heart the mandala, vase, and torma are visualized as the palace. Inside the palace, the deities are visualized in accordance with the textual tradition of activity for peaceful or wrathful deities. The deities of whatever practice you are doing are created from their respective seed syllables. The colors and implements of the deities and their ornaments and styles are clearly visualized. For the peaceful deities, visualize crowns, earrings, long necklaces, short necklaces, bracelets, anklets, skirts, hand implements, and so on. For the wrathful deities, visualize gaping mouths, bared teeth, a voracious manner, hand implements, and the eight articles of the charnel ground. Moreover, meditate on this as appearance without substance, like a reflection in a mirror. After the introduction to the true nature and conferral of empowerment, the wisdom being[17] comes and becomes inseparable from you, the sacred pledge being.

"As for the creation of the deity for the recitation practice:[18] Meditating on the yidam deity purifies the extreme of nihilism, and meditating that the deity's appearance is without substance eliminates the extreme of believing in permanence. By realizing the essential unborn nature that is free from extremes, you won't fall into either extreme. Within that state, the recitation of the essence mantra will be in accordance with whatever practice you are doing. Recite the mantra with the visualization of light emanating and gathering, or without any visualization. While you recite the essence mantra, visualize in accordance with whatever kind of deity it is. If it is a peaceful deity, visualize its tongue as a vajra; if it is an enriching deity, visualize it as a jewel; if it is an overpowering deity, visualize it as a lotus; if it is a wrathful deity, visualize it as a sword; and if it is a spontaneously present deity, visualize it as a wheel. If you meditate in this way, accomplishment comes swiftly.

"During the recitation practice, recite without any interruption by normal human words. Don't utter very loudly, but just so as to be audible from your own collar. Recitation for the sake of someone else's activities, however, should be loud. If it is a wrathful mantra, recite it like lightning. During the recitation, do not put your rosary down, or spit out saliva, or wash your mouth out, or put pointed objects in your mouth. Do not change cushions or move your seat. Also, during the recitation, do the fifty vowels and consonants three times and recite the *ye dharma* mantra once.[19] This will compensate for additions or omissions in the mantra recitation.

"In the evening when you are about to fall asleep, visualize *om* on the in-breath, *ah* on the pause between breaths, and *hung* on the out-breath. As you fall asleep, these will be drawn up by the breath-awareness and sleep will become a continuous recitation of the ritual service. In one day, you do twenty-one thousand breaths from the time of waking. Then do the recitation of the vowels, consonants, and the hundred syllables.

"Thus are the extremes of both nihilism and eternalism cleared away: like flowing water, the continual recitation eliminates the nihilism extreme, while knowing that the mantra sound is empty eliminates the eternalism extreme. These two being cleared away, the extremes become empty, like an echo. By doing such a creation phase and recitation meditation, you gain the spiritual power of obtaining your desires, Pemasal."

"Then what is the completion phase like?"

"Princess, the completion phase is like this. The world and its contents are absorbed into the palace. The palace then dissolves into the deities, the entourage dissolves into the main deity, the main deity dissolves into the vital seed syllable, and that in turn becomes a state of no-visualization; meditate that it vanishes in the realm of space.

> Imagining your body as the deity's body,
> There are no normal, ordinary concepts;
> That is the sacred pledge being.
> That which is immanently present since forever,
> That is the wisdom being.
> Thus there is no being or nonbeing, no arising or ceasing,
> Nor any fixation on the deity.
> The sacred pledge and wisdom are not two.
> From just the creation itself is completion.
> In the clarity of creation is the emptiness of completion;
> In method, creation is wisdom.
> Thus its character is empty of essence.
> Dwelling there, free of the extreme of emptiness,
> Knowing interdependent relationship, is the phase of completion.
> Thus sealed by profound wisdom,
> The Secret Mantra is especially profound.

Princess, practice like this."

"What is the nature of the view?"

"Princess, the nature of the view is approached like this. First, the view of general Dharma; second, the view of the absolute itself; and third, the view of supreme Ati.[20]

"First, the view of general Dharma can be learned from the individual traditions of the various vehicles.

"Second, though there are countless names of views, the essence of the view of the absolute itself is this. The fundamental nature of the knowable is that it does not arise, cease, or abide. In its empty essence is its abiding nature.

Appearance is unimpeded; being empty, it is clear. It cannot be indicated by words, by saying, 'It is this.' It transcends objects of going or coming, permanence or extinction. That essential emptiness without extremes is free of all beliefs of eternalism or nihilism. It is the great view of innate awareness.

"Third, the view of supreme Ati is this. When seeing the objective appearance of the six consciousness groups, one knows that appearances have no intrinsic nature, like stars and planets reflected in the sea. In the present, dwelling within reality itself, everything is realized as empty of intrinsic nature. This essence, the mysterious innate awareness, if actually seen, is a view that is free of fixated mental fabrication. There is no confusion about before, after, or in between, for it remains in the unborn. Engage in such a view, Pemasal."

"What is the procedure for meditation?"

"This is the nature of meditation. When this very essence of the above view is realized and internalized, to abide within that state is called 'meditation.' Moreover, to meditate dwelling in radiant emptiness, in the essence free of extremes, the body should be in the seven-point posture of Vairochana.[21] Then, meditate on the innate nature, radiant emptiness, complete as soon as you think of it. Stay free of thought, without attachment. Do not enter into a mental fixation about meditating. In the state with no concept of emptiness, unpolluted radiant knowing, whatever arises is naturally free.

"How do you meditate on that? Outwardly, there are the reflected appearances; inwardly, there are the perceived appearances of the sense organs and six consciousness groups; and secretly, there is the arising of the mind's dynamic energy. The instant that you fixate on the mode of being of any of it, recognize whatever occurs as thought and rest in a state free of elaboration, without fixation.

"When meditating on the true nature in this way, all kinds of subtle or obvious thoughts arise. Don't chase after thoughts of the past, or go out to greet thoughts of the future, or fool around with thoughts of the present. Rest in the continuity of whatever arises, without grasping. The one who thus rests is also empty of essence, like ice melting in water. If you abide in this state without any frame of reference, the experiences of bliss, clarity, and non-thought will arise. Endowed with essence, nature, and compassion, you will reach the perspective of the three kayas. Relying on that calm abiding (*shamata*), practice Cutting Through Resistance and Direct Crossing. Based on the four lamps, and experiencing the four visions, you will reach the place of extinction and become buddha in this life.[22]

"Until this is firmly attained, engage in the straight path of physical and verbal virtuous activity and exert yourself in the yoga of four sessions. Those are the sessions at dawn, in the morning, in the afternoon, and in the evening. In keeping the sessions of these four times without fail, you will maintain constant effort and pursue meditation. If you apply yourself to meditation in this way, you will attain the state of buddha in this life, Pemasal."

"What is the fundamental basis of conduct?"

"Princess, engage in the fundamental basis of conduct in this way. Do not come under the power of ordinary mind. To act in accordance with reality itself is to pay no heed to the ordinary purposes of this life, but to contemplate death and impermanence, to discard all worldly deeds, and to resist the power of deluded distractions. With the yogic discipline of no-needs having arisen in your being, keep to isolated places and mountain retreats. Give up whatever thoughts you have and reject all other activity. The conduct that is dharmic in nature is the conduct of the altruistic mind of awakening. With this, meditate on the beings of the six realms as your parents and act out of compassion and love.

"When you act within the meaning of reality itself, which is your own purpose, while acting within the meaning of meditation in true nature, then the force of conduct arising from it will be unimpeded. So without accepting or rejecting, abandoning or practicing, leave the fixation of performing actions in its own ground. When free of the act and performing the action, the dynamic energy of innate pristine wisdom will be perfect. Train in this conduct, Pemasal."[23]

"What is the way of attaining the fruition?"

"Princess, this is the way of attaining the fruition. There are two kinds of fruition: common and excellent. The common fruition is that, according to how you have practiced, your life span, merit, entourage, enjoyments, disciples, fame, power, magic, clairvoyance, and capability—all of these—happen without the need to hope for them but occur according to your wishes.

"The excellent fruition is this. Based on the creation and completion of recitation practices accomplished through all kinds of means and insight, the essence of the original innate nature is actualized. Gaining the pristine primal level,[24] you attain stability in the absolute essence without delusion. The two extremes of rejecting and accepting are exhausted. This is the fruition of reaching the level of exhaustion of all phenomena.

"After attaining the level of a nonreturner, there is no fixation on even the dharmakaya. Transcending all extremes, the level of primordial purity is the most excellent ultimate fruition."[25]

Then the princess inquired about her lives, saying: "Gracious One who knows the three times, what kind of births will I have after this? What sort of place and country? What kinds of karmic connections? What growth and decline, well-being and mishap, and so on? And finally what Dharma will I practice?" I, the master, responded as follows.

"Alas, listen to me, Princess. This is the succession of your lives. After passing from this life, for some years you will abide in the presence of the goddess Guhyajnana (Secret Wisdom) in the pure realm of Riwotala. Your father, Trisong Detsen, will dwell for some years in the presence of Manjushri in the pure realm of Five-Peaked Mountain. Then, after thirteen generations, he will take birth as one called Lord Nyang Ral[26] in a place called Tamshul in Lhodrak. He will open the door of the secret profound treasure from the side of the cliff of Sinmo Barje and reveal thirteen profound treasure troves.

"At that time, Princess, your birth will be in the new town of Lower Drak in Central Tibet. You will be born in the Dog year as the daughter of the father Sangye and the mother Getsoma. Both of them will die early on and you will become an orphan. At a young age you will encounter the Dharma. You will be known as Samten Kyi. When that very Lord Nyang Ral is taking out the treasure trove at Samye, by the compelling force of previous prayers, you will meet him there and he will guide you and take you as his wife. Three children will be born. Listening to the condensed essence of the most profound instructions of Orgyen, myself, you will practice them and realize the nature of awareness. Then you will be known as the Wisdom Woman Sangye Kyimo. Your entourage and possessions will increase and you will become a holder of the Secret Mantra doctrine.

"Your next birth will be in Layak, in Lhodrak, in a village of the area called Dzar. Your father's name will be Tsurpa Sangye and your mother Rinchen Zangcham Kyi. You will be born as their daughter in the female Monkey year and be called Pema Drön. At that time, Lord Nyang Ral will be born as the son of Pangru Kartön and Chimza Drönma Kyi. He will have the name Guru Chökyi Wangchuk. He will come to the area called Pangdrong and, beginning with Namkhai Chen, will take many of my profound treasures from their treasure sites. While working for the benefit of beings to be tamed, he will recognize that you are endowed by profound previous karmic connections and will take you as wife. Three children will be born. In order to uphold the Buddha's doctrine, you will build the *vihara* called Guru Temple and establish many beings in the virtuous Dharma.

"The life after that will be in the country called Tsangi Yeru, in the place called Trongsa. Your father will be the mantra adept Gezang, and your mother Drinchuk Samten Kyi. You will be born as their son, Rinchen Drak. After practicing the profound instructions and doing the recitation practice of the fierce mighty Iron Hair Hayagriva, you will meet that deity five times. Very great powers and abilities will be yours.

"In the next life you will be born in Lower Nyal in Drinthang as the son of humble parents of a lineage of mantra adepts, whose names are Rinzang and Dolcham. Born as Lendrel in the female Iron Hare year, you will have good faculties and a bright sensibility. At the age of fifteen you will encounter my profound treasure, revealing the *Dakini Innermost Essence* from the Danglung Cliff and the cycles of the *Planet Rahula* and *Vajrapani Suppressing Fierce Ones*. You will lead all those connected with you to the place of Great Bliss.[27] Since everybody will come under the power of evil, this success will last only a short while, and before you reach the age of fifty obstacles will set in. However, the benefit of your Dharma for sentient beings will endure for a long time.

"Then in Upper Dralung in Central Tibet, in a small area called Ngamshö, you will take birth in the Snake year as an intelligent boy named Tsuldor,[28] the son of Tenpa and Sönam Kyi. Skill in the five sciences will well up from the space of intelligence. Mainly teaching the explanations and practices of both Sutra and Tantra, and thoroughly dispensing the teachings to all without bias, you will ensure the continuity of the Buddhist doctrine. Finally, at a later time, you will be born in the Bumthang region."

"What were the lives before those?"

"Princess, listen, karmically endowed one. As for the lives before all of those, though you wish me to explain the birth succession, there is no limit, no way to say, 'This is the beginning of cyclic existence.' Until the attainment of buddhahood there is no limit, no way to reach the end of cyclic existence. Nobody knows—don't you understand? As for the sequence of births of sentient beings, even I cannot find the limit of their rebirths. Nevertheless, before those lives of yours, I do know something more, but there is no point in making you inadvertently gloomy."

With tears welling up and short of breath, the princess again pleaded, "Great Master, all together, what are my lives?"

"Before those lives, you were born as the elder queen of the King of Maguta. Then after seven lives as a human, you were born as yourself, the daughter of a king. By the force of your prayers to meet me, Padma, there will be a sequence of six births, Princess, some of them female and some of them male. Of those births that are of noble, fine family, the three as male will be the series of treasure-revealers. The two female ones also will engage in two treasure teachings."

"At the final birth, when born in Bumthang, what will be the places and countries, what family and background, and what will be the names of the parents?"

"The manner of your final birth[29] is this. It will be in the center of the place called Chökor in Bumthang, in an isolated place that looks like the fringe of an umbrella, in the middle of the place surrounded on three sides by forest, at a small place called Baridrang. You will be the son of Döndrup Zang of the Nyö clan and the nomad Palkyi Dzo. Born in the Horse-Snake year,[30] you will be named Pema.

"Your body will be stocky and your skin red, your torso adorned with five birthmarks, and between the two shoulder blades on the back will be a red mole marked like a curved knife and lotus. On the back of the right hand the decoration of the veins will look like an *ah*, and at the heart will be a relic the size of a pea. You will experience visions, and the desirous mind will be destroyed. You will speak harsh words like the neighing of a horse. Doing various Dharma and non-Dharma activities, you will receive much criticism and slander, but altruism will inspire you, and you will guide whomever connects with you to the supreme way."

"In this final birth, what are the times of revealing the profound treasures and how many treasures will be revealed?"

"Princess, faithful one of virtuous mind, the profound treasures that you will encounter are such. In the Monkey year, when you are twenty-seven, the sacred *Quintessence of the Mysteries*[31] will be taken out from the Burning Lake. Then, as you will find a series of addresses, your empowered treasure teachings will be these: *The Total Union of Intention, The Supreme Intention, Jewel Ocean* from the teaching of the Mind Section, *The Lamp That Illuminates the Darkness, Refuge of All Cyclic Existence, The Most Secret Essence, The Complete Supreme Meaning, Dakini Innermost Essence, Vajrasattva Clear Light Tantra, The Great Tantra of Seventeen, The Secret Tantra of the Sun, The Small Child Tantra, The Nine Cycles of the Most Secret*, and the cycles of instruction on completion phase.[32]

"Then, the nine cycles of yidam recitation practice: *Yamantaka, Hayagriva, Vajrapani, Kilaya, Amitayus, (Eight Herukas) Most Secret Mirror of the Mind, Iron Hair Hayagriva*, and both *Peaceful Guru* and *Wrathful Guru*. These are the nine cycles of the supreme most secret.[33]

"The cycles of the dakinis are, similarly, *Ocean of Shortcuts, Wrathful Black One, Red Varahi, Vajrayogini*, and *Sarasvati*. These are the five Dharma precepts of the dakinis.[34]

"These are the cycles of the protectors from the *Blazing Meteorite Vajra Tantra: Maning, Ekadzati, Black Vitality Devil, Excellent Planet, Red-Black Phungje, Vajrasadhu, Lion-Faced Demon Master, Glorious Goddess*, and *Pekar*. These are the cycles of the protectors.[35]

"There are many other miscellaneous cycles. All those profound treasures, none excluded, will be revealed by you in your final rebirth."

"Great Master, what karmically endowed individuals will come to uphold those profound treasures?"

"The individuals to uphold the treasure teachings are these. One called Drakpa will come from Yarlung, one called Shönnu Darma will come from Kongpo, and Könchok, Sönam, Gyaltsen, Senge, Tashi, and Palden, these six karmically endowed ones will come from Kham. Dharma masters from Kongpo will be Chöjor, Göndor, Namgyal, Kundrak, Sönam, Paljor, Rinchen Senge, and Dorje Palden. These will be the eight Dharma masters of Kongpo. Five Dharma masters of Tsang will be Shakyapa, Gangzangpa, Chölungpa,

Lodröpa, and Tulkuwa. Drupnyak and Kudrak will be the two Dharma masters from Central Tibet. Lodrö and Kundrak will be the Dharma masters of Latö. One named Sönam and one named Norbu, and Longyangpa and Palden, these four will be the Dharma masters of Lhodrak. Zöpa, Yidam, Tulku, and Tapkhe, these four will be the Dharma masters of Nyalo. Gyamtso, Rinchen, and Tashi will be the three Dharma masters from Bumthang.

"Aside from those, Dharma masters from various other places and many karmically endowed individuals will appear. Keeping the Dharma lineage, they will enhance the benefit for beings and keep the living vitality of the Buddha's doctrine."

"In that final life of mine, what benefit will I accomplish for sentient beings with my body, speech, mind, qualities, and activities? How long will I live, and then what pure realm will I be born in?"

"Princess, faithful one, listen to me. The countries where you will benefit beings with your body are throughout Lhodrak and Bhutan. Your speech will benefit those karmically endowed disciples and all those of faith impartially. Your mind will benefit faithful men and women and all objects of compassion without exception. Your qualities will directly benefit those receptive spiritual heirs and will clear up the doubts of all beings. Your activity will benefit all beings impartially, since you will apply whatever is effective impartially to whomever comes into contact with you.

"In Bhutan, Central Tibet, Tsang, Kongpo, and Kham you will be the unrivaled supporter of the Secret Mantra doctrine. If you do not come under the power of evil conditions and obstacles through involvement in the faults of sacred pledge breakers and so on, you will reach the end of your life span as this noble person at seventy-six. If you accomplish longevity through confession, fulfillment, and so on, and do my, Padma's, most profound practices, you could even live until the age of eighty.

"When you reach the end of this noble life, you will be surrounded by an entourage of a hundred ranking scholars[36] and a gathering of your inner circle entourage. Ten thousand people with karmic connection, twelve hundred with connection through prayers, eleven spiritual children connected through the profound crucial meaning, seven spiritual children that keep the mandala, three who have emerged as heart sons, thirty karmically endowed patrons, as well as many of the faithful will come.

"Those who have made a connection through the Dharma and empowerments will be reborn at the level of awareness-holders if infractions or flaws in their sacred pledge don't occur. People who have made a connection through money and food will be born wealthy and powerful in the next life. Even those who have only seen, heard, thought of, or touched you will be born as subjects to be influenced. Anyone who has been involved with you physically, if they do not turn back on the path, will attain the state of awareness-holder after abandoning their female bodies. Whoever has a connection, even a worm, will begin the spiritual path."

"In the future, when finding these treasures, what about the noble people who will hold the lineage, spiritual sons and daughters, faithful patrons, attendants with a connection, field of disciples, and propagation of Dharma empowerments? What sort of happiness and suffering, heights and depths, acclaim for activities, obstacles, conditions, and so on, will befall me?"

"Princess, at a future time, those who are now connected with you, the princess—male and female Dharma practitioners, masters, household servants, subjects, attendants, cooks, close friends, and maids, all the women connected with you, and the skeptical men and women who criticize you— some of them will be born as the children of lineage holders, some as princes and princesses, some as monks and disciples, some as faithful patrons, and some as attendants and servants. Of those women connected, some will be wives and *mudra* partners. The subjects and attendants will come into the realm of those to be influenced. Of those who are skeptical now, some will become the disciples of evil incarnations, some will forswear their sacred pledge, some will be rivals, some critics, and some skeptics. Of the entourage connected with you, some will possess faith and the sacred pledge and some will not; all types will come. At that time, girls of noble race will be attracted and all will become disciples, since you will have the name Pema. Finally, in the pure realm of Chamara, they will come to dwell together with me, without unity or separation. They will all be of harmonious signs and family.

"Because of some bad sorts who do not keep their sacred pledge, some evil will occur that causes obstacles to your life span. It is important to be discerning so as not to make mistakes. Vow-breakers, charlatans, con artists, and those clever in the ways of the world will appear. Since, as is said, 'If the Dharma is profound, the evil is profound,' it is important that the auspices be correct. Therefore, although you are certainly karmically endowed, it is possible that the auspices might come together or might not, so it is important to examine them minutely. There will come a mixed crowd of pure and impure among those to be tamed who are karmically endowed. Nevertheless, you will influence their attitudes.

"As for yourself, there will alternate prosperity and misfortune, heights and depths, since in all lives one does some virtue and some wrongdoing. The propagation of the Dharma, as explained before, will ultimately be widespread. As for acclaim, there will be both positive and negative reports and various undeserved criticisms. Every kind of malicious accusation will be leveled. As for evil forces, many will come causing anger and passion. Whatever you think, meditate with compassion. Take careful account of your own conduct. By the power and efficacy of profound prayer, negative connections will nevertheless be brought under your control. Since the evil obstacles that may occur are not known, avoid pledge-breakers and such. There will be many people bearing passion, anger, and bad food,[37] so be meticulous. Reject methods that rely on mudra partners of bad family. Persevere in feast fulfillment, confession fulfillment, and restoring fulfillment, and exert effort in the longevity practices. The sentient beings of the degenerate, bad times would look for faults even if the Buddha came. Having taken care of your own welfare, maintain compassion for beings for the sake of others. That is the practice of all victorious ones."

The princess, her face cleansed by tears, asked, "After completing the beneficial activity for the subjects to be influenced, will I be able to go to Chamara or not? Will my karmically endowed spiritual children go with me wherever I am born? Will those connected with me be born after me or not? If I go to Chamara, what fruition of the four kinds of awareness-holders[38] will I obtain?"

"Princess of excellent virtuous mind, captivating goddess, through good karmic connections you will meet me again and again from now on, and each time the previous karmic connection will grow. You, stricken by moving tears of devotion, your supplications made in heartfelt faith will always be achieved. With my great compassionate affection, how could I not grant blessings, excellent child? We will actually meet in meditative experiences and dreams. When you have brought out your destined treasures, you will live without obstacle, benefiting beings, until the age of sixty-eight, or, if obstacles to your life are removed, until the age of eighty or seventy-six.

"Finally in Chamara, in the presence of Orgyen, you will attain the body of the spontaneous presence awareness-holder. At that time all those who have the karma of being connected with you will attain various states of development on the levels and paths, and will definitely come to dwell together with you. By the great force of your prayers now, at that time they will come together in the pure realm. Having achieved pure appearance, you will accomplish boundless benefit for beings with your emanations in a hundred million worlds, through deeds of body, speech, and mind, for as long as the three realms of cyclic existence are not empty."

"Orgyen Rinpoche, before that happens, when the one named Pema is engaging in the treasure teachings, what other Dharma connections will there be aside from those destined teachings? What signs and proofs will there be of correctly engaging in knowledge?"

"Princess, listen, beloved child. In that last life of yours, when you are involved in my profound treasures, aside from those that are your own destined Dharma, there are some others, new and old, oral and treasure, that you will be impartially involved with and reveal. In particular, in the two lives,[39] you will discover *The Great Completion Supreme Dharma*, three cycles of *Radiant Expanse Innermost Essence*, *The Union of Samantabhadra's Intentions*, *Jewel Ocean*, *Perfection of Supreme Meaning*[40] and all the treasure teachings that I hid in Tibet, more profound than which do not exist, like the heart's blood.

"In the creation and completion phases of all of them you will exert effort and take up practice. You will comprehend every kind of knowledge without study due to the karmic propensity of your previous training. This intellectual insight means that you will be learned in the meaning of both Sutra and Mantra, and since training was previously accomplished, the realizations will arise from within. You will not have to feign your conduct, and because you will comprehend arising, freedom, and hidden faults, you will cultivate the potential of means and insight, and your debates will remain unrepudiated, revealing this brilliant awareness.

"You will be unskilled in relations with people, and heedlessly you will speak the unequivocal words of your experiences. Being a hero endowed with means, women will gather around you. With the voice of Brahma, you will enchant disciples. With a fine youthful body, you'll say anything at all. Being very volatile yourself, others will not take your perspective. You will practice the Dharma in unpredictable ways and perform the secret conduct. In your effort to possess the abilities and signs, you'll engage in all kinds of deeds without pretense. At that time, when you gain all good qualities, all kinds of evil obstacles may be conjured up. Be precise in your investigation and foresight."

"If those are the precepts for training, how does one engage in proper Dharma?"

"Princess, this is how to engage in the Dharma properly. With the fierce heartache of death and impermanence, recollect the sufferings of the ocean of cyclic existence. A sense of urgency arises in your being, and with that yogic discipline, respectfully attend an authentic lama with the devotion that sees the lama as the actual Buddha, and obey the lama's precepts without transgressing them. With a longing not impelled by concern for body or life, in a state of nonattachment to anything you might have, you would offer even your own heart if it would please the lama. Even without obtaining instructions, just stay to please the lama, attending for many months and years.

"After hearing many profound instructions, practice them strenuously just as instructed, with total resolution of mind, and with understanding you can begin training. Guard your sacred pledge as you would your own eyes, and, without breaking even the most minor of the lama's commands, listen to whatever is advised and practice it diligently. Those are the first most important things.

"Afterward, when doing the practice, develop enthusiasm. Don't be corrupted or touched by the stains of the eight worldly concerns. If you keep to the crucial points of the profound instructions, experiential realization will cause definite renunciation and dissatisfaction with worldly matters to arise. Never be separated from that heartfelt repulsion toward cyclic existence. If you put aside your own purposes, altruism arises. With high realization, meticulous behavior, and great repulsion, the mode of being arises from within. Cultivate sacred outlook impartially toward all. Having engaged in the view, meditation, and fruition properly, you will reach the ultimate view of emptiness and compassion. The great purpose of both self and others will be accomplished.

"To so cherish the Dharma is indeed important. Those lacking that authentic approach, the 'Dharma practitioners' of the degenerate times, do not engage in proper view and conduct. With no time to listen, they long to meditate. With no time to meditate, they long to explain. Not matured themselves, they long to empower others. Not free themselves, they teach experiential guidance to others. Those with no meditation do fake meditation. Those with no realization offer fake realization. Those with no freedom offer fake freedom. Those with no experience make a lot of noise about emptiness. Their outer appearance is of venerable scholars, proclaiming themselves. Doing their recitations, they portray a false image of erudition. Those with no qualities label the faults of others. What are their names? Chöjé, Rinpoche, Tokden, Siddha, Loppon, Khenpo, Gomchen, Yogin, Monk, Geshe, and Sangha.[41] They are labeled with these pure names, these Dharma practitioners dressed up in fancy red cloth and silk. Many a one has been seen here in Tibet.

"Generally, in this bad, degenerate time, the signs that evil blessings have struck will be that a charlatan is preferred to a fine individual and that a gift of a morsel of tasty food is preferred to heartfelt explanation of instructions. Without realization in subjective meditational experience, practitioners will look to assemble the conducive external conditions. Since there are so many kinds of savages and criminals, no one will be able to be a great meditator in the mountains, so in general those great meditators will have no realization. The monks will have no discipline, the realized ones no sacred pledge, and the mantra adepts no powers. Disciples of bold lamas will gather around to sell their own fame. Girls without vows will secretly sleep with the clergy. Delinquent boys will sleep in secret with nuns. The crevices in the walls of monasteries will be full of the corpses of the clergy's illegitimate infant boys and girls.

"They will say they are practicing Secret Mantra but will have no quality of the path of means. They will say they have discipline but will keep no vows. The profound esoteric instructions will be sold for wealth. Diligence will all go to creating curses and adversity. Dharma language will be broadcast by lay people, and in the philosophical language of emptiness, all women will be esteemed. Keeping their teacher secret, disciples will broadcast their own greatness. Many will be those who desire Dharma, but few who desire a lama. The fortunate noble person whose karma from previous training has awakened, just the few who have not regressed before the end of their aspirations, the few who truly practice the Dharma, will be scattered outside of Tibet and few will remain."

"If those are the points of training to engage in Dharma, what is the procedure for the practice of Dharma activities?"

"Princess, girl, daughter of my heart, here is the procedure for practice of the meaningful supreme Secret Mantra.

"First, there is the meditation of all appearance as the deity. Meditate that all appearing form is the nature of the deity. The wisdom being and the sacred pledge being, those two should be known as inseparably one.

"Second, there is the resounding of sounds. Meditate on all sounds in the external world, as well as the language of beings within that world, as being the sound of the mantra being recited.

"Third, there is all the mental activity that causes thoughts and memories to move. Within emptiness without fixation, meditate at ease in the state of knowing that there is nothing to be done about existence.

"Fourth, there is the procedure for circumambulation. Whenever you go anywhere, imagine that in the empty space to your right, on a seat made up of a thousand-petaled lotus, sun, and moon, is your own root lama surrounded by a multitude of victorious ones. Surrounding are the boundless buddhas of the ten directions and the host of yidam deities, heroes, and dakinis, in immeasurable numbers. Imagine that all beings, led by yourself, circumambulate them, purifying obscurations. By meditating in this way, boundless qualities will arise.

"Fifth, there is the procedure for sitting. Wherever you stay, in any place whatsoever, meditate that it is the palace of the yidam deity. Within it, perceive yourself as the yidam deity. In the state of great uncontrived mind itself, think that you will stay until cyclic existence is emptied. This is the special procedure for profound sitting.

"Sixth, there is the procedure for reclining. Perceiving yourself as the yidam deity, recline in a comfortable bed with the intention of grasping luminosity and dreams. After meditating on the lama in the center of your heart, lie on your right side with your hand under your head and abide in uncontrived mind itself, free of thought. If you recline in that state of reality itself, luminosity will arise. It is the quality of profound sleep.

"Seventh, there is the procedure for getting up. When you get up from bed in the morning, visualize clearly according to the words of the creation phase. With no frame of reference to yourself, from within emptiness, think that the illusory form of compassion is produced to engage in the benefit of beings to be influenced. Meditation causes emptiness and compassion to be fully present. With that, having abandoned all thoughts of ordinary being, you arise as the nature of the yidam deity.

"Eighth, there is the procedure for going to eat, drink, and feast rituals. Visualize yourself as the yidam deity and imagine that in front of you is the vessel, a qualified skull cup, vast and wide. Visualizing the essence of the five meats and five nectars, imagine your hand as the vajra ladle and, saying *om ah hung*, stir the contents. The root and lineage lamas are in your throat, the yidam deities in the heart, and the dakinis, heroes, and Dharma protectors in the navel. Others are everywhere, like a burst sack of sesame seeds. Creating this field of visualization in yourself, and imagining that you are offering the feast to it, partake of the food and drink yourself. Then, throw the leftover food in front, saying *om ah hung*. Visualizing the karmic debts of the six realms, give it away. Then, thinking that the victorious ones are pleased, seal the practice with the dedication prayers. If you do this, it will not be ordinary food; the gathering of the two accumulations will be boundless; and it will become the sublime accomplishment of prosperity. This is the sublimely profound procedure for eating and drinking.

"Ninth, there is the procedure for washing away flaws and obscurations. Visualize yourself as Vajrasattva and imagine in the heart on the mandala of the moon the letter *hung* encircled by the hundred syllables. By your recitation of the hundred syllables, imagine that stainless, pure water flows down. As you recite, begin to urinate. First, fill your palm and offer it as 'first fruits,' then drink a handful of it and, with what is left over, wash yourself clean. Meditate that flaws, infractions, and mental obscurations are all purified. By doing this, all flaws and obscurations are purified. Your senses are clarified, and your constitution is invigorated. This is the profound procedure for washing.

"Tenth, there is the procedure of the path. If you pursue the path properly with intense diligence, the immediate and ultimate qualities will be measureless, for the Vajrayana is the especially eminent, profound path of means and auspicious connections.

"Eleventh, there is the procedure for meditating on the true nature. All abiding should be free of the delusion of distraction. When abiding within the true nature practice, the body should be arranged in whatever position is comfortable. Then phenomenal appearance, the conceptualizations of the objective appearance of the six consciousness groups, and the activities that arise from the mind naturally are dispatched as innately free without fixation from the mind's mode of being. This is the procedure for meditating on the true nature.

"Twelfth, there is Cutting Through Resistance (*trekchö*) and Direct Crossing (*tögal*). At this time of manifesting the practice, make the three unmoving states[42] the basis and, without wavering, cut through the resistance of fixating on whatever arises. Then, without meditation and without distraction, naturally resting in the expanse, open the door to the four radiant lamps and reach the level of exhaustion, the final practice of the four visions. That is the procedure for Cutting Through Resistance and Direct Crossing.

"Thirteenth, there is abiding in the expanse of reality. Combining the expanse and awareness, the wisdom vase body empowerment is the fruition of the three bodies inseparable. Abide within the unborn dharmakaya, the innate abiding of dharmakaya: this is the procedure.

"In this way, value these thirteen procedures in whatever Dharma and practice you do: in all of the common and special practices, and in particular those that follow me, Orgyen, in the practice of the profound treasure Dharma."

"How should I meditate on the protection circle in order to protect myself from obstacles?"

"Princess of good family, child of my mind, when engaging in the meaning of the profound Secret Mantra, the meditation on the protection circle is crucial in order to protect against outer and inner obstacles. There are two aspects of this: peaceful and wrathful.

"First, there is the peaceful protection circle. Meditate that you are the Great Compassionate One, Avalokiteshvara, white in color, with one face and four arms, as big as a mountain, filling the whole place. Visualize this with the clarity of it being insubstantial appearance, in a state without shifting, moving, or changing, at all times and situations. The obstructing forces of the six realms are all invoked. With immeasurable compassion, thinking, 'I will achieve the welfare of all beings,' meditate on the aspiration of awakening. Whatever obstructing force sees you will feel joy and devotion, and in that state will want to achieve your welfare. With such joyful thoughts, causing you an obstacle would be impossible.

"Second, there is the meditation of the wrathful protection circle. Meditate that you are the Mighty Great Padma Hayagriva, large and heavy of limb, fierce and terrifying, standing in advancing posture with one leg up, in awesome splendor. In the midst of the hair on the head is a green horse head that neighs three times. Imagine the eight classes of gods and demons brought under control. Think that one neigh imposes the command and commitment. Three neighs crush obstacles and forces, and, like ashes carried away by the wind, they are scattered out of sight in the ten directions. A tent of weapons emanates from your heart. Above, below, and in every intermediate direction it becomes a weapon tent of vajras, axes, swords, wheels, crosses, and such. Imagine that all the obstructing forces are terrified and panicked and are blown away to the other side of the outer ocean, where even the wind of the eons won't free them. Then meditate that in all the intermediate places, from all your hair follicles and pores, appear many miniature wrathful beings to protect you, carrying weapons and vibrating like stars. Practice like this and nothing can enter to create obstacles. This very profound protection circle should always be employed when doing practice."

"When one is meditating on the protection circle, what should the main practice be? What is more important, one's own or others' welfare? And commonly, by what activity should one achieve it?"

"Listen, you enchanting princess. To mainly pursue your own welfare, accomplish the three kayas and practice the instructions of the secret guidance. To pursue the welfare of others, the benefit of beings, give guidance and empowerments and accumulate actions for others' sake. If you desire to meet me, practice the mystery and always supplicate me. If you desire to attract oathbound ones and dakinis, exert yourself in feast rituals and fulfillment amendments. If you desire to attract the Dharma protectors as subjects, do the creation phase, recitations, and torma rituals. To engender the physical experience of bliss-emptiness, rely on a mudra partner. If you desire to eliminate obstacles to long life, avoid recreants who have broken their sacred pledge. If you desire to bring beings under your control, meditate on the aspiration of awakening and give up prejudice. If you desire greater prosperity, offer whatever feast rituals there are to the lama. If you desire to engender physical strength, exert diligence in acquiring vitality through longevity practice and through a qualified woman.

"Give up concentrating on this life and practice the absolute. Contemplate the proximity of death and cultivate the attitude of needing nothing at all. Direct your mind to what is transcendent and make the Three Jewels your sublime refuge. This will cause the qualities to arise from within; realization will manifest, and, if meaningful, the energy of compassion will arise. Insofar as someone is connected with you, whatever you touch will become meaningful.

"Until that is the case, apply yourself enthusiastically in seclusion. If you do that, then whatever you do for the welfare of yourself and others will ultimately be achieved and you will become a glorious guide of beings. These are my personal instructions. Hold every one of them in your heart, Princess."

"Oh, Orgyen Rinpoche! Please tell me about the times and the spread or decline of the doctrine in terms of human activities at the end of the teachings of my final life."

"Princess, faithful one, listen to me. Toward the end of the life of your final birth, during the increase of the five degenerations, the doctrine will decline. Human life span will be about fifty in that age of swords. It will be the time when the nine gongpo⁴³ brothers arrive in Tibet from China. Gongpo spirits will enter the hearts of all people, so it will be a time of various perverse actions. The doctrines of both Sutra and Mantra will decline, so although it seems about to increase, accomplishment will be very rare. When children won't listen to their parents, it will be a time of empty anarchy and chaos.

"At that time, in Lower Yarlung, the karma will ripen for the royal lineage. Hor-like non-Hors⁴⁴ will invade and there will be eighteen great clan chiefs. They will disagree among themselves and their fighting will cause armies to agitate like oceans in Central Tibet and Yor. Both Lhasa and Samye will be involved in the fighting. After an uprising of subjects from Tsang, Lhodrak will be permanently destroyed and Bumthang decisively affected. A Hor camp will be established below Lhotö Deu and above Lhomé Kharchu. From Kong in the east, toxic lakes of armies will overflow. They will make a fortress at each passage. It is a time when the hidden lands will open up on their own, when the earth cannot keep its treasures and overflows itself, a time gripped by the disease of despair.

"It will be a time when theologians are generals and clergymen are commanders; when monks can't keep discipline, and Secret Mantra practitioners can't keep their sacred pledge. It will be a time of internal strife among monastic orders, when practitioners seek refuge in lay people, when women are regarded as high, when lay people speak the language of Dharma, and girls give advice. It will be a time of wearing incongruous hats and clothes. The learned clergy will stay among the masses, women will buy poison to apply,⁴⁵ and lamas will wander around like dogs. It will be a time when the Secret Mantra strays into Bön, the doors to empowerment conferrals are suppressed, esoteric instructions are explained to crowds, and charlatans confer fake empowerments. Noble beings will cultivate fields. Dharma practitioners will have gross attachments and aversions, nuns will be nannies,⁴⁶ and noble beings will renege on their oaths. It will be a time when half the people die from weapons and plagues, and epidemics rage without cure; a time when the ebb and flow of the elements is out of balance, with many deadly hailstorms on the crops.

"The omens of these things occurring are a thundering in the sky, the comet of Pöd coming five times from the north, Crystal Mountain Cliff of Yarlung cracking, and the mountain of Zotang Gongpo burning. When vultures land on Skull Mountain, the times will be beset by all kinds of disorder.

"At that time, pity the poor Tibetans! The retribution for the royal decrees and royal lineage will be disgrace, for the temples and monastic orders it will be suppression, and for the patriarchy it will be disruption by internal strife. Nevertheless, temporarily at that time some happiness and joy will be possible. Certainly many individuals with qualities of learning and religion, such as spiritual adepts and so on, will appear. However, the growth and decline of the doctrine will be like the sun in spring.

"There will be lay people giving perverse advice, fighting among factions, fighting in the mountains of the great meditators, recreant masters, practitioners full of passion and aggression, and internal strife among mantra adepts. With all that inappropriate behavior, the protectors of the world and the gods and spirits who favor the Buddha's doctrine will avert their faces inside Supreme Mountain and the dark evil forces will face outward. Each year it will grow worse. At that time, fakes with no treasures will pretend to be treasure-revealers and try to help beings with the teachings of their nontreasures. This means that discernment will be of utmost importance. Dharma and non-Dharma, authentic and inauthentic, must be carefully distinguished.

"The import of this is to not misidentify the authentic lama but to seek one who truly holds the transmission of the victorious ones. After requesting the complete instructions from such a one, in a secluded place follow the practice that was granted. If you apply yourself to the practice, the blessings of the Lama Jewel will enter, purifying the obscurations of body, speech, and mind, and you will gain the fruition of the three kayas."

"Please give me a method to eliminate obstructions and benefit the doctrine."

"Princess, you of virtuous mind, listen. Here is a method for benefiting the doctrine. In the first month of spring of the new year, during a favorable astrological transit, collect the five precious substances,[47] five grains, five fine silks, and five medicinal substances. Gather the three whites and three sweets[48] and foods with essential vitality. In an amulet box made of the earth element that has been thoroughly baked in the fire and decorated with the implements of the five buddha families, pour the substances and bind up the openings. Go to places in the four directions of east, south, west, and north, and on the mountaintops and high peaks hide the vases of substances as treasures. Proclaim the truth to the gods and spirits of the mountains. They bear witness and will obey your command. Also say a prayer of your desires:

Gods, *menmo* goddesses,[49] planetary forces, *tsen* spirits,[50] evil forces, *nagas*, and earth lords of this mountain; all of you gods and demons of phenomenal appearance, by my hiding of this profound treasure, make it rain during the rainy season, make it always a most prosperous year, stop the spread of diseases in humans and cattle, pacify the fighting of the time, diminish the era of weapons, and make everything happy and auspicious for all beings.

Saying this, you address the eight classes of gods and demons equally. If you do this each year, deadly hailstorms and famines will be prevented in that area, the current fighting armies will be pacified, disease and plagues will not occur, and all beings will be well and happy."

The princess prostrated and circumambulated and said, "All this that the Guru has told, these questions and answers, this girl will not forget and will put into practice." Then the daughter of the king, the girl Pemasal, took Orgyen's feet and placed them on her head, saying, "Lord Guru Rinpoche, so that I will always have a meaningful connection, please look after me in all my lives and pray that I will be born finally in Chamara." As she said that, her face filled with tears.

"You, princess endowed with faith," I replied, "from now on until you attain buddhahood, I will look after you wherever you are born. You, Princess, and all beings, male and female, will enter the door of the profound ripening and liberating Secret Mantra due to the power of the prayers that I will make. All those connected in whatever way now, in the future, on the peak of the Glorious Mountain of Chamara, will come before me and all the male and female awareness-holders. When every one of all those karmically endowed ones has gathered there, we will speak of the ripening and liberating creation and completion and will turn the wheel of the Dharma day and night.

"Realizing the crucial point of intrinsic awareness, may we come to abide in the state of dharmakaya, inseparable from the primordial lord Amitabha in the Land of Bliss in the west."

After I made this prayer, the princess said, "Orgyen Padma, lord of beings in the three times, I supplicate forever your uninterrupted kindness. Wherever I am born, wherever I live, always regard me with the compassion of a mother for a child. From now on until I attain buddhahood, hold me with compassion, never being apart for even an instant. Write down the words of this dialogue that is like refined gold, and hide it as profound treasure so that I may meet with it again in the future, in my final life."

She requested this, and so I, Orgyen, wrote this down and hid it in the Mendo Cliff in Lhodrak. In the future may my child named Pema, who has the yogic discipline, find it. With this prayer I hide it in Mendo.

SAMAYA GYA GYA GYA MATATVA TER GYA BE GYA TE GYA KATAM
ITI

sacred pledge; sealed sealed sealed; matatva; treasure seal; hidden seal; entrusted seal; keep quiet; iti!

I, Pema Lingpa, brought this forth from the Lion-Faced Cliff of Mendo in Lhodrak.

The Dialogue of Princess Trompa Gyen and the Guru

FROM *LAMA JEWEL OCEAN*[1]

Homage to Padma, the awareness-holder.

WHEN ORGYEN PADMASAMBHAVA was dwelling at Samye Chim-phu, Princess Tsomo and twenty-one ladies requested instructions from him. Among them was a girl, pleasing and beautiful to behold, more like a child of the gods than of humans, Princess Trompa Gyen. She took her mother's jeweled goblet with lotus designs, filled it with grape wine, and offered it to Orgyen, saying:

> Alas, Orgyen Rinpoche! In general, all women, but especially myself,
> have accumulated bad karma in previous lives and have taken the form
> of a woman.

> With such a poor body as this,
> We have no hope besides our fathers,
> But fathers do not hold girls dear.
> We have no love besides our mothers,
> But mothers and daughters go separate ways.
> Our thoughts are with our brothers,
> But brothers barter sisters as merchandise.
> Fathers, mothers, and brothers confer,
> While girls are left to cyclic existence.
> Hold me with love and compassion,
> I pray from my heart!

> Our minds seek virtue in the Dharma,
> But girls are not free to follow it.
> Rather than risk a lawsuit,
> We stay with even bad spouses.

Avoiding bad reputations,
We are stuck in the swamp of cyclic existence.
Orgyen Padmasambhava,
Hold me with love and compassion,
I pray from my heart!

In youth we forget the divine Dharma
And make bad karma while housekeeping.
In old age we remember the divine Dharma,
But our powers have deteriorated.
Orgyen Padmasambhava,
Hold me with love and compassion,
I pray from my heart!

Deceived by devils on the way,
We err when stepping out.
Chased by the winds of bad karma,
We enter the swamp of cyclic existence.
Orgyen Padmasambhava,
Hold me with love and compassion,
I pray from my heart!

Girls, having little intelligence,
Must ask a man for counsel.
But ascending champions are rare,
So we find no guide toward the Dharma.
The power of descending evildoers is great,
So we listen to everyone's deluded advice.
Orgyen Padmasambhava,
Hold me with love and compassion,
I pray from my heart!

Leaving our happy homelands,
We wander in a man's distant country.
Though we accumulate wealth ourselves,
It is the new wives who use it.
Orgyen Padmasambhava,
Hold me with love and compassion,
I pray from my heart!

Though despair and remorse arise,
There is no one to teach the true goal.
Though tears flow uncontrollably,
They say it is just a girl's acting.
Orgyen Padmasambhava,
Hold me with love and compassion,
I pray from my heart!

Though remorse is born from the heart,
There is no one to show compassion.
Though we plan to enter the Dharma,
Doubts creep into our minds,
So there is no way to enter the Dharma.
Orgyen Padmasambhava,
Hold me with love and compassion,
I pray from my heart!

Women, who are so stupid,
Do not come to understand the Dharma.
Girls, who are so angry,
Are caught in deceit, hypocrisy, and cheating.
Orgyen Padmasambhava,
Hold me with love and compassion,
I pray from my heart!

Distracted by worldly activities,
We have no chance to meet a lama.
If we do stay with a lama,
His wife comes yelling.
Orgyen Padmasambhava,
Hold me with love and compassion,
I pray from my heart!

Though we stay in strict, isolated retreat,
We encounter vile enemies.
Though we do our Dharma practices,
Bad conditions and obstacles interfere.
Orgyen Padmasambhava,
Hold me with love and compassion,

I pray from my heart!

From the full ripening of previous accumulations,
We have taken this current bad body.
Sublime father, Orgyen Padma,
Close the door to rebirth as a woman!
Orgyen Padmasambhava,
Hold me with love and compassion,
I pray from my heart!

Next time let me obtain a male body
And become independent,
So that I can exert myself in the Dharma
And obtain the fruition of buddhahood.
Orgyen Padmasambhava,
Hold me with love and compassion,
I pray from my heart!

Consider my meaning in your heart!
Hold me with compassion!
So I can escape the suffering of afflictive emotion,
Rescue me from the swamp of cyclic existence!
Orgyen Padmasambhava,
Hold me with love and compassion,
I pray from my heart!

I, Orgyen, considered this and thought, "This girl is not beset by doubts or a divided mind. She has given rise to heartfelt remorse over cyclic existence. She seems to have a sincere yearning to practice Dharma. If I do not teach her a Dharma that will affect her deeply, remorse about cyclic existence will not continue to arise and the Dharma will not stay in her mind." Thinking this, I answered her with this song:

Listen and consider this, Trompa Gyen.
As for what helps, relatives will not help.
Having forsaken the true goal, divine Dharma,
You prefer neurotic cyclic existence.
Having abandoned homeland, you roam in a man's country.
Having forsaken your parents, you rely on a husband.

Having forsaken your siblings, you honor another's loved ones.
Having forsaken your own priorities, you serve another.
Alienated one who has abandoned parents,
Faithful one who endures these unpleasantries,
You are the earliest to rise in the morning
And the last to sleep at night.
Your painful, heavy load of work increases
As you slave to provide food and clothes.
You exert yourself day and night
At all of this busywork,
But when your bad-tempered husband arrives
You cannot even complete the work.
He'll rage, "You ugly old woman."
You suffer but get no gratitude.
Your stiffened back carries the load of karmic ripening.
Now, having obtained this very human body,
Which is like arriving in the golden land of jewels,
Will you return empty-handed, Trompa Gyen?
Dharmaless woman abandoning homeland,
Wageless woman serving men,
When the lord of death gives orders,
The counsel of your own lord won't help.
Eloquent girl, what will you do?
If you attend your husband, an actual devil,
You don't attend a lama, a true friend.
Even though a girl thinks of following the lama, the true friend,
She'll change her mind later, and then what will happen?
Even though a girl thinks about Dharma,
Hoarded wealth won't give her a chance.
You, stingy one, what will you do?
When you are wrapped up in your death shroud,
You'll leave behind your fine, soft clothes and go.
What can your workers do about it?
When you leave your body and it's hidden in a cemetery,
However fine your mansion, you'll leave it behind and go.
What can your builders do?
When the time has come to go all by yourself, alone,
The gathering of family and parents won't help.
What can those relatives do?

Listen and consider, Trompa Gyen!
Although you are the daughter of a king,
Once you enter a man's door you are a servant.
If you try to put off the backbreaking pain of work,
You will come back beaten and sore.
Then you will remember the suffering of cyclic existence.
But remembering won't help; it's just too late.
If your good judgment is not lost to a man,
You might still follow a lama above,
And give in charity below.
A girl should value her own worth.
Stand up for yourself, Trompa Gyen!
Girl, do you recognize me or not?
In case you don't recognize me,
I am Orgyen Padma.
You are a master of mundane work.
You are distracted by the day's work
And then fall into stupid slumber at night.
You are a slave busy with food and clothes morning and evening.
Your human life continually vanishes into nothing.
I am the one who has rejected mundane actions.
I am the renunciant yogi, Padmasambhava.
In the daytime I meditate on guru yoga.
Morning and evening I do practice sessions and torma offerings.
At night I dwell in the state of radiance.
I always maintain alert relaxation of the six groups of consciousness.
A yogin endowed in this way
Has a view higher than the sky,
Meditation clearer than the sun and moon,
And conduct more precise than sand grains.
I am the undying vajra body.
For me, passing away is nondual.
Though I am like all men and women
Who obtain the human body,
Unlike, alike—what is the difference?
Do you understand, do you comprehend, Trompa Gyen?
If you understand, it's more joyful than a hundred pounds of gold.
If you don't understand, at least connect with the Dharma.

Trompa Gyen said:

Padmasambhava, knower of the three times,
Kind one whose kindness is difficult to express,
The deeds of this life are just a dream.
Whatever one does has no real meaning,
And once those actions have become the cause for bad karma,
It's like falling and falling into the abyss of delusion.
Without interference from mundane phenomena,
Father, hold me with compassion
And teach me a sublime, profound method
For escaping this cyclic existence.
Establish me in the Dharma in this life.
If you do not establish me in the Dharma,
I will commit suicide and stay dead,
Praying to you to obtain a male body
With power to practice Dharma in the next life.

Princess Trompa Gyen implored from the bottom of her heart, and I thought,
"The princess has given rise to sincere remorse over cyclic existence. I must
teach her some Dharma."

Alas, Trompa Gyen, daughter of the king!
If weariness with this cyclic existence has arisen
And you want to pursue the Dharma now
In order to purify the obscurations of previous actions
And accomplish buddhahood later,
Turn your back on mundane cyclic existence
And make death and impermanence your inspiration.
Without needing anything, just thinking of this,
Devote yourself to dharmic pursuits.
To the lama who teaches you the Secret Mantra,
Offer the mandala of whatever comes your way.
With faithful devotion in thought, word, and deed,
Seek the presence of an authentic lama
And request the profound esoteric instructions.
Then, in a place with no conditions for delusion,
Such as a rock cave in an isolated mountain retreat,

Practice those profound instructions
And resolve them in your own mind.

The princess asked for profound instructions to resolve her mind, and I responded in this way:

"Karmically endowed Trompa Gyen, to take up the practice of profound Secret Mantra, assume the physical posture of Vairochana, and as soon as you think of it, whatever root lama you are devoted to appears on a sun-moon seat above your head, surrounded by buddhas and bodhisattvas of the ten directions. Meditating like this, pray to that lama with devotion. Imagine that a river of blessings flows down. All the wrongdoing and obscurations of body, speech, and mind ooze out from your soles and toes like dirty washing water, black and flowing out. The lama's blessing enters you and your body becomes like a crystal ball. Then meditate that the victorious ones in the ten directions are gathered into the lama's heart. Then the root lama dissolves down from the crown of your head and your body disintegrates like an old house. Rest in the open state of the completion phase. After the meditation in this state without reference point, with a loving mind toward all beings, recollect immeasurable compassion, saying, 'From this point on I will practice to become Buddha for the sake of beings.' Motivated by this recollection, remain in isolated mountain retreat. Make the three unmoving states the basis, and remain in the state of true nature until the realization of the ultimate Great Completion."

"What is the procedure for training in conduct while engaging in the state of true nature?" asked the princess.

"Faithful Princess Trompa Gyen, listen to this procedure for training. Don't feign the pure conduct of a brahmin.[2] By developing the potential of coupling means and wisdom, reveal the indisputable, irrefutable intrinsic awareness. Be precise in the conduct of harmonious relationships. Employ the words of spontaneously arising experience. Magnetize with the power of a skillful hero and captivate others with the voice of Brahma.

"Without that kind of conduct, you would have only your body, your youth, and the repeated words of others. You would enjoy secret activity with various false pretenses. Though possessed of signs and ability, secretly you would have no great discernment about your actions. Then, even if you became learned, until meditative stability is achieved, all sorts of interfering evil would come to afflict you. So with the foresight of deep discrimination, come to a precise understanding of the conduct."

Then She asked, "What are the experiences and feelings during the realization of view, meditation, conduct, and fruition in the practice of the profound spiritual path?"

"Faithful Princess Trompa Gyen, the supreme view, meditation, conduct, and fruition are this. The basic character beyond extremes is essentially empty. The mental discernment of this all-important emptiness does not get beyond verbal realization. Yet when that realization is free of fixation, simultaneously empty and radiant, then the realization of the basic character is stabilized. Whatever occurs is the play of dharmakaya, and from that all phenomena arise as the ornament of intrinsic awareness. For the individual who reaches the limits of unborn space, there is no discipline to be kept and no keeping of it. Purity and purification are not two. But those who do not have such realization, who are obscured by the accumulation of neurotic emotion and the five acts of immediate consequence, should purify obscurations in this way:

"In the space one cubit above your head, upon a sun, moon, and lotus, is Lama Vajrasattva. He is white, with one face and two hands, the right one holding a golden vajra and the left a silver bell facing his hip. He wears a jeweled crown on his head and jeweled ornaments on his body, and he sits with crossed legs. Create this in such a way that you cannot get enough of looking at him, like the sun rising on snow mountains. On a sun and moon in his heart, visualize a white *hung* encircled by the hundred-syllable mantra. Light radiating from this syllable invokes the lamas, yidams, dakinis, and all the buddhas of the ten directions. They dissolve into the letters and become nectar. Imagine that this fills the inside of his body and falls from his right big toe like milky nectar into the crown of your head. The entire inside of your body is filled like a milk bag. Your infractions, wrongdoings, and obscurations are expelled through the soles of your feet like used washing water, black and flowing out. Then recite the hundred syllables:

Om benzra satto samaya manu palaya benzra satto tenopa tikta dridho mebhawa suto kayo mebhawa anu rakto mebhawa supo kayo mebhawa sarwa siddhi metrayatsa sarwa karma sutsame tsittam shriyam kuru hung ha ha ha ha ho bhagawan sarwa tathagato benzra mamemuntsa benzri bhawa maha samaya benzra sato ah³

After hundreds and thousands of recitations, the world and its contents all dissolve into Vajrasattva. Vajrasattva dissolves into the letter *hung*. The letter dissolves into your head and arrives at the heart. The heart dissolves from the edges into the center and into the *hung*. The *hung* melts into red-tinged white nectar. It completely diffuses into the channels and elements of the body, filling it with the nectar of stainless pristine wisdom. Your own body, speech, and mind mix inseparably with Vajrasattva's. With that thought, rest in an uncontrived state free of embellishment. Then recite the usual confessions and give rise to the knowledge that all infractions and obscurations are purified.

"This is the special amendment of infractions of the inner supreme way. If you do this, the karmic obscurations of a thousand eons will be purified; all the infractions and breaks in the sacred pledge and even the five acts of immediate consequence will be purified. If a yogin strives at this, then the fruition of buddhahood will be attained in this lifetime."

"What is the method of prayer?" asked the princess.

"Princess, although the seed of Buddha exists primordially in you, without the lama there is no one to show it to you. Therefore, the lama is better than the buddhas of the three times. Visualize that facing you in the space in front of the top of your head, upon a throne supported by eight lions, on a seat of a thousand-petaled lotus, sun, and moon, is the brilliant form of your root lama. In the lama's heart, light radiates from the letter *hung* and there appears to the lama's right the Jewel of the Buddha, and to the left the Jewel of the Sangha, in front the host of yidam deities, and behind, the dakinis and protectors all around. Pray to the lama with immeasurable devotion, purified by tears of longing and with the hairs on your body standing up, thinking, 'I have nowhere to put my hope, nowhere to look, other than you.' Then do the sequence of prayers to the root and lineage lamas.

"Now for the essence of mind. The innately radiant emptiness of the expanse and awareness is the stainless dharmakaya awareness. Innate radiance without fixation shines from that; it is the pristine wisdom of compassion. It is the perspective of all the victorious ones, Great Completion, the pinnacle of the meaning of Secret Mantra. Whoever practices this will reach the ultimate fruition accordingly; they will gain the fruition of the three kayas. Princess, practice in this way and you will accomplish buddhahood in this life."

The princess took up the practice in the Cave of Virtue. Opening the channels of meditative experience and realization, she realized that all of phenomenal existence is the dharmakaya. She understood that cyclic existence is the ornament of intrinsic awareness. She saw that neurotic emotions are the five wisdoms. She comprehended that the world is illusory in nature. She saw that whatever arises is the play of dharmakaya. She understood that one's own mind is the Buddha. She realized the hidden faults in the aims of this and the next life. She achieved the true goal. Contemplating this, she came before Orgyen and said:

> Victorious one of the three times, guide of beings,
> Compassionate one without compare,
> Gracious one, there is no way to repay your kindness.
> You have given me profound instructions
> That are the essential meaning of the supreme Secret Mantra,
> And I have practiced them.
> The understanding of the mode of being has arisen from within.
> I have discarded the suffering of cyclic existence.
> The coming and going of thoughts is purified in its expanse.
> Suffering is free in its own ground, without rejection.
> I know that my mind is the Buddha.
> Thank you, Rinpoche.
> From now until the next life, we will not be separated.
> Hold me with compassion!

In this way she gave thanks, and I said:

> Beloved Trompa Gyen!
> Whatever realization or meditative experience occurs,
> Do not get lost in being a great learned clergy person.
> The nature of all phenomena is nonself.
> Rest within the great unembellished state.

Then the princess, out of sheer joy, wrote down the dialogue and gave it to Orgyen. And I, Padmasambhava, attached it as an appendix to *Lama Jewel Ocean* to be concealed in Mendo Cliff.

I, Pema Lingpa, drew this out of Mendo Cliff in Lhodrak.

SAMAYA GYA GYA GYA TER GYA BE GYA TE GYA

sacred pledge; sealed sealed sealed; treasure seal; hidden seal; entrusted seal

The Dialogue of Master Namkhai Nyingpo and Princess Dorje Tso

FROM *LAMA JEWEL OCEAN*[1]

Homage to the Guru.

M ASTER PADMASAMBHAVA and Master Namkhai Nyingpo were practicing at the Conch Palace of Kharchu in Lhodrak,[2] and at the cave of Palgyi Phukring (Glorious Long Cave). One evening before midnight, while Master Namkhai Nyingpo was sleeping, a girl wearing six bone ornaments, with the golden down on her face glowing, appeared to him and said, "Master Namkhai Nyingpo, if you desire to gain the special supreme spiritual powers, practice by attending a wisdom dakini. That dakini, furthermore, will be in the town Kyangbu Tsatok in Shang Tanak.[3] She is fifteen or sixteen years of age and is endowed with the thirty-six signs of a dakini. You should practice by attending her."

Saying this, she vanished. Then Master Namkhai Nyingpo thought to himself, "Is this an obstacle of gods and demons, or a dakini's prophecy? I just don't know. The Guru who knows lucidly everything in the three times abides in magical retreat like a mandala of Iron Kilaya in the cave of Palgyi Phukring. I must go and ask him in person."

Arriving when the dawn was just barely clearing away the darkness, he said, "Great Master, last night this sign came to me. Is it a prophecy or an obstacle?"

Guru Padmasambhava replied, "Well, since it is a dakini prophecy, you must discern whether or not there is karma and destiny. Go, and take this single-strand crystal rosary of mine."

The master rose the next morning when the throne and parasol of the sun rose, and came to the upper bank of the Yeru Tsangpo. When the sun was warm he arrived at Kyangbu Tsatok in Shang Tanak. It was a very large town, and in front of it was a big work yard. There were fifteen women weavers in the work yard. In the midst of them was one girl with the complete thirty-six marks of a dakini, very wonderful, fine, and alluring. There was also a grand old man of impressive bearing and a young person with a crooked mouth and a handsome nose. The master said to them, "Give me, a yogi, some alms."

Whereupon the old man said, "Master, great meditator, what monastery do you come from? Who is your lama? On what yidam do you meditate? What essence mantra do you recite? What holy Dharma do you practice? And who are you anyway?"

The master intoned the melody of the *rulu* essence[4] and spoke these words:

> Body is the body like an immutable vajra.
> Speech is the Brahma speech of unimpeded equanimity.
> Mind is unchanging, beyond telling, imagining, or uttering.
> Homage to Vajradhara, the spontaneously present three kayas.

> You ask about my lama—
> There were twenty-five learned ones.
> You ask about my holy Dharma—
> It is the holy Dharma of Great Completion.
> You ask about my yidam—
> It is the yidam Palchen[5] in union.
> I recite the rulu essence of syllables.
> I am joyful anywhere, happy anywhere.[6]
> Place and country do not matter.
> Since I do not worry about articles of livelihood,
> Give this yogi some alms.

The old man said, "Master, your lama and your yidam and your holy Dharma are all especially exalted. Now, what is the fruition of your practice, and ultimately the conviction of your view and experiences of meditation?" He replied:

> My view is the nonexperience of view:
> I have the conviction of the view of space without limit.
> My meditation is no experience of meditation:
> I have the conviction of meditation dawning of itself.
> Leave your busywork and get on with it!
> Give this yogi some alms.

Then the old man said, "Your view, meditation, conduct, and such are all very good. Now, for the minds of us worldly folk, since attachment to the phenomena of this life is primordially unborn, please give us a Dharma instruction that will help us to mentally forsake cyclic existence and give birth to the realization of impermanence, an instruction that is easy to understand and yet will lead us to ultimate buddhahood."

Master Namkhai Nyingpo responded, "In general, beings of the three realms of cyclic existence, and in particular this gathering of fortunate men and women, have not ever gained the stronghold of unborn mind, no matter what they may reject or accept of birth and death from the limitless time of cyclic existence until this present human form.

> Cyclic existence is like a waterwheel;
> Give up the ceaseless activity.
> Birth, aging, sickness, and death are like the rhythms in a flour mill;
> Give up this inexhaustible activity.
> Suffering is like the ripples in water;
> Give up the continuing sequence of activity.
> The body is like a scarecrow in a field;
> Give up this precarious activity.
> The mind is like a passing rainbow in the sky;
> Give up this disintegrating activity.
> Leave your busywork and get on with it!
> Give this yogi some alms!

Exceptional faith was born in all those gathered at the work yard, regardless of their age, and tears poured forth. They did prostrations and circumambulated the master, offering special articles of sustenance. Then, from the midst of that work yard, the youth with the crooked mouth said, "Great master, sir, there are those who say that sooner or later everybody dies. But we young folk here, since we have no cause to die in the next year or two, may be joyful and sporting. There has been time for it until now; won't there be more time for it later?" The master responded:

> Beings of the three realms of cyclic existence in general,
> And this gathering of youthful men and women in particular:
> You with these fine bodies,
> In one or two years' time,
> Will be like old bows destroyed by the smoke.[7]
> Contemplate this and practice the divine Dharma.
> These fine brows of yours,
> In one or two years' time,

Will be twisted like fresh palm leaves.
These fine hairstyles of yours,
In one or two years' time,
Will be like the white heads of thistles.
This fine clothing of yours,
In one or two years' time,
Will be like tattered furniture thrown outside.

You won't get upright, you'll get bent over.
You won't get better, you'll get older.
You won't get taller, you'll get shorter.
Old age is like the grass on fire:
Is there any way but for it to get shorter?
This illness is like the southern clouds of summer:
Is there any certainty that they won't come suddenly?
The devil of death is like the shadows of evening:
You run and run away from them, yet they come closer and closer.
This death is like the disappearing oil of a lamp:
Don't you know there is no way to control it?

It's time to practice the holy, divine Dharma!
It's not just time, it's rather a bit late.
Thinking about this, practice the divine Dharma.
Think about Dharma and arouse faith.
Leave the toil of food and dispatch charity.
Leave the toil of sleep and practice virtue.

Faith arose in all those in the work yard, and they offered him a mountain of provisions. The day lapsed into evening, and the workers got ready to leave. All the cattle and sheep were herded into corrals. The girl with the marks and signs of a dakini picked up her load to go. The master, in order to check whether or not the girl possessed karma and destiny, threw Padmasambhava's single-strand crystal practice rosary into the sky. It melted into the top of her head like snow in hot sand. Seeing that she was endowed with karma and destiny, he followed the girl and said, "The yogi needs a place to sleep for the night."

"There is no place at our house," she replied. "My old mother and father are very powerful, but I will ask and get their answer. Wait here," she said and closed the door.

At this point the workers said, "Wherever the master meditator stays and whoever serves him is fine. But he has seen that this girl with a lovely face is the most beautiful and attractive and has gone after her. He bears only the appearance of a genuine yogin, someone calling himself a Dharma practitioner with mere words, but their meaning is rarely applicable." With that kind of talk, they indulged in backbiting slander.

Then the girl said from the window, "I asked my parents, and they said that you may not stay here." The master, in order to respond to those who had slandered him, said:

I, a beggar yogi of the kingdom,
Have everything I need or want myself.
My dwelling place is indefinite:
Sleeping in doorways is fine for me.
My clothes are indefinite:
Wearing a corpse's clothes is fine for me.
My food is indefinite:
Eating dry flour is fine for me.
Shang Tanak may well be a great place,
But in order to usher the karmically endowed into the Dharma,
We will leave here today, I swear.
Think about this, you who dwell inside.

The master sat there in the doorway doing his evening practice of meditative absorption, chanting the melody of rulu, and such. The girl entered her parents' bedroom and saw that all the household business was finished. She said to the maid, "That master great meditator chanting down there has genuinely impressed me. Let us two sleep here." So they arranged their pillows and beds at the head of the steps to sleep. Then the girl said to the master, "Your melody was most pleasant. Do a spiritual song." So he sang:

You, white lioness of the high snow mountains,
Sticking close to the face of the white snow mountains,
When you come right down for food,
Not noticing the descending mists,
You risk being caught under the collapsing snow.
Spring up from the risk of sinking and be heroic.
It's time to flee to the white snow peaks.
It's not just time, it's rather late.

Stallion prancing over the meadow lawns,
Sticking close to the grassy meadows,
Not noticing the overflowing hollows,
You risk sinking into the mud of the hollows.
Leave the meadow lawns and ascend.
It's time to flee to the path of ecstatic freedom.
It's not just time, it's rather late.

You, mistress of the house up yonder,
Sticking close to your illusory wealth,
Not noticing that you are wandering in cyclic existence,
You risk falling into the three bad existences.
Throw away material possessions and be diligent.
It's time to flee to the path of Great Vehicle awakening.
It's not just time, it's rather late.

The girl said to her maid, "The master's song is so very pleasant. I must hear it again. But if he sings it one more time from here, my parents will notice, so we two should go to that enclosed work yard." She closed the door and said to the master, "Great meditator down there, I want to practice the holy, divine Dharma, but I cannot give up my kind parents, or my accumulated wealth and possessions, or my fine ornaments and clothes, or my loving relatives, or my native country. For you, a master, it makes no difference. For me, a girl, it makes a great difference. Please stay in this part of the country and by all means practice the holy divine Dharma. Please look after me with loving compassion. I will offer you all the necessary sustenance." The master replied in this way:

Objectively regarded, you three siblings
Are like guests in the marketplace:
Although you arrive together, you depart separately.
Without relations, practice the divine Dharma!

Objectively regarded, accumulated wealth
Is like the wealth of honey possessed by bees:
Accumulated by oneself but enjoyed by others.
Indeed wealth is an illusion—practice the divine Dharma!

Objectively regarded, constructed mansions
Are like the mansions built in child's play:

First constructed, then inevitably destroyed.
Native home has no essence—practice the divine Dharma!

If you desire from your heart to practice the divine Dharma,
If you desire in your spirit to practice the divine Dharma,
Then your homeland is the devil's prison.
Turn your back on it and practice the divine Dharma!

It is the cause of the bondage of great attachment;
Resolve attachment and practice the divine Dharma!

To this, she retorted:

Considering the compassion in practicing Dharma,
Does it really help to turn one's back on one's parents?
Considering the value of obtaining the precious human body,
Does it really help to ignore this dubious body?
Considering bringing the faithful into the Dharma,
Does it really help to be without vital sustenance?
Considering the service to lama and Dharma friends,
Does it really help to be without a practice of protocol?

The master thought to himself, "This girl is very self-satisfied with her wealth, possessions, and relatives. Even if she practiced Dharma, it seems that deep remorse would not arise." He said:

The flower that grows in the springtime,
When taken by a seasonal frost,
Dries up and vanishes, does it not?
Think of that, and practice the divine Dharma.

The sprout that grows in the millet field,
When sliced with a sharp sickle,
Is cut through and vanishes, does it not?
Think of that, and practice the divine Dharma.

The field with its valuable grain,
When it ripens in the fruiting season,
Falls uselessly on its own ground and vanishes, does it not?

Think of that, and practice the divine Dharma.

This body of combined flesh and blood
Is on loan from the four elements, and when it dissipates
The body separates from the mind and vanishes, does it not?
Think of that, and practice the divine Dharma.

Old age, sickness, and death, these three
Follow in our wake and touch the heart.
Think of that, and practice the divine Dharma.

Hell beings, hungry spirits, and animals, these three
Await us on the highway like an ambush.
Think of that, and practice the divine Dharma.

This life, the next, and the intermediate, these three,
Are all lined up like spirit stones.
Although rich now in our hoarded enjoyments,
Like being overcome by an adventitious thief,
We depart naked without a trace, do we not?
Think of that, and practice the divine Dharma.

Even a haughty king
Wanders forth alone like a pauper.
Even a powerful minister
Is chained to the bed like a prisoner.
Even an indolent queen
Is food for ants and worms.
Parents are the guides to cyclic existence.
Wealth and possessions are the tether to misfortune.
Relations are the fetters to cyclic existence.
Think of that, and practice the divine Dharma.

Dorje Tso thought, "What the master says is true. No matter what, I must practice the holy, divine Dharma." Coming out beyond the threshold, she grasped the master's hands and placed his feet on her head. "I will turn to the Dharma no matter what. Please take me with you," she pleaded. "Certainly it is not well to be attached to wealth and possessions. But shouldn't we take some money and things for Dharma provisions?"

The master replied, "If you are able to practice the Dharma, you don't need Dharma supplies. The gods will provide sustenance."

The girl took off the pigeon-sized turquoise from around her own neck and gave it to her maid, saying, "Don't tell anyone that I have run away to the Dharma. Take good care of my parents." Then, without a word, she went off to serve the master.

The two of them left early in the morning, and when the tip of the sun rose, they came to the banks of the Yeru Tsangpo. There, the master brought out a bag full of *tsampa* from his pack, took water from a skull container and began preparing a meal. But an army had followed them, and the whole area was suddenly filled with the chaos of charging horses, men wielding arms, little children crying, and old folks carrying canes. Coming from nowhere, an unidentified priest threatened the master, saying, "You have perpetrated an evil deception and taken away our dear child who is like a goddess. We will eat flesh and gulp blood."

In order to test whether or not the girl had a stable mind, whether there was a great or small chance of her reverting, and whether or not she had conviction, the master said, "Girl, if you feel regret and have not mentally forsaken your past, it's better to turn back." He continued:

> Of birds caught in snares,
> Many flee but few escape.
> Of antelope caught in traps,
> Many flee but few escape.
> Of fish caught in nets,
> Many flee but few escape.
> Of girls who run away to the Dharma,
> Many flee but few escape.
> Girl, you have turned back.
> I, the old man, will flee and depart.
> If we do not die, a time will come to meet.
> At that time, if destined for Dharma, it may work.

The girl replied:

> You, Master Namkhai Nyingpo,
> Have you been to India or not?
> Have you served an authentic lama or not?
> Are you a Tibetan adept or not?

Have you achieved mastery in mantra or not?
If you have magical powers, reveal them now.
If now you do not take this girl,
She risks sinking in the swamp of cyclic existence,
Carried off by the devil of bad karma.
If at this point you do not take this girl,
She will jump into the Yeru Tsangpo and depart.

Since she seemed to be of stable mind and not about to change, he decided to take her. He said to the army that had come after them:

The wind that leaps at the sky—
Wanting to chase it is most tiresome.
The controlled breath and mind—
Charging it with horses is most tiresome.[8]
The king of birds who soars in the skies—
Being a frog trying to catch it is most tiresome.
When we get to a great plain,
We will emanate as a pair of wild ponies and go.
When we get to a great lake,
We will emanate as two golden ducks and go.
When we get to a great mountain pass,
We will emanate as a pair of wolves and go.
You men who would follow us
With your charging horses, how pitiful!
These dear weeping children, how pathetic!
These old men with their canes, how ridiculous!
You will turn and run without getting the girl.

"You old beggar fraud! Where will you flee? Where will you escape?" they yelled and threatened. The master replied with this verse:

In order to root out negative forces,
We will emanate as a pair of wild ponies and go.
In order to bring the three realms under control,
We will emanate as a pair of vultures, lord of birds.
In order to be free of the waters of cyclic existence,
We will emanate as two golden ducks and go.

Having thus spoken, they emanated as golden birds and flew over the Tsangpo. The emanations dispersed when they landed, and the pursuers were convinced.

"Oh my goodness! Girl, no man could overtake you, only gods and demons. So we will all turn back," they said, admitting defeat.

Then the master and the girl went to the Conch Palace of Kharchu in Lhodrak. The master conferred on Dorje Tso the outer, inner, and secret empowerments. Manifesting the mandala of Glorious Yangdak, he introduced the yidam deity and entered meditative absorption. The master's throne was built on the right of the mandala and the girl's throne on the left. Doing the recitation of the rulu formula while abiding in the accomplishment practice, the master dwelled without wavering in the absorption of the great equalness of reality itself, emanating love. The girl practiced the rulu formula for many years. At one point, by the force of her youth, she felt remorse over her lack of playmates or companions. To bring her lament to the master's attention, she inserted this into the sound of the rulu recitation:

> When first I came from my country,
> I was not attached to the face of my father.
> When first I came from my country,
> I was not attached to the face of my mother.
> When first I came from my country,
> I was not attached to any place or personal lineage.
> At first I was not attached to any of my three siblings.
> At first I was not attached to any wealth or enjoyments.
> At first I was not attached to any of these three: country, homeland,
>   or house.
> At first I was not attached to any of these three: playmates, companions,
>   or friends.
> Alas, when I came here my natural life was cut off.
> Now the remorse I feel is unparalleled.
> If you have any possible compassion,
> Take me to the country of my birth.

As the master sat listening, he saw that it was true that she was still young. He sang this song:

> Relatives and pure lands are many indeed.
> But when the time of one's death comes,

Though many surround you until you die,
After you die you yourself must go alone.
Think of that and recite rulus.

Though looking to your loving father,
When sudden illness strikes,
The unbearable tears that fall
Will not affect the disease at all.
Be decisive and recite rulus.

Though wealth and possessions are nicely hoarded,
When the time of death has fallen,
Not even one needle and thread can be taken with you.
Be decisive and recite rulus.

Though the constructed mansion is nice and tall,
The dead have no power to stay inside.
You get no more than a coffin fit for one.
Be decisive and recite rulus.

For a few days this helped her mind. Then once again she felt remorse awaken in her heart, and she sang this lament:

The acclaim of Lhodrak Kharchu,
From a distance, unseen, is very loud.
When you've been there and seen it,
It is a big, empty place without people.

The acclaim of the Conch Palace
From a distance, unseen, is very loud.
When you've been there and seen it,
It's an empty cave with no door.

The acclaim of Namkhai Nyingpo,
From a distance, unseen, is very loud.
When you've been there and seen him,
He is an old charlatan monk, an old swindler.

The acclaim of the yidam Palchen,

From a distance, unseen, is very loud.
When you've been there and seen it,
It's the drawn shape of a deity's body.

The acclaim of the eight-syllable rulu,
From a distance, unseen, is very loud.
When you've been there and seen it,
It's the endless braying of a donkey.

The girl thus requested to revisit her homeland, and again the master replied:

Girl, don't speak nonsense, recite rulus!
The acclaim of Lhodrak Kharchu
Is of a sacred site visited by awareness-holders.
The acclaim of the Conch Palace
Is of a sacred site to gain supreme spiritual power.
The acclaim of Namkhai Nyingpo
Is indeed of a yogin with spiritual power.
The acclaim of the yidam Palchen
Is of the embodiment of all buddhas.
The acclaim of the eight-syllable rulu
Is of the sound of the unborn bodhisattva.
Settle this up and recite rulus!
Develop enthusiasm and recite rulus!

For a few days this helped her mind. But after a few more days, she could not disperse the deep feeling of remorse and again requested:

When you see pieces of wool
And white feathers
You think they are alike.
Pieces of wool carried away by the wind
On the side of a red cliff flutter and flutter.
White feathers carried away by the wind
On the tops of the foliage dangle and dangle.
Pellets carried away by the water
In the river's eddies swirl and swirl.
The confused girl who is I
Emerges from the doorless cave longing and longing.

Regarding this regretful girl,
No messenger on a racing stallion comes to the rescue.
Is the retribution of full ripening true or not?
If the retribution of wrongdoing is true,
Then I send the retribution to Master Namkhai Nyingpo.
Send this girl home!

The master thought, "Since this girl is young, although she stays here at my place, she is not concentrated enough to practice. I must offer her to Master Padmasambhava." So thinking, he went to the cave of Palgyi Chakpur,[9] dragging the girl there by the hem of her dress, and offered the master this praise:

On the northwest border of Orgyen,
On the island in Lake Dhanakosha,
On the pollen-bed of a lotus,
You attained wonderful, supreme spiritual power.
Renowned as the Lotus Born,
In the youthful manner of an eight-year-old,
To you, Tötrengtsal, I bow and offer praise.
The acclaim of Dorje Tsogyal,
Is of a lady of noble lineage with faith in the Dharma.
She has a beautiful face and all thirty signs of excellence.
She is sweet-voiced, bright, insightful,
And as fragrant as the utpal flower,
The finest companion for attaining enlightenment.
Great being, I offer her as your consort.
Compassionate one, please accept her.

After making this offering he left. The girl thought, "What? This Master Padmasambhava is not someone who was born as a mortal person but appeared from a lotus. He is said to be an emanation body. Even now he appears as youthful as an eight-year-old, with a white complexion like the sunrise on snow mountains, and is adorned by all the signs and marks. I cannot get enough of gazing on him. How fantastic to meet such a person. Master Namkhai Nyingpo also is so gracious. Now I have a fine companion for this life, and in the next I will attain enlightenment."

Thinking this, she felt immeasurable joy and delight. The Guru, comprehending through his clairvoyance, thought, "This girl has engendered a great fantasy of attachment to me. I had better do something to reverse this."

After Dorje Tso had fallen asleep, there came an old man with hair whiter than a conch and eyes paler than blue, his head at the same level as his shoulders, drool and snot reaching his chest, and eye bags hanging down to his cheeks. This frightful, nauseating magical appearance was there when the girl woke from her slumber. She reconsidered, "This Master Padmasambhava can be really incredible. But now he has become an old man like this. It is probably an apparition of Master Namkhai Nyingpo. Perhaps it is best if I stay with him rather than with this." And so she returned to Master Namkhai Nyingpo and said, "Master, sir, please put me into the practice."

While she was abiding in the practice of Glorious Yangdak, diligently reciting the rulu formula, the black devil Trakme[10] came near her, waiting in ambush for her life force like a cat for a mouse. As she was about to go to sleep, the master uttered underneath his rulu formula:

> Girl, at dusk, *thum thum*, don't fall asleep,
> There is danger of a sacred pledge corrupter coming for your life force.
> At midnight, *thum thum*, don't fall asleep,
> There is danger of devilish obstacles.
> At dawn, *thum thum*, don't fall asleep,
> There is danger of interference from smell-eaters.
> In the morning, *thum thum*, don't fall asleep,
> There is danger of interference from tsen spirits.
> At noon, *thum thum*, don't fall asleep,
> There is danger of interference from mamos.[11]
> In the afternoon, *thum thum*, don't fall asleep,
> There is danger of the obstacle of ogresses.
> Develop diligence and recite rulus.
> Develop enthusiasm and recite rulus.

By his proclaiming that, the obstacle was cleared away and the girl practiced with devotion. The special meditative experiences and realizations arose, and the excellent indications and signs occurred. She thought, "All places are the nature of dharmakaya. Before now, the wool covered my eyes. Now I need not be like that." Intoning the rulu melody, she said:

> This world, a container for objective appearance,
> Is the palace of the pure deity.
> Internally the sentient beings of devilish minds
> Are the host of Heruka Yamantaka's ogres.

> The habitual patterns of various sounds and talk
> Are the sound of the eight-syllable rulu recitation.
> Ideas and expressions, awareness's memories and thoughts,
> Are arising in the expanse of innately occurring dharmakaya.
> In the mandala of the sublime mystery,
> Bestow the spiritual power of sublime bliss.

At some point during that time, with a feeling of great joy, a sudden intuition came over her, a heartfelt desire to go outside the retreat house. Going outside, she saw that the red cliff called Phongring in front of the house had become the body of Palchenpo. Beholding his visage, she gained the supreme spiritual power. The girl then offered this praise to Palchenpo:

> In the charnel ground mandala of sublime mystery,
> The Conqueror Palchen Vajra Heruka
> Is terrifying in subduing enemies and evil forces
> With wild, abusive, and terrifying displays,
> Compassionate, voracious, tranquil, and so forth.[12]
> The great body of extremely immutable material
> Holds up the Supreme Mountain, looking terrifying,
> Wears charnel ground ornaments, looking heroic,
> Laughs at the White Palace, looking humorous,
> And terrifies with blue face in the center, looking wrathful.
> Like that you come, King of Wrath, with your terrifying form.
> I prostrate to the voracious form of Palchen.

Praising him thus, the dakini Dorje Tso attained both ordinary and supreme spiritual power. Meanwhile, Great Master Padma and Master Namkhai Nyingpo had both flown into the sky and had landed on the upper side of the mountain and were happily sitting in the sun. The girl would have to go around from the bottom of the valley to reach them. So she too, carrying their cushions, flew to the side of the two masters.

Dorje Tso accomplished immeasurable benefit for beings. In the snowy fastness of Tibet, she spread the doctrine of the deep and vast holy Dharma and completed the remedial activity of subduing all devilish emanations.

Virtue!

The Heart of the Matter:

The Guru's Red Instructions to Mutik Tsenpo

FROM *LAMA JEWEL OCEAN*[1]

I, Padmakara,
Was born on a lotus as the son of a king.
When I was eight years of age, faith arose.
I circulated around India, east and west, like water.
I met Garab, Shri, and all the awareness-holders;
Tasted the empowerments and instructions like salt water;
Solved the view of hearing, contemplating, and meditating;
Reached the limit of the perspective of Supreme Great Completion;
Completed the welfare of beings in India and elsewhere.
Through the force of karma I went to central Tibet.
Through the force of prayer I accomplished the king's wishes.
To the prince Mutik Tsenpo I gave the especially profound Jewel *Ocean*.
I conferred Dharma fortune on the captivating Lady.
I hid it as a most profound treasure for future benefit.
It is Padma's instruction to his spiritual son.
May the future destined one discover it.

SAMAYA GYA GYA GYA
sacred pledge; sealed sealed sealed

PRINCE MUTIK TSENPO[2] supplicated Master Padmasambhava, "Alas, Orgyen Rinpoche! I request a teaching that is short, pithy, and never before taught, something from your own experience that is easy to understand, pleasant to maintain, and personally effective to my practice."

Orgyen replied, "King, offer a mandala. I will give you an instruction." So the prince arranged heaps of turquoise on a golden mandala and offered it. Then the Master spoke:

"Prince, since it is the crucial point of the body, you should sit cross-legged with your spine straight as a stack of gold coins and your hands in the meditation position. Since it is crucial for the channels, gaze with your eyes into space. Since it is crucial for the vital winds (*prana*), hold in the lower wind and press with the upper wind. Since it is crucial for the vital drops (*bindu*), visualize a red drop from the syllable E in the emanation chakra in the navel. Then visualize a white drop from the syllable *pam* in the great bliss chakra in the head. Since it is crucial for the consciousness, visualize that red fire blazes up from the *e* and melts the white drop into light, which then falls to the dharma chakra in the heart, where the white and red drops combine. Concentrate there. Since mind is the crucial point of awakening (*buddha*), the white and red drops become smaller and smaller. After they are gone, do not do anything at all with the mind."

The king practiced for a while in that way, and the experience of the great perspective of the basic mode of reality arose. He had no sensation of having a body, and he felt that appearances were unhindered and free and that he was immortal. He said to Orgyen, "Oh, Great Master, sir. I have practiced as you instructed. Appearance and mind combined, and I felt that there was no cause of mortality. What is this conviction?"

Orgyen replied, "Great Dharma King, it is merely the lama's blessing entering your mind. Now again go into retreat and don't conceive of anything at all. Whatever appearance[3] occurs, practice with this also in clarity-emptiness without fixation."

As he practiced without fixation in clarity-emptiness, it occurred to the prince that appearance is empty. Emptiness is appearance. Appearance and emptiness are inseparable. And the thought occurred that buddhas and sentient beings are not two things. And he thought that whether one practices the ten nonvirtues, or the ten virtues, there is no cause for their consequences to come. He reported these experiences to Orgyen. The Guru said:

"Prince, you are fooled by fixation to the validity of your experience. To think that appearance and emptiness are inseparable, you need to be free of attachment to this appearance. Are you? If you think that buddhas and sentient beings are not two things, you need to render service and homage to sentient beings the same as to buddhas. Do you? If you think that the full ripening of practicing the ten nonvirtues won't come, you need to forbear those acts, such as murder and so on, when inflicted on yourself by others. Can you? If you think that there is no consequence of practicing the ten virtues, then you must not feel joy when others benefit you through the ten virtues, such as saving your life. Do you have that?

"Stay yet again in retreat and make this body of yours like a corpse. Rest your voice like a mute. Place your mind like the sky. When you practice in an isolated place like that, the experience of clarity-emptiness is a radiant transparency without outside or inside. Whether you close your eyes or not, this clarity-emptiness arises. The emptiness experience is without attachment to anything at all, external or internal. Emptiness pervades evenly with nowhere for the mind to abide. In the bliss experience, body and mind both melt like butter, becoming tranquil and welling with bliss. There is no attachment to the growing clarity of the various appearances. Consciousness rises like the sun in space, and the body is like the mists. Unwaveringly, you recognize yourself and others.[4] Just as you know by yourself the meaning of mind itself, you'll think that others have awareness of knowing."[5]

The prince said, "Orgyen Rinpoche, having practiced those matters, what is it like at the time of fulfillment?"

Orgyen responded, "Great Dharma King, sir. As for the time of fulfillment of those matters, the Great Completion has three parts: the time of spontaneous presence, the time of the unimaginable, and the time of great bliss. Of those, this is the time of spontaneous presence. If you abide there, the time of spontaneous presence is unimaginable, and there is naturally occurring great bliss. But, again, cyclic existence is clever at deceit, and awareness is gullible. Develop a vast, open mind without attachment to the meditative appearances. Then there is no qualitative difference between buddhas and sentient beings other than awareness or nonawareness.[6] 'Intellect,' 'mind,' 'awareness'; there is just a single essence. The nonaware intellect of sentient beings abides in pieces. The mind of buddhas abides pervasively. It has developed vastness like the sky. The sky arises without limit, empty without limit: no limit in the west, no limit in the north, beyond limits in all directions. Such are the limits of naturally occurring awareness.

"At this point mind has no production—however you place it, it abides persistently in one-pointed clarity-emptiness. You think that this must be the so-called one-pointed[7] state itself. Then there is no attachment to any external object, and the mind abides nowhere. You think that this must be what's called 'free of embellishment,' what else is there? Feeling that whatever you do it is the same, that there is nothing to reject or accept, you think that certainly this is the so-called one taste itself, what else is there? Meditating is that, not meditating is that. Since there was never anything to practice or to meditate on, you think this is the so-called no-meditation itself.

"The two form kayas do not arise from dharmakaya, because the various appearances that arise are like the clear radiance of a lamp.[8] The inhalations and exhalations of the breath occur without sensation. Without you doing anything, various expressions arise. It is unchanging like the essence of the sky.

The concept of duality doesn't arise at all. You think, 'this is it,' the final measure of experience. Other experiences occur, such as clarity, vibrancy, pervasiveness, tranquility, welling, shimmering, a clarity experience like the sun, an emptiness experience like the sky, or an experience of bliss like the ocean. The experiential appearances are all different, like the ripples in the sea or the clouds in the sky.

"If the true nature of things is devoid of experience, what have you experienced? Who is it who experiences? What are you so pleased about? If I don't have even a little experience, do you think you will find something better? These experiences of yours aren't experienced this way even by the buddhas of the three times. Fixated on experience, you are an evil demon. Since it all occurs through effort, it is contrived experience. There are still ups and downs to come. Your experiences won't stand up to circumstances. They are just the husks of positive thinking. You haven't cut through the bones of discursive thinking. It's like having an internal disease. At some point, even feeling good won't help. You still haven't reached the depths. The ashes of confusion will rekindle. When you believe that your meditation experience is paramount, you become complacent. Attached to your brief absorptions, you think there is nothing beyond that, and you cling to a measure of absorption. The bones of discursive thought are not broken. The husks of meditative appearances are not removed. The stains of ignorance are not purified. Each meditative experience will be accompanied by specific attachment to it, but you will see it only as good. Thus it has become obscured. Being without attachment to anything is the meaning of immutability. By obscuring that and being attached, the crucial mutability will result only in error.

"Furthermore, if you are attached to the validity of clarity and hold it to be paramount, you will see the form realm. If you are attached to the reality of the emptiness experience of nonthought, the highest resulting place is the formless realm. And if you are attached to the validity of the bliss and believe that it is paramount, the highest you will attain is the place of the desire realm, nothing more. It is taught that you will not attain the sublime spiritual power of the Great Completion, unsurpassable enlightenment."

"Orgyen Rinpoche, if nothing more than that is obtained, then what is the meaning of attaining the unborn?" asked the great Dharma King.

"Once those errors have been eliminated, the meaning of attaining the fruition of the unborn is this: it is taught that the meaning of all our efforts is to attain effortlessness itself. Great Prince, don't be attached to the value of the mental appearances of incidental meditative experiences. Don't watch the mind of deluded appearances. Don't create desire or aversion for actions.

Don't get anxious about realization. Whatever the mind wants to do, let it. Rest mind itself like the center of the sky. Without attachment to the reality of the clarity, look at the essence of clarity-fixation itself. When there's attachment to the validity of the experience or thought of nonthought, look at the root of thought experience. When there's attachment to the validity of bliss, look at the one who is fixated on that bliss. If you practice in that way with the arising of those previous experiences, the husk of conceptual mind will be peeled away and you will realize ordinary mind unobscured by either faults or qualities. Then you will be free of the roots of anything to meditate on or anything to be deluded about. You have the realization that there is nothing to arise from meditation, and also nothing to be deluded about in not meditating. You have the realization of ordinary mind without faults and qualities, wide awake and naked, wide open and starkly free. You realize that all the phenomena of samsara and nirvana are as child's play. That so-called dimension of reality (*dharmatakaya*) that is the unconditioned primordial true nature *is* that same wide-awake state that is free of either meditation or delusion, like pure gold. Now, don't be obscured by desire for this state. This single desire will carry you to an undesirable place. Not experiencing meditation and not experiencing departure from it, never depart from the meaning of no-meditation. By maintaining that, you will attain the ordinary and supreme spiritual powers. If you are unable to do that, there is no one more useless than you."

The king said, "If no one is more useless than I, then at least with regard to shame about sacred pledge and such, I have nothing to transgress."

"Prince, are you displeased?"

"Somewhat displeased," he said.

"Well, if you are displeased, you have hopes. If you are pleased, you have fears. If you have hopes and fears, you have dualistic fixation. That obstructs nondual pristine wisdom great bliss, the fruition free of stains. Don't regard anything as good or bad. Rest without regard for anything at all through nondualistic yogic discipline. If you maintain just that, the thought of good and bad doesn't arise at all. Wherever mind has gone, it's gone. However it stays, it stays. For instance, to abide within the state of nonaction is like the traces left by a bird flying in the sky. Once free of the burden of striving, you have reached the great bliss of the realm of reality.

"King, practice the teachings of Secret Mantra like that. Until you have attained such stability, live as taught in the *pitakas*. Meditate as taught in the Secret Mantra. Have the view of the Great Completion. Hold mind itself as a jewel. Rely on many fortunate disciples. Always offer to the lamas and dakinis, even if you don't feel like it. Realize that all phenomena of apparent existence are like an illusion, and maintain that mind itself is unborn and undying."

In order to liberate the prince Mutik Tsenpo, I, Padmakara, have spoken *The Guru's Red Instructions, the Heart of the Matter*. Now it is finished. May the spiritual children who are karmically endowed encounter it.

SAMAYA GYA GYA GYA
TER GYA BE GYA TE GYA KA GYA SANG GYA

sacred pledge; sealed sealed sealed;
treasure seal; hidden seal; entrusted seal; command seal; secret seal

May I, Pema, fulfill my karma and aspirations.
Tulku Pema Lingpa extracted this from Mendo Cliff in Lhodrak.

A Strand of Jewels:
The History and Summary of Lama Jewel Ocean[1]

Embodied union of every Joyful One in all directions and times,
Manifest in peaceful or wrathful emanation, appearing to whomever
    is to be tamed,
Supreme Lama, unified principle of all, to you I bow.
I, the tantric awareness-holder Padma,

Through the immeasurable five bodies[2] and eight identities[3]
Composed many practice methods for the sake of future times.
The union of their most quintessential essence
Is none other than this most profound union, *Jewel Ocean.*
Only this heart's elixir, this vital drop of life,
Will advise the hearts of those with karma at the final time of conflict.
Samaya gya gya gya
(Sacred pledge; sealed sealed sealed)

I N THE CITADEL of naturally occurring primordial purity in the
totally pure realm of reality, the self-contained great expanse that
does not fall in any direction, the principle of the vase body of pristine wisdom is glorious Samantabhadra, masculine and feminine, devoid of any
essential existence.

From the radiance of awareness-emptiness, the body without back or front
manifests facing in the ten directions. From the responsiveness of that such-
ness and that principle, body emanates as Vairochana, speech as Amitabha,
mind as Akshobhya, quality as Ratnasambhava, and activity as Amoghasiddhi.
Such is the intention to benefit beings.

Further, the principle of Samantabhadra's speech is the dharmakaya
Amitabha: in the western pure land of Sukhavati, the naturally occurring

citadel of the realm of reality without an appearance of outside or inside. In the expanse of the five pristine wisdoms, upon the sun and moon seat beautified by entwined peacocks, dwells Buddha Amitabha, red in color, with one face and two hands and all the adornments of the sambhogakaya, sitting cross-legged, with hands settled in equipoise.

Such a buddha, intending to act for the welfare of beings, evokes and manifests the five emanations of body, speech, mind, quality, and activity. The body emanation, in the pure land of Sukhavati, emanates as the body of the Dharma-protecting king, Amidhewa, and acts for the welfare of beings. The speech emanation, acting for the welfare of beings, emanates as the form of Mahakaruna, with one face and four arms, in the Lotus Lake. The mind emanation, acting for the welfare of beings, emanates in the form of the Conqueror Lord Amitayus. The quality emanation, acting for the welfare of beings, emanates in the form of five kinds of Tötrengtsal.[4] The activity emanation, acting for the welfare of beings, emanates in the form of one such as myself, Padmasambhava. This is how the welfare of beings is enacted.

On the tenth day of the monkey month of the male Fire Monkey year, one red letter *hri* with a *tsekdrak*[5] radiated from the heart of Amitabha. As it struck the lake Drimé Dangden (Immaculate Radiance) on Kosha Island in the northwest country of Oddiyana, a lotus flower grew up with one thousand petals and twenty-five anthers. Upon that, I, Padmasambhava, appeared in the mode of an eight-year-old mendicant. From above, all the gods made offerings and gave praise. The lake spirits and the eight classes of gods and demons prostrated and circumambulated. The steadfast earth goddess gave me the name Tsokyi Dorje (Lake-Born Vajra).

While I was coursing in the profound meaning of reality itself, there was a king of Oddiyana called Indrabhuti, who had one thousand courtiers and five hundred queens but not a single son. The king thought, "I do not have the son so necessary in this world. One must take the essence of all the illusory things and thereby accomplish one's goals for the future."

With that thought, he had four storehouses for distributing charity constructed on the four sides of his palace. Summoning people from all directions, he gave in charity. Eventually all the charity houses became empty and the wealth ran out. But those in need of charity did not run out. While the king was sitting around being gloomy, the religious minister Trigunadhara[6] said to him, "Oh, Great King, sire, wouldn't it be better to practice generosity by obtaining a jewel from the island of precious wish-fulfilling jewels that lies on the other side of the great outer ocean?"

The king replied, "Minister, let us do as you have suggested. Gather all the subjects and subordinate rulers, and we will convince them of this advice to obtain a wish-fulfilling jewel."

The minister brought together the queens, ministers, and subjects, the entire entourage. Then the king spoke: "Oh, hear this, queens, ministers, and entourage. I have given indiscriminately in charity and the treasuries have been emptied, and yet the eagerness of the needy has not been exhausted. We must satisfy their desires. To that end, what capable person will volunteer to go retrieve a jewel from the island of wish-fulfilling jewels that lies on the other side of the outer ocean? The best would be merchants with previous experience of the place. Whoever has such familiarity must volunteer."

From amid the crowd an old, balding, squint-eyed man stood up and said, "Great King, to retrieve a wish-fulfilling jewel, one must cross the ocean. Give me a ship, with metal reinforcements, four sails for the four corners, four iron anchors attached with iron rope, a white conch shell to kill the noxious sea creatures,[7] a white she-goat for milk to revive the conch mollusk, and all the necessary equipment. We will sail under a favorable astrological sign."

The king provided all the equipment just as the merchant had requested. Commencing the journey on the full moon of the snake month, they arrived at the island of jewels in three months, on the fifth day of the first month of autumn. "Has the time come to take the jewel or not?" asked the king.

"Great King," the merchant replied, "to the west of here is a three-tiered mountain of precious gems. Crossing over to the other side of that, there is a castle made out of five precious substances. Go to the front of the door, and you will find a golden pestle. Pick it up and knock on the door three times."

The king did exactly as instructed. A beautiful young girl came out and said, "O King, what do you desire?"

"I desire a wish-fulfilling jewel that grants whatever one needs and desires," he said. The girl went inside, fetched a wish-fulfilling jewel, and offered it to the king. Then the king returned, and when he approached the merchant, he showed him the jewel to see if it was good or bad.

"King, this is the jewel that grants whatever one needs and desires," the merchant assured him. "You should pray."

The king offered prayer, and his blindness was cured. The king was then called Eyesight Gained [since he had regained his eyesight]. Then the lord and his subjects returned to their own country. They prayed to the jewel, and it rained upon them whatever they needed and desired. The suffering of poverty of all beings was alleviated. At that time, the king came to be known by the name of Ratsagausha.

Now, the minister Trigunadhara came to the shores of Dhanakosha. On

Kosha Island was a lake called Immaculate Radiance. In its center he saw a new lotus flower on a stem, beautiful to behold and delightful, with one thousand petals. On top of the twenty-five anthers was a beautiful boy child, resplendent and radiant with light. When news of this came to the king's ears, he came to the cliff overhang of the lake and saw the lotus for himself. He saw Precious Orgyen sitting there, vivid and brilliant, and he said, "If my wish-fulfilling jewel is a true one, then through the power of my prayers to you, may this boy child on the lotus come to be my son."

Thus he prayed, and I, Orgyen, was placed on the same seat as the king. I was invited into the palace and installed as prince. I was named Padma Gyalpo (Lotus King) and given five royal princesses as brides, among them the Princess Bhasadhara. I stayed for twenty-five years, and the Dharma was established in the kingdom.

Then one time I went outside and miraculously reached the top of the palace. An innately occurring sound came from the depths of the sky. I looked up and from among the white clouds there appeared a young male child making a symbolic gesture with his right hand and revealing this prophecy: "Hail, noble son. Abandon this royal kingdom and engage in the welfare of the beings throughout the world." Saying that, he disappeared. Thus Orgyen obtained the prophecy bestowed by Vajrasattva.

Then, singing a vajra song and dancing, I dropped the trident from my hand from the roof of the palace and it killed a minister's child, so that, in accordance with the law, I was banished to the charnel ground called Cool Grove.[8] At Cool Grove charnel ground, I, Padma Gyalpo, lived for five years by extracting vital essence in the practice of corpses, medicinal poison, and so on. I also became proficient in the five areas of knowledge.

Then I went to the palace of King Dza[9] on the meteorite tip of Mount Malaya and obtained the empowerment of the volumes of Precepts. In the Blazing Bonfire charnel ground, from the emanated one, Garab Dorje, I obtained the empowerment of *Direct Anointment of Majesty*[10] and received the entire instruction in the tantras of the Secret Mantra, outer, inner, and secret. Again in the Forest Latticework Cave, Princess Gomadevi gave me the outer, inner, and secret empowerment and for instruction, the complete five most essential tantras. At Rugged Grove,[11] I received the cycle of Ati yoga, including the Space Section, male, female, mother, and child, from Guru Shri Singha. In Akanishta I met Vajradhara face to face and obtained the empowerment in the energy of innately occurring awareness.

Then I visited the Eight Great Charnel Grounds and fully received the complete empowerment in the *Eight Transmitted Precepts*,[12] as well as all of the oral transmission and esoteric instruction in the tantras of the *Eight Transmitted Precepts*, from the eight great awareness-holders: Manjushrimitra, awareness-holder of body; Nagarjuna, awareness-holder of speech; Humkara, awareness-holder of mind; Vimalamitra, awareness-holder of quality; Prabahasti, awareness-holder of activity; Dhanasamskrita, awareness-holder of Mamo; Devachandra, awareness-holder of Mundane Worship; and Shantigarbha, awareness-holder of Wrathful Mantra. Returning once again, I became a lama of the eight awareness-holders.

Then I went to the Ragarati charnel ground, accomplished the practice of Amitayus, and became an awareness-holder of immortality. At the mountain of Kasarpani, I turned the Dharma wheel of Mahakaruna that tames beings. When in Bodhgaya, I cultivated the fields of the doctrine. I conquered the six kinds of teachers of devils and extremists so that the doctrine of the inner religion illuminated the darkness like a beacon.

Furthermore, the precepts of the tantras of the Great Completion naturally occurred and fell to me: dharmakaya Samantabhadra bestowed them by a mere blessing; sambhogakaya Vajrasattva bestowed them through the medium of intention-symbol; and nirmanakaya Garab Dorje bestowed them through the medium of words and poetics.

This is how it was bestowed through the medium of blessing by dharmakaya. The place is the expanse of space, the totally pure realm. In the primordially pure, innately occurring citadel is Glorious Samantabhadra. In a state without any real existence, like space, there manifests form, face, hands. This is Vajrasattva, in the place Akanishta, in the state of intentionality with no point of reference. It has blessing naturally; this is the bestowal.

This is how it was bestowed through the medium of the intention-symbol by the sambhogakaya. In the citadel of Dharma in the place Akanishta, based on that very Samantabhadra and the Great Compassion of that principle, Glorious Vajrasattva in the manner of an eight-year-old boy came to the top of a stemmed lotus flower. From Vajrasattva's heart the whole mandala of the Vajra Expanse opened up, and all the tantras of innately occurring Great Completion were bestowed through the medium of the intention-symbol.

This is how it was bestowed through the medium of words and poetics. In the country of Oddiyana in the northwest, in the citadel of nine levels called Torchokchen, there was a princess nun, Sudharma, the daughter of King Uparaja and the mother Nangsal Öden. She had devoted herself to monastic life and upheld the pure foundation of discipline. One night in a dream there came a white man made of crystal carrying a jeweled vase decorated with the seed syllables of the five families: *om, hung, tram, hri, ah*. He placed it on the princess's head and poured nectar onto her tongue. Thus she dreamed. Because of this amazing sign, between nine and ten months later the princess gave birth from between two right ribs to a boy with all the marks of a buddha. The gods rained down a shower of flowers and uttered many words of auspiciousness. He came to be known as Garab Dorje. At that time, on the meteorite mountain of Malaya, it was time for the precepts of the Great Completion to be naturally transmitted. Garab went to the Mountain of Supreme Manifestation and stayed in meditation for thirteen human years. His mind, endowed with the essence of pristine wisdom, went to Akanishta and received all the teachings of the Great Completion in their entirety from Glorious Vajrasattva. Vajrasattva bestowed them by merely showing a symbolic mudra, and sixty million four hundred thousand tantras were assimilated in his mind. Then, in the Blazing Mountain charnel ground he stayed in meditation in the play of the Great Mystery.

At the same time, in a place called Pososha country in China, Shri Singha was born as the son of Khyimdak Geden and Nangsal Khyendenma. His training was enhanced by the qualities of previous lives. When he was in meditation in the charnel ground of the Mute Lady's Garden, Mahakaruna actually revealed his face and gave him this prophecy: "If you desire the ultimate meaning, enlightenment's fruition, in one life and one body, then go to the Blazing Mountain charnel ground."

So Shri Singha went to the Blazing Mountain, and there he met Garab Dorje. Shri Singha said, "Great Master, if it would so please you, impart to me the profound quintessence of the innately occurring Great Completion."

Garab Dorje bestowed in their entirety the outer scripture collections and the inner Secret Mantra in its fruition: all the instructions of Ati yoga, through the medium of words and poetics. Then he went to the great charnel ground of Rugged Grove and stayed in meditation.

During that time, I, Orgyen Padma, was staying at the great charnel ground Sosaling, and was given a prophecy by the five kinds of dakini: "Great Master, go to Rugged Grove charnel ground. One whom you will meet there has the instructions to buddhahood." So I, Padmasambhava, went to Rugged Grove. I met the great awareness-holder Shri Singha and requested him to kindly give me an instruction. Shri Singha thoroughly bestowed the complete outer, inner, and secret instructions. Most important, he bestowed the entire secret tantras of Ati Great Completion, Space Section, male, female, and nondual, without leaving anything out.

Then the awareness-holder Shri Singha said, "Train your mind in the Three Baskets (*tripitaka*)." So I trained and mastered the Sutra Collection in the east, at Bodhgaya. In the south I trained and mastered the Discipline (*vinaya*). In the west I trained and mastered the Abhidharma. Then I mastered the Perfection of Wisdom (*prajnaparamita*) in the north. The mind training in the teachings of the Secret Mantra was like this: I studied and mastered the Three Baskets in the country of Oddiyana. The two sections of Tantra and Mind I studied and mastered in the country of Zahor. In Naradzara I studied and mastered Kilaya. In Singhala country I trained in Hayagriva and mastered it. I trained and mastered the Kriya in Badura country. In Nepal I trained in Yamantaka and became a master. Mamo was practiced in Marutse country and mastered. In the Vajra Seat of Bodhgaya I mastered the *Eight Transmitted Precepts* as well as Guhyasamaja father and mother tantras.

Then there are the famous Eight Identities of the Guru. I went to glorious Oddiyana in the west, and from the island of Lake Dhanakosha, I gained wonderful, supreme spiritual power. Then was I known as Padmakara (Lotus-Arisen).[13] In the Cool Grove charnel ground, supreme among the ten sacred sites of the heruka, I gained the spiritual power of the various qualities and became known as Padmasambhava (Lotus-Born). Near the city Vaishali, in the charnel ground of Raga Rakta, I gained the spiritual power of omniscience and became known as Loden Chokse (Intelligent Boon-Seeker). In the charnel ground Grove of Delight in the east, a sacred site where dakinis gather, I gained the spiritual power of controlling the three realms. My name then was Padma Gyalpo (Lotus King). In the charnel ground of Sosaling, before the tiered stupa of Maheshvara, I gained the spiritual power of taming beings and was known as Nyima Özer (Rays of Sun). The country was in the east of India, in the center of the country of the Zahor king. There I gained the spiritual power of wrathfully taming beings and was known as Shakya Senge (Lion of the Shakyas). In the central land of Magadha, at Bodhgaya to the north, I gained the spiritual power of subduing the extremists. I became known then as Senge Dradrok (Lion's Roar). The country was the Snowy Land of Tibet, where, at Taktsang Senge Samdrup, I gained the spiritual power of violent annihilation. Dorje Trolö (Vajra Wrath) was my name.

As these Eight Identities of the Guru, I wandered without direction throughout India, experiencing the empowerments and instructions of the awareness-holders like water absorbing salt. Possessed of learning and contemplation, I totally resolved the view of reality.

Then I perceived that the realm of Zahor should be subdued. There was one daughter of King Vihardhara who appeared outwardly in the form of a dakini, inwardly as Lady Tara, secretly as Vajravarahi, and most secretly as the play of Samantabhadri. Such was the wisdom dakini, and with her the pupils were living in the monastery observing the discipline, when I, Orgyen, arrived from the vault of the sky along the path of a rainbow in space, alighted at the palace, and sat down cross-legged. When the princess and the pupils saw me, they set up a large golden throne. They invited me to take my seat inside the palace, and prostrated. The princess said, "Sublime man, unequaled sovereign, lord of Dharma, what excellent sacred site or pure land have you come from? From what race do you come and what is your origin? What is your intention and your great purpose in coming to this place?"

I, Orgyen, replied, "Just now I have come from the pure land in the west. My race is that of Samantabhadra, Amitabha, Heruka. My origin is birth from a lotus, unhampered by a womb. My name is Padmasambhava. My intended purpose here is to establish the princess in the Dharma."

Then the princess offered a mandala of gold and silver, saying, "Great Master, I request the profound quintessence of the Great Vehicle Secret Mantra, the swift path, convenient to practice, an instruction that will benefit sentient beings."

I, Padmasambhava, thoroughly taught the Princess Mandarava and the pupils the entire teaching of Mahakaruna that tames beings. I also bestowed the three Innermost Essences, and all the Supreme teachings without exception. Headed by King Vihardhara, all the kingdom of Zahor was established in the Dharma. We two, the princess and Padmasambhava, went to a cave in the mountains of the highlands and stayed doing practice. A time came when I realized that I had completed my work for the welfare of beings in India. The time had arrived to tame the kingdoms of the Himalayas.

"Alas, Princess," I said, "to the north of here, on the other side of thirteen black mountains, lie the kingdoms of the Himalayas inhabited by cousins of the monkey. The time has come to tame them. If you have not finished your practice of the instructions, finish up now."

The princess protested, "As long as I am alive, even until I am an old woman at death's door, please stay here to protect the kingdom of Zahor. If you don't listen to me and we go to Tibet, what kinds of patrons for life's necessities will we find there? What kinds of great spiritual heirs who hold the Dharma lineage will we find there? What kinds of sacred sites for doing practice will we find there? And what kinds of women practitioners like me will we find there?"

"Princess, when I go to Tibet, the patron of life's necessities will be the son of King Tridé Tsepo[14] and Mashang Kongjo, born on the eighth of the first autumn month, the dragon month. He is an emanation of Manjushri, arising as one called Trisong Detsen. He will become a Dharma king and establish the Himalayan kingdoms in happiness. The great spiritual heirs who will hold the Dharma lineage are Sangye Yeshe, Gyalwa Chokyang, Namkhai Nyingpo, Nyak Jnana, Kharchen Tsogyal, Palkyi Yeshe, Langchenpal, Berotsana, Mutik Tsepo (aka Mutik Tsenpo), and so on. There will be many such great heirs to hold the Dharma lineage, but most of all, based on the power of my prayer, the descendants of the sovereign, the eight Lingpa Dharma masters, and many other treasure-revealers will appear. From now until the human life span is thirty years they will protect the doctrine of the Dharma.

"Regarding the sacred sites for practice, there is the body practice site of Drakyi Yangdzong, the speech practice site of Samye Chimphu, the mind practice site of Lhodrak Kharchu, the quality practice site of Yarlung Sheldrak, the activity practice sites of the three Senge Dzongs, the mamo practice site of Shampoi Gang, the subduing-all-violence practice site of Nesing Chugyun, the wrathful mantra practice site of Yamalung, and the union of joyful ones practice site of Utse Riksum. Moreover, there are prophecies for Taktsang, Yerpa, Tidro, twenty-one snow mountains, nine lakes, four hidden lands, five ravines, Kurje Cliff in Bhutan, Namkha Dzong, and many more such great sacred sites.

"As for women practitioners such as yourself, when I leave here and go up there, there will be, in Nepal, a Nepali girl named Shakyadhewa and Nepali subject Kalasiddhi and, in Tibet, the woman Yeshe Tsogyal, Dorje Tso of Tanak, the Bhutanese woman Tashi Khyedren, the princess Bumden Kyi from Bumthang and the daughters of the king—many such women practitioners will be there."

At the time I was saying this, the Dharma king Trisong Detsen was thirteen years old. His father, Tridé Tsepo, had passed away. When he was between the ages of fifteen and seventeen there was hostility and fighting in the country. At the age of twenty-one, in the year of the Rat, he conceived the idea of constructing Samye Monastery. He reflected, "My forefather Songtsen Gampo had also built many temples, such as Ramoche in Lhasa, and set up many self-appearing images, foremost among them the Jowo Shakyamuni. After blessing all the lands of Tibet, he taught the three renditions of *The Sutra of Jewel Chest Design,*[15] long, medium, and short, thus founding the holy Dharma. I, too, here in Tibet, which is as though filled with dense and dark gloom, must make the doctrine of the Buddha shine like the sun, by building temples, which are the support of enlightened body; translating holy scriptures, which are the support of enlightened speech; and establishing monastic orders, which are the support of enlightened mind."

So he gathered together all of his subjects, entourage, ministers, and subordinate kings and gave this speech:

"Listen, kings, ministers, subjects, and attendants. My forefather Songtsen built the temple of Ramoche in Lhasa and the other extremity-subduing and further-subduing temples, and established the Buddha's doctrine. I too was thinking whether I should build a crystal stupa at Zhang high enough to see China, or construct a copper conduit big enough to hold the upper Tsangpo River, or build a miniature temple. Please confer and advise me."

This was the king's command, and the ministers came to agreement and submitted their advice, "O Great King, you wouldn't find the crystal or copper to make either the crystal stupa or the copper conduit. It is better to construct the temple. Apply the measurements for its construction."

"Let us make it an arrow-shot in length in each direction," said the king. The ministers drew aside and secretly conferred among themselves. They agreed to empty the insides of an arrow and fill the arrow with gold dust or sand.[16] Then Taralugong filled the inside of an arrow with sand and handed it to the king. The king shot the arrow in the four directions and thus marked the building site of Samye. Then to bless the land and construct the temple of subduing the land, the king invited from Zahor the tenth-level bodhisattva, the regent of Shakyamuni, Acharya Shantarakshita, also known as Khenpo Bodhisattva. He came and blessed the site. Starting with the Triple-Storied Central Temple,[17] the temple foundations were laid. But what was built each day by humans was taken down each night by gods and demons. Mountain stones were carried back to the mountain, river rocks returned to the river. At that point the king became discouraged and said, "Although I was born a king, I must have impure karma, or else the people of Tibet have little merit, or else the buddhas and bodhisattvas of the ten directions have little compassion. Otherwise, why can't this sort of virtuous activity be accomplished?"

Khenpo replied, "These most fierce and noxious gods and demons of Tibet are not subdued by the great tranquility of my mind. There is one person now living in India who has a connection from previously formulated prayers. His name is Orgyen Padmasambhava. He is not afflicted by the duality of birth and death. He forces the eight kinds of gods and demons into his service. If you bring him here, the king's ambitions will be accomplished."

Then the king dispatched three envoys, Bamitrisher from Yarlung, Dorje Dudjom, and another to India to invite the Master. At this time, I knew intuitively that these three envoys from Tibet were coming to invite me there. The Indian road is very difficult to traverse, so I thought it better to depart first, at least as far as Nepal.[18] Traveling on a rainbow road in the sky, I arrived at the Eyi Temple in Nepal. For seven days I did the practice of Vajra Kilaya, Razor of Life, and hid many treasures at the Eyi Temple. Then the three envoys arrived. When they met me, they offered a measure of gold and prostrated. I told them, "All of my experience is golden, I have no need of your illusory gold," and threw all the gold into the sky. The envoys were astonished and anxious. I reflected that because there is much greed in this land of Tibet, gold is highly valued. Pouring out a handful of pebbles, I told the three envoys to hold out their robes as an apron. They held out their robes and all the pebbles turned to gold as I poured. Overflowing their robes, the gold fell to the ground. The envoys were astounded, and then they conducted me to Tibet.

The king, ministers, and subjects came out a long distance to greet me and accompany me to glorious Samye. The Dharma King Trisong Detsen offered me all his illusory wealth and said, "Alas, Great Master, this bad, desert land of Tibet, a primitive borderland, is controlled by fierce gods and demons. They are causing obstacles to the construction of my temple. Please demonstrate how to bind them with oaths and construct the temple."

Then I, Padmasambhava, staying in meditation in the Tamarisk Grove of Red Rock, bound the eight kinds of gods and demons of Tibet to oaths, and each of them offered me the essence of its life and promised to serve as slaves. On the full moon of the first month of spring in the Tiger year (810), on the day of the star Victory and the planet Saturn, we laid the foundation of the one hundred eight temples of Samye, starting with the Triple-Storied Central Temple. With the Four Great Kings[19] as my foremen, the gods and demons built more at night than the humans did in the day, and it rose up. The Triple-Storied Central Temple, the Triple-Realm Copper Shrine, the Flourishing Virtue Sand Shrine, the Golden Orphan Shrine,[20] the Aspiration of Awakening Shrine, the Sutra Mantra Shrine, the Translation Shrine, the Purification Shrine, the Amitabha Shrine, the Hayagriva Shrine, Aryapalo, Yaksha Subduing, upper and lower, the Magical Power Shrine, the four stupas, the Treasury Shrine, and the iron mountains—all these were successfully built and completed in the year of the Horse (814).[21] In the Sheep year the consecration and inauguration were done, and unimaginable, amazing omens occurred.

The three queens presided over the three Lady Shrines, and the great Dharma king stayed in the Triple-Storied Central Temple. Every month special services were held. To Queen Margyen[22] was born the son Murum Tsenpo[23] and the princess Nujin. To Mandhe Zangmo was born the son Mutri Tsenpo,[24] princess Trompa Gyen, and Lekjin Zangmo, the three siblings. Murum Tsenpo was exiled to the borderlands, so Mutri Tsenpo would inherit the kingdom. But Queen Margyen became jealous and poisoned him. During this time, Shantarakshita translated the Sutra literature and I translated the Mantra literature. Khenpo and Master together brought from India many of the outer

Baskets, and inner and secret Mantra transmissions. The Dharma king gathered together Vairochana and the other children of Tibet. They studied linguistics with us, Khenpo and Master, and then were dispatched to India. During this outpouring of translators to India, all the teachings of the outer Baskets and inner and secret Mantra, the supreme fruition, were received from Shri Singha and other wise Indian pandits. When they returned to Tibet, they caused the teachings of Sutra and Mantra to leap like sacred fire in the gloomy darkness of Tibet.

During that time a princess was born to Jangchub Drön who was given the name Pemasal. After that a son was born and called Mutik Tsepo.[25] While Mutik Tsepo was still growing, the Dharma King Trisong Detsen passed away. I thought that Mutik Tsepo was too young and that he would not be able to take command of the kingdom. So I kept the king's death a secret, and it was said that he was in retreat. I, Orgyen, held the kingdom for twenty-five years. Then, when the secret was revealed, Mutik Tsepo was entrusted with the kingdom.

All the profound teachings were written down and arranged as body treasure, speech treasure, mind treasure, and all the extra and miscellaneous treasures. They were then hidden as treasures in the mountains, cliffs, and temples of the Himalayas and were entrusted to the treasure lords. I opened the mandala of *The Compendium of the Most Secret Precepts*[26] in the Triple-Storied Central Temple; the king, lord, and the subjects made aspiration prayers for those treasures, that in the future, when the human life span becomes thirty years, the profound treasures would be a refuge for the doctrine. Then I said to Mutik Tsepo, "Great Prince, now one hundred eleven years have passed. The welfare of the beings in the Himalayas has been accomplished. Now I go to Chamara in the southwest to suppress the *rakshasa.*"[27]

When I said that, Mutik Tsepo fainted and collapsed like a felled tree. Tsogyal splashed water on him to revive him, and he said, "Lord, Knower of the Three Times, Padmasambhava, you, Orgyen, how can you not compassionately take care of me, the king, who is like an orphan without a father? I beg you, stay in Tibet as long as I live."

The king, in his misery, thus pressured me, so I thought I should take him to Zablung of Shang to do some training and to dispel his sadness. I said, "Oh, Prince, let's go to Zablung and stay there for a few years."

So we three, Orgyen and Tsogyal and the prince, went to Zablung in Shang, the place with ground like a carpet of skeletons, a sacred gathering site of mamos and dakinis, a place where supreme and ordinary spiritual powers fall like rain. We stayed in Zablung surrounded by the snow mountains. At that

Burning Lake (Mebartso) with an underwater cave in the Tang River of
Bumthang where Pema Lingpa discovered his first treasure. Photograph by
Marilyn Downing Staff (travel@asiatranspacific.com).

Gangteng Monastery (Gangtey Gonpa), Sang-ngak Choling, in the Phubjika Valley in the Black Mountains, the main seat of the Pema Lingpa tradition in Bhutan. Photograph by Stephen Barrie (Dolphin Spirit Pictures).

The main temple and courtyard of Gangteng Monastery.
Photograph by Marilyn Downing Staff (travel@asiatranspacific.com).

Lama dances that originated as a treasure discovery of Pema Lingpa.
Photograph by Cheyenne Ehrlich.

Lama dance. Photograph by Marilyn Downing Staff
(travel@asiatranspacific.com).

Rimochen Temple in the Chel Valley of Bumthang, built against the cliffside where Pema Lingpa discovered several important treasures (see Appendix B). Photograph by Natasha Diganello.

Kunzangdrak Temple, founded by Pema Lingpa high on the hillside. Photograph by Sarah Harding.

The actual site of a treasure discovery in the cliff-side near Kunzangdrak.
Photograph by Sarah Harding.

Current incarnations of the Pema Lingpa tradition: Tukse Rinpoche (mind),
Sungtrul Rinpoche (speech) and Gangteng Tulku Rinpoche (body).
Photograph by Natasha Deganello.

A stupa and mantra wall near Tamshing Monastery in Bumthang (seat for the
three Pema Lingpa incarnations). Photograph by Sarah Harding.

Konchok Sum Temple, also known as Tselung Lhakhang, in Bumthang, site of
several important treasure discoveries. Photograph by Sarah Harding.

The Ninth Gangteng tulku, Rikdzin Kunzang Pema Namgyal.
Photographer unknown.

time I said to the prince, "Great Dharma King, listen to me! All conditioned phenomena upon this earth are impermanent, like a dream. The end of birth is death. The end of gathering is parting. The end of accumulating is depleting. The end of building is collapsing. The end of acting is emptying. To all buddhas are their individual disciples. To all sentient beings are their individual sufferings. The likes of me, Padmasambhava, have completed the destiny of influencing India and other places and the welfare of beings in the Himalayas. Padmasambhava will go to Chamara. Prince, do not worry about it. For all of my children who have devotion, it is the same whether I stay or depart. Pray to me, Mutik Tse, and I will know all the aims of this and future lives. Practice the instructions you have received."

Prince Mutik Tsepo implored me, "Great Master, then please bestow a teaching never before taught by a previous victorious one, that no translator has yet translated; a Buddhadharma for right now, at this juncture; the profound quintessence of Orgyen's own mind; a means of accomplishment of the three roots—lama, yidam, and dakini; an especially profound, grand, comprehensive guidance."

In response to this request, I, Orgyen, granted the Dharma king Mutik Tsepo the pith of the crucial meaning, extra profound, quintessential, vital life of esoteric instruction from the expanse of my heart. Having revealed all the teachings of the Mind Section, I established him in the instruction of *Lama Jewel Ocean*. Mutik Tsepo accomplished the three bodies of the lama, and practiced Cutting Through Resistance and Direct Crossing, thus realizing that all apparent phenomena are like the illusion of dreams. He actualized the perspective of the realm of reality and perceived the meaning of the unborn.

Then Mutik Tsepo said, "Great Master, my sister Princess Pemasal will not reach her full life span. There is only a short time to keep her company. In your compassion, please care for her Dharma destiny with this instruction that you have bestowed on me."

Orgyen said, "Oh, let it be so. Tsogyal, put it all down in writing."

So Tsogyal wrote down the instructions of *Lama Jewel Ocean* without mistakes or omissions, using blood from her nose and six essential ingredients on paper that changes color, and handed it to the master. At Chimphu we went through it three times to check for mistakes, and then sealed it in a rhinoceros-skin box. Prince Mutik Tsepo asked, "If you are going to hide this instruction as treasure, where will you hide it? When is the time of its revelation? What noble beings will hold these teachings, and how will they benefit sentient beings?"

I replied, "These teachings of the Mind Section will be hidden as treasure in the Lion's Face, to the north of the White Cliff which is like three hearth-stones, at the confluence of two rivers, in the cliff called Mendo in Lhodrak, which is west of here at Samye. It will be revealed when eight hundred seventy years have passed; when, in the Himalayan kingdom here, the doctrine of the nine gongpo brother spirits has emerged, the people's leaders spread the fighting of greed and aggression, and the religious discipline of all sections of the Dharma has been destroyed. Many will then have the realization of impropriety and non-Dharma. Lay people will wear the dress of the clergy; clinging to red and yellow, they'll conduct themselves in wrongdoing. Earth lords and planetary forces will spread evil. There will be many incurable contagious diseases. Offerings will be made to demons, rakshasas, and gongpo spirits as if they were deities. The fortresses of gods and spirits will be used as bunkers. The chapels of Kyirong will hold military camps. That will be the destined time for the cycle of *Lama Jewel Ocean* to be revealed and reinstated.

"At that time your present sister will be born in the area of Bumthang to the southwest of here, in a low valley like two palms joined in prayer, a secluded place like the fringe of an umbrella, surrounded by forest and meadow, a small area that is like a firepit. This one named Pema will be born as the son of the father Döndrup and mother Pema in the male Iron Horse-Snake year. His body will be stocky and his skin red, his torso adorned with three white birthmarks, the mark of the letter *ah* on the back of his right hand, the mark of a birthmark like an eye on the inside thigh, and at the heart a relic the size of a pea. He will experience visions, and the desirous mind will be destroyed. Doing various Dharma and non-Dharma activities, he will speak harsh words like the neighing of a horse. He will receive much criticism and slander, but altruism will inspire him. All those connected with him will become awareness-holders. When he is twenty-seven years old, he will encounter my, Padma's, profound treasure: this treasury of the Mind Section, *Jewel Ocean*. That noble being will reveal it and confer all the empowerments, guidance, and instructions, ripening the beings and establishing them in the path of freedom. The karmically endowed ones who will hold this teaching will be one man known as Dvatruk from Yarlung, Dharma of Dvak Kong, Dorje of Nyal, Gyatso of Bumthang, Sönam of Lhodrak; some other karmically endowed children will come who will hold this teaching. It will spread for the welfare of beings in Central Tibet, Tsang, Kong, Kham, Bhutan, and Lhodrak. The doctrine of this treasure teaching will spread until the human life span is thirty years."

I, Orgyen Padma, and Tsogyal, have come together to Mendo in Lhodrak on the eighth day of the spring month of the Tiger year. Imprinting an *ah tam* in the cliff for immutability, the entire instruction of *Jewel Ocean* sealed in the maroon rhinoceros-skin box, stamped with seven layers of seals, is hidden as treasure. Outwardly, it is entrusted to Sokdak Khyakpa Karpo; inwardly, to the obedient ones (*kasung*); and secretly to the dakinis.

You, Treasure Lords!
If the wrong time or treasure-thieves occur,
Take control of their life-force faculties.
In the future, the final life of Pemasal,
May the one named Pema find it at the right time.

With this oath, the treasure is hidden.

In the middle period of the five degenerations of the doctrine, according to the aspiration prayers of Orgyen and the prophecy of the dakinis, I, Pema Lingpa, extracted this from Mendo Cliff in Lhodrak on the full moon of the first month of autumn in the year of the female Fire Hare (1507).

SAMAYA GYA GYA GYA TER GYA BE GYA TE GYA KA GYA
SANG GYA DAM GYA ZAB GYA

sacred pledge; sealed sealed sealed; treasure seal; hidden seal; entrustment seal; command seal; secret seal; sacred seal; profound seal

May my, Pema's, activities and prayers be accomplished.

Appendix A
Incarnations of the Pema Lingpa Tradition

COMPILED BY JOHN ARDUSSI

THE INFORMATION in this appendix has been compiled from many sources, written and oral. The main ones are listed at the end. The sequence of Pema Lingpa's prior incarnations (and those also of the First Gyalse or Gangteng Tulku) are indicated here with letters (no official numbering scheme for them is found in the original sources). As for their seats, the Pema Lingpa incarnates acquired monasteries in both Bhutan and Tibet, and traveled frequently between them during the course of their teaching in the two countries.

PELING SUNGTRUL RINPOCHE
(PAD-GLING GSUNG-SPRUL)

Seats:

1. Gtam-zhing Lhun-grub-chos-gling Monastery, in Bumthang, Bhutan.
2. Lho-brag Guru Lha-khang in Tibet, beginning with the Second *Gsung-sprul* Bstan-'dzin grags-pa and shared with *Rgyal-sras* Padma-'phrin-las.
3. By recent appointment of HM the Druk Gyalpo, *Gsung-sprul Rin-po-che* currently resides at Sgra-med-rtse Theg-mchog-rnam-'grol O-rgyan-chos-gling Monastery near Tashigang, E. Bhutan.

Previous Incarnations:

A. Lha-gcig Padma-gsal
B. Rig-ma Sangs-rgyas-skyid
C. Jo-mo Padma-sgrol-ma
D. Sngags-'chang Rin-chen-grags-pa
E. Padma-las-'brel-rtsal (1291-1319)
F. Klong-chen-pa Dri-med-'od-zer (1308-1363)
G. Thod-dkar

Pema Lingpa and His Incarnations:
1. Padma-gling-pa (Childhood name: Dpal-'byor) (1450-1521)
2. Bstan-'dzin-chos-grags-dpal-bzang *aka* Bstan-'dzin grags-pa (1536-1597)
3. Kun-mkhyen Tshul-khrims-rdo-rje (1598-1669)
4. Rdo-rje-mi-bskyod-rtsal *aka* Ngag-dbang Kun-bzang Rol-pa'i-rdo-rje (1680-1723)
5. Kun-bzang-tshe-dbang *aka* Bstan-'dzin Grub-mchog-rdo-rje (1725-1762)
6. Kun-bzang Bstan-pa'i-rgyal-mtshan (1763-1817)
7. Padma-bstan-'dzin, *aka* Kun-bzang Ngag-dbang-chos-kyi-blo-gros (1819-1842)
8. Kun-bzang-bde-chen-rdo-rje *aka* Nges-don Bstan-pa'i-nyi-ma (1843-1891)
9. Bstan-'dzin Chos-kyi-rgyal-mtshan (1894-1925)
10. Padma-'od-gsal-'gyur-med-rdo-rje *aka* Thub-bstan Chos-kyi-rdo-rje (1930-1955)
11. Kun-bzang Padma Rin-chen-rnam-rgyal (b.1968)

Peling Tukse Rinpoche (Pad-gling Thugs-sras)[1]

Seats:
1. Lha-lung Me-tog-lha-nang Theg-mchog-rab-rgyas-gling Monastery, in Lho-brag, Tibet. (This former Karmapa monastery was given by the Fifth Dalai Lama in 1672 for use by the Pad-gling incarnates. The seat was used by both the Pad-gling *Thugs-sras* and *Gsung-sprul,* who sometimes include the epithet Lha-lung in their title).

2. Gtam-zhing Lhun-grub-chos-gling Monastery, in Bumthang, Bhutan (this seat is also shared with the Pad-gling *Gsung-sprul*).

Dawa Gyaltsen (Zla-ba Rgyal-mtshan) and His Incarnations:
1. Zla-ba-rgyal-mtshan (b.1499)
2. Nyi-zla-rgyal-mtshan[2]
3. Nyi-zla-klong-yangs[3] (fl. early seventeenth century)
4. Bstan-'dzin 'Gyur-med-rdo-rje (1641-ca.1702)
5. 'Gyur-med-mchog-grub-dpal-'bar-bzang-po (ca. 1708-1750)
6. Bstan-'dzin Chos-kyi-nyi-ma (ca. 1752-1775)

7a. Kun-bzang 'Gyur-med-rdo-rje Lung-rigs-chos-kyi-go-cha (ca. 1780-ca. 1825) (enthroned at Lha-lung)

7b. Bstan-'dzin Ngag-dbang-'phrin-las (resided at Rdo-rje-brag)

8. Kun-bzang Zil-gnon-bzhad-pa-rtsal (rebirth of 7a)

9. Thub-bstan-dpal-'bar (1906–1939)

10. Theg-mchog Bstan-pa'i-rgyal-mtshan (1951–) born in Dra-nang, Tibet.[4]

PELING GYALSE RINPOCHE (PAD GLING RGYAL-SRAS) AKA GANGTENG TULKU (SGANG-STENG SPRUL-SKU)

Seats:

1. Sgang-steng Gsang-sngags-chos-gling Monastery, near Wangdiphodrang, Bhutan

2. Traditional winter seat: Phun-tshogs-rab-brtan-gling Monastery, after its completion in 1682.

Previous Incarnations:

A. Bodhisattva Tsunda (Skul-byed)

B. *Mkhas-pa chen-po* Ldan-ma Rtse-mangs *aka* Rnam-grol-ye-shes

C. Lha Bla-ma Ye-shes-'od

D. *Mkhas-mchog* Kun-dga'-grags-pa (student of Rngog Lo Blo-ldan-shes-rab)

E. *Myang-sras* Bstan-'dzin-yon-tan

F. Legs-pa-rgyal-mtshan *aka* Dbang-phyug-dpal-'bar

G. 'Jam-dbyangs Khyab-brdal-lhun-grub (son of the Lho-brag La-yags rgyal-po)

H. *Gter-ston chen-po* Dri-med-gling-pa (from Bumthang, Bhutan)

I. *Mkhan-chen* Tshul-khrims-dpal-'byor (born in Lho-brag[5])

Pema Trinle (Padma-'phrin-las) and His Incarnations:

1. Padma-'phrin-las (1564-1642?)

2. Bstan-'dzin-legs-pa'i-don-grub (1645-1726)

3. 'Phrin-las-rnam-rgyal *aka* Kun-bzang-padma-rnam-rgyal (d. ca. 1750)

4. Bstan-'dzin-srid-zhi-rnam-rgyal (1761?- ca. 1796)

5. O-rgyan-dge-legs-rnam-rgyal (d. 1842?)

6. O-rgyan Bstan-pa'i-nyi-ma (ca. 1873–1900?)

7. O-rgyan Bstan-pa'i-nyin-byed (brother of Zhabs-drung 'Jigs-med Chos-

rgyal, 1862-1904)
8. O-rgyan 'Phrin-las-rdo-rje
9. Rig-'dzin Kun-bzang Padma-rnam-rgyal (b. Dec. 17, 1955)

SOURCES:

(a) Gter-ston Padma-gling-pa [1450-1521]. n.d. *Bum thang gter ston padma gling pa'i rnam thar 'od zer kun mdzes nor bu'i phreng ba zhes bya ba skal ldan spro ba skye ba'i tshul du bris pa* (autobiography). Reprinted in *Rediscovered Teachings of the Great Padma-gling-pa*, vol. 14. Thimphu: Kunsang Tobgay, 1976.

(b) Rje Mkhan-po X Bstan-'dzin-chos-rgyal [1700-1767]. 1745. *Rgyal kun khyab bdag 'gro ba'i bla ma bstan 'dzin rin po che legs pa'i don grub zhabs kyi rnam par thar pa ngo mtshar nor bu'i mchod sdong*. 123 folios. Biography of the Second Rgyal-sras Sprul-sku Bstan-'dzin-legs-pa'i don-grub (1645-1726). Reprinted in Kunsang Topgay, *Biographies of Two Bhutanese Lamas of the Padma-gling-pa Tradition*. Thimphu, 1975. Lists all of the incarnations prior to Rgyal-sras Padma-'phrin-las.

(c) Pad-gling Gsung-sprul VIII Kun-bzang-bstan-pa'i-nyi-ma [1843-1891]. 1873. *Pad gling 'khrungs rabs kyi rtogs brjod nyung gsal dad pa'i me tog*. Reprinted in Kunsang Tobgay, *Rediscovered Teachings of the Great Padma-gling-pa*, vol. 14. Thimphu, 1976.

(d) 'Jam-dbyangs Mkhyen-brtse-dbang-po [1820-1892]. n.d. *Gangs can bod kyi yul du byon pa'i gsang sngags gsar rnying gi gdan rabs mdor bsdus ngo mtshar padmo'i dga' tshal*. Reprinted in S.W. Tashigangpa, *Mkhyen-brtse on the History of the Dharma*. Leh, 1972. A history of selected Nyingmapa lineages, including those of Lhalung.

(e) Gu-ru Bkra-shis (= *Stag-sgang Mkhas-mchog* Ngag-dbang-blo-gros). 1813. *Chos 'byung ngo mtshar gtam gyi rol mtsho*. Beijing: Krung go'i bod kyi shes rig dpe skrun khang, 1990. Information on many Nyingma lineages including the Thugs-sras of Lhalung.

(f) Bdud-'joms-'jigs-bral-ye-shes-rdo-rje [1904-1987]. 1975. *Pad gling 'khrungs rabs rtogs brjod dad pa'i me tog gi kha skong mos pa'i ze'u 'bru*. Reprinted in Kunsang Tobgay, *Rediscovered Teachings of the Great Padma-gling-pa*, vol. 14. Thimphu, 1976.

(g) Bla-ma Gsang-sngags [b.1934]. 1983. *'Brug tu 'od gsal lha'i gdung rabs 'byung tshul brjod pa smyos rabs gsal ba'i me long*. Thimphu: Mani Dorji. Biographical study covering some of the families descended from Padma Gling-pa and his relatives.

(h) Interview 5/28/02 with H.H. Gangteng Tulku at Gangteng Monastery, by the author.

(i) Interview 5/30/02 with H.H. Peling Sungtrul Rinpoche at Drametse Monastery, by the author.

Appendix B

Contents of Pema Lingpa's Collection of Treasures
(Pad gling gter chos)

COMPILED BY HOLLY GAYLEY

VOLUMES 1–2: Ka/Kha
Lama Jewel Ocean
Bla ma nor bu rgya mtsho
Revealed from the Lion-Faced
Cliff at Mendo in Lhodrak

VOLUME 3: Ga
Drag po che 'bring chung gsum
Wrathful Guru Cycles; Greater,
Middling, and Lesser

*Bla ma drag po dmar chen me lce
   phreng ba*
The Great Red Wrathful Guru,
   Necklace of Flames
Revealed from the indestructible
   rock outcropping at Kurje in
   Bumthang

Bla ma drag po 'gro ba kun 'dul
Wrathful Guru, Tamer of Beings
Revealed from the throne-like
   base of Lion Cliff in lower
   Bumthang

Drag po me rlung 'khyil pa
Wrathful Fire Twister
Revealed at the eastern side of
   Lion Cliff at Tharpaling

VOLUME 4: Nga
Rdzogs chen kun bzang dgongs 'dus
Great Completion, The Union of
Samantabhadra's Intentions (Vol-
ume One)
Revealed from the stupa at Chim-
phu near Samye

VOLUME 5: Ca
Klong gsal gsang ba snying bcud
The Quintessence of the Mysteries
of Luminous Space (Volume One)
Revealed from the Burning Lake
by the foot of the Long-Nosed
Cliff in Bumthang

VOLUME 6: Cha
*Snying tig yang gsang rgyud bu
chung ba*
The Small Child Tantra of the
Most Secret Innermost Essence
(or The Small Child Tantra)
Revealed from the Lion Cliff at
Rimochen in Bumthang

VOLUME 7: Ja
Thugs rje chen po mun sel sgron me
The Great Compassionate One,
The Lamp That Illuminates the

Darkness
Revealed from the indestructible
enclosure of the Copper Cave of
Rimochen

VOLUME 8: Nya
Tshe khrid rdo rje'i phreng ba
The Diamond Necklace of
Longevity Instructions
Revealed from the Lion-Faced
Cliff at Mendo in Lhodrak

VOLUME 9: Ta
Phyag rdor dregs pa kun 'dul
Vajrapani Suppressing Fierce Ones
Revealed from a cracked rock in
the variegated cliff in Lhodrak

Bdud rtsi sman sgrub
Elixir Medicine Sadhana
Revealed from Rimochen in Bum-
thang

VOLUME 10: Tha
*Bka' brgyad yang sang thugs kyi me
long*
The Most Secret Eight Transmitted
Precepts, Mirror of the Mind
Revealed from Tselung Lhakhang
in Bumthang

VOLUME 11: Da
Mgon po ma ning
The Protector Maning
Revealed from the Meteorite Blaz-
ing Cliff at Mendo in Lhodrak

Nag po skor gsum
Three Black Cycles

Revealed from the back gate of
Tselung Lhakhang in Bumthang

Gshin rje kha thun nag po
Black Yamantaka

Phra men phag sha nag po
Black Sow-Headed Tramen

Mu stegs gu lang nag po
Black Heretic Maheshvara

Las phran skor
Cycle of Minor Activities
Revealed from the back gate of
Tselung Lhakhang in Bumthang

VOLUME 12: Na
Tshe khrid nor bu lam khyer
Longevity Instruction, Applying
Jewels on the Path
Revealed from the indestructible
rock outcropping at Kurje in Bum-
thang

Rta mgrin dmar po dregs pa zil gnon
Red Hayagriva, Overwhelming
Fierce Ones
Revealed from Mendo in Lhodrak

Rta mgrin nag po lcags ral can
Iron-Hair Black Hayagriva
Revealed from the red rock mete-
orite cliff in Yamdrok

VOLUME 13: Pa
Bka' 'bum yid bzhin gter mdzod
Pema Lingpa's Collected Writings,
A Wish-Fulfilling Treasure Trove

VOLUME 14: Pha
Pad gling gi rnam thar
Biographies of Pema Lingpa (and
his subsequent incarnations)

VOLUME 15: Ba
Rdzogs chen kun bzang dgongs 'dus
Great Completion, The Union of
Samantabhadra's Intentions (Vol-
ume Two)

VOLUME 16: Ma
Phur ba yang gsang srog gi spu gri
Kila, The Most Secret Vital Blade
Revealed from the Lion-Faced
Cliff at Mendo in Lhodrak

VOLUME 17: Tsa
Klong gsal gsang ba snying bcud
The Quintessence of the Mysteries
of Luminous Space (Volume Two)

VOLUME 18: Tsha
'Don cha'i skor bdud 'jom sogs
gsung
Liturgical cycles by Dudjom
Rinpoche et al.

VOLUME 19: Dza
Dbang gyi mtshams skor
Ritual Arrangements for Empow-
erments

VOLUME 20: Wa
Bla ma nor bu rgya mtsho'i kha
skong
Appendix to Lama Jewel Ocean

VOLUME 21: Zha
Orgyan padma 'byung gnas kyi
'khrung rabs sangs rgyas bstan pa'i
chos byung
The Biography of Padmasambhava, A History of the Buddha's
Teachings

Endnotes

NOTES TO PREFACE

1 For a thorough discussion of the terma (*gter ma*) tradition see Janet Gyatso, *Apparitions of the Self: The Secret Autobiographies of a Tibetan Visionary* (Princeton: Princeton University Press, 1998). Also, Tulku Thondup, *Hidden Teachings of Tibet: An Explanation of the Terma Tradition of the Nyingma School of Buddhism* (Boston: Wisdom Publications, 1986).

2 *gter ston rgyal po lnga*, five "kingly" treasure-finders, emanations of King Trisong Detsen, were Nyang Ral Nyima Özer (1136–1192), Guru Chöwang (Chökyi Wangchuk, 1212–1270), Dorje Lingpa (1346–1405), Pema Lingpa (1450–1521), and Do-Ngak Lingpa (Jamyang Khyentse Wangpo, 1820–1892). Guru Chöwang and Dorje Lingpa also discovered important treasures in Bhutan.

3 Dakini script is symbolic writing indecipherable to all except the destined treasure-finder or treasure lords, and is associated with the particular lineage (of six) called "the lineage of the dakinis' seal of entrustment." See Dudjom Rinpoche, *The Nyingma School of Tibetan Buddhism* (Boston: Wisdom Publications, 1991), 1:745. All of the termas translated in this book had a few lines of such script left in them.

4 Written by Loppon Padma Tshewang and translated by Chris Butters in *The Treasure Revealer of Bhutan: Pemalingpa, the Terma Tradition and Its Critics,* Bibliotheca Himalayica, ser. 3, vol. 8 (Kathmandu, Nepal: EMR Publishing House, 1995).

5 Jamie Zeppa, *Beyond the Sky and the Earth: A Journey into Bhutan* (New York: Riverhead Books, 1999).

NOTES TO THE INTRODUCTION

* I would like to thank Stanley Tambiah and Janet Gyatso for reading and commenting on an early draft of this introduction. A special note of appreciation to Gangteng Tulku and Sarah Harding for inviting me to Bhutan and involving me in this project.

1 Personal interview, Bumthang, 30 May 2001. Translated by Sarah Harding.

2 On the term charisma, see Max Weber 1978, especially vol. 1: 241–54, and Edward Shils 1975: 127–275. For a discussion of charisma in relation to Buddhist saints, see Stanley Tambiah 1984: 321–47 and Reginald Ray 1994: 23–31, 421–23.

3 Up to the present, the categories of Buddhist saints considered by scholars have included the *arhat, bodhisattva,* and *mahasiddha.* This introduction represents a first attempt at defining the tertön as a category of Buddhist saint. For previous discussions of Buddhist saints, see Tambiah 1984 and 1987, Ray 1994, Bond 1984, Lopez 1984, and Robinson 1979 and 1996. For excellent anthologies of saints through a comparative lens, see Hawley 1987, Kiechefer and Bond 1984, and Stephen Wilson 1983. It is important to note that tertöns are not an exclusively Buddhist phenomenon in Tibetan and Himalayan regions, even though the discussion in this introduction focuses on tertöns as a category of Buddhist saint. For a discussion of tertöns in the Bön religion, see Karmay 1972, Kvaerne 1974, Gyatso 1992 and 1996, and Kapstein 2000.

4 I borrow the term "predetermined emissary" from Janet Gyatso (1998: 147).

5 The degree to which the activities ascribed to Padmasambhava by the Nyingma tradition are historical or legendary has been explored by Matthew Kapstein in *The Tibetan Assimilation of Buddhism: Conversion, Contestation, and Memory* (2000).

6 For an analysis and list of biographies of Padmasambhava, see Anne-Marie Blondeau 1980.

7 Weber identifies charisma with innovation; he states that "charisma is *the* great revolutionary force." (See Weber 1978: 241, 245.) The definition of the charismatic individual provided by Edward Shils likewise emphasizes innovation. Shils links innovation to a "source remote in time or timeless" in a formulation particularly relevant to the case of tertöns. He states, "The charismatic person is a creator of a new order as well as the breaker of a routine order. Since charisma is constituted by the belief that its bearer is effectively in contact with what is most vital, most powerful, and most authoritative in the universe or in society, those to whom charisma is attributed are, by virtue of that fact, authoritative... The bearer and the adherents of charismatic authority, in contrast [with other forms of authority], tend to think of their norms as legitimated by a source remote in time or timeless, remote in space or spaceless" (1975: 129). As we will see, the tertön establishes new ritual cycles and religious communities associated with them, based on the authority of both a remote time, the eighth century, and the timeless realm of a primordial buddha. However, unlike what is proposed by Shils, it is key to the revelation process that the past and present are linked by place. So, while the atemporal dimensions of a primordial buddha may not have a specific locus, the revelation process explicitly claims that activities of Padmasambhava in the past occurred at the very site of revelation.

8 In addition, sacred objects discovered as treasures (*rdzas gter*) are considered to be relics of Padmasambhava; as such they are also called terma. This type of terma typically consists of statues and ritual implements. The sacred objects among Pema Lingpa's terma are housed at Gangteng Gompa, the principal seat of the Peling tradition in Bhutan today. In September 2002, due to the renovation of Gangteng Gompa, these terma were briefly displayed.

9 Not all treasures are attributed to Padmasambhava as a source. The Bön religion in Tibet had its own treasure tradition traced to their founder Shenrab. Within the Nyingma school itself, Padmasambhava and Yeshe Tsogyal are the principal figures associated with the terma tradition; they are credited with hiding away the

bulk of the treasure caches for future generations. However, in the *Rinchen Terdzö*, Jamgön Kongtrul also lists other figures: Vimalamitra and Vairocana, as well as a number of Padmasambhava's disciples such as Nub Sangye Yeshe, Namkhai Nyingpo, and Nanam Dorje Dudjom. From the twelfth century onwards, Padmasambhava became increasingly the dominant figure within the treasure lore. For a discussion on these points, see Gyatso 1996: 150, 162.

10 Quoted from Gene Smith 2001: 240.

11 On the cosmopolitan nature of Tibet at its zenith of empire, see Kapstein 2000, especially 58–65.

12 See Pommaret 1994 and 1999 for a discussion of the Mön people in Bhutan. Dorji 1997 provides a genealogy of the names for Bhutan.

13 For short biographical accounts of these tertöns, see Dudjom Rinpoche 1991. Karmay 2000 discusses Dorje Lingpa's treasure activities in present-day Bhutan.

14 Kongtrul's anthology is titled *Lives of the One Hundred Tertöns* or *Gter ston brgya rtsa'i rnam thar*. It consists of a compilation of short biographies for more than one hundred and fifty tertöns.

15 The most standard list for the Five Tertön Kings is as follows: Nyangral Nyima Özer, Guru Chöwang, Ratna Lingpa, Pema Lingpa, and Do-ngak Lingpa.

16 Thank you to Gene Smith for lending me his outline of this anthology. The table of contents for the *Rinchen Terdzö* has been electronically inputted and the entire anthology scanned; it is available at www.tbrc.org. For an overview of its contents, see Gyatso 1996.

17 Orgyen Lingpa's *Padma bka' thang* first appeared in translation as *Le Dict de Padma*, translated by Gustave-Charles Toussaint. It is also available in English as *The Life and Liberation of Padmasambhava*, translated by Kenneth Douglas and Gwendolyn Bays (1978).

18 Douglas and Bays 1978: 630.

19 Tertöns also achieved recognition based on prophecies from within one of their own treasures.

20 Aris 1988b: 41.

21 *Lung bstan gsal byed 'od kyi dra ba* (*Pad gling gter chos*, vol. 1: 139–49). See Appendix B.

22 Interestingly, ordinary works by Pema Lingpa occasionally are marked by *gter tsheg*, thus blurring to a certain extent the line between revelation and ordinary modes of authorship.

23 This prophetic frame entails an inner and outer frame of several lines that bracket the contents of each text regardless of its contents or genre. The outer frame of a text consists of the opening homage, often to Padmasambhava, and a colophon, when there is one, usually a single line at the end of the text that provides the details of the discovery in the first person voice of Pema Lingpa. Within that is an inner frame that sets the stage for the contents of the text. In the inner frame, the voice shifts to a first-person narration by Padmasambhava himself. The content

of any text is thus framed as the words of Padmasambhava whether or not he continues to act as an explicit narrator throughout the text.

24 In Pema Lingpa's treasures, the discovery date is not a prominent feature. It may be recorded only in the internal catalogue (*them byang*) or alternately appear in the colophon of a single text per treasure cycle.

25 The prophetic aura is enhanced by two final framing devices. In the first of these framing devices, the author's pledge is directly followed by a "seal of commitment," which adds a prophetic thrust to the aspiration. It reads "*samaya gya gya gya*" or "sacred pledge, sealed sealed sealed." This seal gives the author's pledge a new weight; it is no longer merely a pledge to compose a text with a specific intention in mind but a commitment to be fulfilled in a distant future. Padmasambhava's intentions are thought to be efficacious, but with a seal of commitment there is an additional solemnity. The promised item, in fact, is the text to follow, which will appear under the conditions stated in the aspiration. This seal marks not just the promise itself but the very thing that has been promised to future generations, the text sealed below. The concluding lines in Padmasambhava's voice are followed by the second seal of commitment, usually more elaborate, which seals the prophecy and also the seals the end of the text. This second seal completes the "prophetic frame" around the contents of the text. It is followed by the tertön's own colophon, naming the site and occasionally the date of the discovery.

The second of these final framing devices occurs at the outset of many of Pema Lingpa's treasure texts. Just before the title is a single strand of what might be dakini script, the symbolic language in which the treasures are said to be encoded. (See Gyatso 1993: 100.) Another strand of this script is often placed between the two parts of the colophon, marking the boundary between the inner and outer layers of the framing structure at the end of the text. The cryptic style of the letters is particularly reminiscent of the dakini script found on the yellow scrolls within the treasure casket. This association further imbues each text with a numinous quality.

26 For discussions concerning origin accounts and the transmission process of terma, see Gyatso 1986 and 1993 as well as Thondup 1986.

27 On contemporary terma, see Germano 1998.

28 Below are some examples of the variation in numbers and phases within the histories in Pema Lingpa's treasures. See Appendix B. In the *Rdzogs chen kun bzang dgongs 'dus* (Vol. 4), there are four stages of transmission according to its history: *rgyal ba dgongs pa'i rgyud tshul, rig 'dzin brta'i rgyud tshul, gang zag snyan khug kyi rgyud tshul, smon lam dbang bsgyur gyi rgyud tshul.* In *Thugs rje chen po mun sel sgron me* (Vol. 7), the history lists five stages: *sangs rgyas dgongs nas brgyud pa, byang chub sems dpa'i thugs rje'i brgyud pa, gang zag snyan gyis khungs nas brgyud pa, dgos ched don gyi nyams len gyi brgyud pa, lung bstan gtad rgya gdams pa'i brgyud pa.* In *Tshe khrid rdo rje'i phreng ba* (Vol. 8), the history lists six stages: *rgyal ba dgongs brgyud, thugs rje brda brgyud, gang zag snyan brgyud, dgos chad nyams len don gyi brgyud, lung bstan gtad rgya'i brgyud, drub thob rnal 'byor brgyud.* In *Bka' brgyad yang sang thugs kyi me long* (Vol. 10), there are seven stages: *rgyal ba dgongs pa'i brgyud, rig 'dzin rig pa brgyud, mkha' 'gro gtad rgya'i brgyud, grub thob rnal 'byor brgyud, gang zag snyan khung brgyud, zab mo gter gyi brgyud, bka' babs lung bstan brgyud.*

29 For an excellent study on the three-kaya theory, see John Makransky, *Buddha-hood Embodied* (Albany: State University of New York Press, 1997).

30 *Lo rgyus stong thun dang bcas pa nor bu'i phreng ba* (*Pad gling gter chos,* vol. 1: 395–429).

31 See Thondup 1986 concerning the importance of the aspirational empowerment (*smon lam dbang bskur*).

32 The histories in Pema Lingpa's treasures use terms for the transmission process of a treasure that are slightly different from the set later standardized by the third Dodrupchen Jigme Tenpe Nyima (1865–1926) in the *Wonder Ocean: An Explana-tion of the Treasure Tradition.* Dodrupchen's account includes three transmissions: (1) the "prophetic authorization" (*bka' babs lung bstan*); (2) the "aspirational empowerment" (*smon lam dbang bskur*); and (3) the "entrustment to the daki-nis" (*mkha' 'gro gtad rgya ba*). Dodrupchen's text has been translated by Tulku Thondup in *Hidden Teachings of Tibet* (1986).

33 Thondup 1986: 106-9.

34 See Gyatso 1986.

35 The phrase "six degrees of separation," the title of a play by John Guare, has entered into common parlance. The counting of degrees of separation here is crudely thus: a dharmakaya buddha, a sambhogakaya bodhisattva, a nirmanakaya figure, Padmasambhava, Princess Pemasal, Pema Lingpa. I use this phrase to demonstrate the close connection between the tertön and sources of authority as conceived within the treasure tradition.

36 These two methods of transmitting the teachings are called *gter ma* and *bka' ma.* For a detailed discussion of the differences between these two lineages, see Gyatso 1993.

37 In the Nyingma tradition, scriptures passed down from master to disciple are des-ignated by the term "spoken" or *kama* (*bka' ma*). For a discussion of the differences between kama and terma, see Gyatso 1993.

38 See Smith 2001: 238–9. For an overview of the canonization process, see Paul Har-rison's article, "A Brief History of the Tibetan Bka' 'gyur" in Cabezón and Jackson 1996. Ratna Lingpa (1403–1478) collected tantric literature from the early transla-tion period into a canon for the Nyingma tradition, called the Nyingma Gyubum (*Rnying ma rgyud 'bum*).

39 See Smith 2001: 239–40 for a short list of famous tertöns found in schools outside the Nyingma.

40 Tambiah explores this dual aspect of the saint in "The Charisma of Saints and the Cult of Relics, Amulets and Shrines." Unpublished paper.

41 This is particularly true for the treasures of Orgyen Lingpa. I am indebted to Leonard van der Kuijp for bringing this point to my attention.

42 See Aris 1979 for a partial translation and summary of two treasures by Pema Lingpa, which cultivated a regional lore concerning Bumthang's own royal period: (1) *Rgyal po sindha ra dza'i rnam thar,* outside of Pema Lingpa's current corpus, and (2) *Sbas yul mkhan pa ljongs kyi gnas yig* (*Pad gling gter chos,* vol. 17: 493–517).

43 This fascinating text, *Gsal ba'i me long*, has been translated in full in Olschak 1979 as *The Clear Mirror of Mysticism*. Michael Aris concludes from the colophon, attributing the text simply to "O-rgyan," that this small text—only thirty folios in length—indeed belongs as a treasure of Pema Lingpa, even though it appears independently of his treasure corpus. The text emphasizes Sindhu Raja's relationship with local deities, his invitation to Padmasambhava, and the erection of an "oath stone pillar" (*rdo ring mna' rdo*) to demarcate the border between Sindhu Raja's Mön kingdom and the Indian kingdom of his foe, Nahuche.

44 See Huber 1994 and Karmay 1996 for important discussions of royal cults and local deities.

45 A temple complex of three massive structures today stands at Kurje where Padmasambhava is said to have left his body print.

46 For other accounts of this hidden valley in Himalayan lore, see Diemberger 1997 and Pommaret 1996.

47 According to legend, Kyikha Rathö was the illegitimate son of Trisong Detsen, born from one of his wives who copulated with a dog and goat. Literally, his name means "dog face" (*khyi kha*) with goat's horns (*ra thod*). This is a derogatory epithet for a figure otherwise known as the prince, Murum Tsenpo.

48 Aris 1979 includes translated portions of this treasure.

49 *Bum thang lha'i sbas yul gyi bkod pa med tog skyed tshal* from Longchenpa's collected miscellaneous writings, *Gsung thor bu*: 235–245.

50 The fire that consumed Taktsang in 1997 reached the international press, and the reconstruction process is still in progress today.

51 Toni Huber translates *byin brlabs* as "field of power" rather than "blessings" to denote an active spatial field associated with a sacred place (1994: 42 and 1999: 15). Huber uses "field of power" primarily in relation to the locus of deities. However, tantric masters are also thought to leave blessings at sites where they were active, especially where they engaged in intensive meditation. The ubiquity of impressions in the landscape identified as hand and footprints in rock left by Padmasambhava in Tibetan and Himalayan regions aptly attests to the belief that individuals with extraordinary capacities can make an indelible mark on a place.

52 There are three sources for Pema Lingpa's life story. (1) Pema Lingpa's autobiography, "A Garland of Jewels Beautifying All with Its Light Rays" (*'Od zer kun mdzes nor bu'i phreng ba*) can be found in *Pad gling gter chos*, vol. 14: 3-510. This text has been studied in depth by Aris 1988b. See note immediately below for excerpts from reviews of his book. (2) "Flowers of Faith: A Short Clarification of the Story of the Incarnations of Pema Lingpa" (*Pad gling 'khrungs rabs kyi rtogs brjod nyung gsal dad pa'i me tog*) follows Pema Lingpa's autobiography in vol. 14. It was written by the Eighth Peling Sungtrul, Kunzang Dechen Nyima (1843–1891) and provides a short account of Pema Lingpa's life (see Chapter 1) and brief biographies of his subsequent incarnations. This text is followed by an important supplement written by Dudjom Rinpoche Jikdrel Yeshe Dorje (1904–1988), *Pad gling 'khrungs rabs rtogs brjod dad pa'i me tog gyi kha skong mos pa'i ze'u 'bru* (Vol. 14: 601–29), which serves as an appendix to the previous account, bringing it up to date to the Eleventh Peling Sungtrul. (3) The contemporary Bhutanese scholar and former

Director of the National Library Padma Tshewang has also compiled a biography of Pema Lingpa, translated by Chris Butters. This can be found in Padma Tshewang et al., *The Treasure Revealer of Bhutan: Pemalingpa, the Terma Tradition and Its Critics* (1995).

53 A detailed study on Pema Lingpa's autobiography can be found in Aris 1988b. In this section, I rely heavily on historical research by Aris, but I disagree with his conclusions about Pema Lingpa. In contrast, I situate Pema Lingpa as an expression of a wider phenomenon, the paradigm of a tertön as Buddhist saint. As such, I attempt to situate Pema Lingpa within his cultural context and demonstrate his important role in Bhutanese history.

Aris portrays Pema Lingpa, and by implication the entire treasure tradition, as a type of pious fraud. He states: "To recognize that the whole cult depended on conscious pretense and fraud does not mean we should therefore take an unsympathetic view of its prime members or of its ultimate purpose... Apart from Pemalingpa's endearingly human weaknesses (not forgetting his qualities of strength too), there is the undoubted fact that his activities as a whole greatly enriched the cultural and spiritual life of his homeland and the regions beyond. The texts he produced, the dances he composed and the works of art he commissioned are among the real cultural treasures of Bhutan to this day" (97). In a similar vein Aris states: "We can only speculate on how Pemalingpa and those who preceded and followed him in the treasure cult rationalized their use of deception. Since in this area lay the most secret of all their many secrets, perhaps hardly breathed even to themselves, absolute certainty will never be reached. Yet it is only in the light of the thought process suggested above [a psychological profile of Pema Lingpa] that one can reconcile the tone of complete and ingenuous sincerity permeating the whole text of this autobiography with the writer's constant use of deception in his daily life" (101). Overall, his depiction of Pema Lingpa is far from sympathetic, labeling him variously a charlatan and a rogue.

The late Michael Aris was a prominent scholar and expert in Bhutanese history, yet his analysis of the autobiography of Pema Lingpa has received criticism by reviewers. In his review of *Hidden Treasures and Secret Lives*, Robert Thurman (1991) criticizes Aris for a "reading of the texts without any hermeneutical sensitization, applying a thick layer of his personal prejudices" which " merely assumes the presupposition that there are no such things as treasure texts buried by ancient Lamas" (376). Thurman summarizes his critique as follows:

Both exercises in debunking the "mystique of Lamaism" seem rather like a secularist setting out to "prove" not only that Moses never parted the waters of the Red Sea, but also that Moses must have been a knowing charlatan to have promoted the fabrication that he had done so. But such a "proof" is a category mistake. The modern secularist does not believe such things, therefore he can confidently assert their impossibility. Some religious persons do believe that God can part seas, without requiring materialistic proof. There is so much interest in the lives of the two lamas that a pseudo-historical analysis as to "did this or that miracle happen or not?"—in the absence of any new data—is a waste of time. And when pursued so aggressively, using language sharply offensive to the Bhutanese and Tibetan believer, it is also deplorable. (377)

In his review, Robert Mayer (1992) makes the following critique:

Yet sadly, as a study of religion, this book disappoints, for several reasons. Firstly, the hagiographies under consideration here are highly complex religious texts, yet Aris' self-confessed lack of adequate Buddhological understanding often distorts his interpretations. For just one example among many: Aris argues at length that Pemalingpa's visionary "journeys" to Buddhist paradises to receive teachings are evidence of Pemalingpa being more "shaman" than Buddhist; yet Nagarjuna and Asanga, those authoritative founders of Sanskrit Buddhism's twin paradigms of orthodoxy, Madhyamaka and Yogacara, received their teachings in precisely the same way. Nagarjuna "traveled" underwater to the Nagas to receive his doctrine, while Asanga "flew" to buddha Maitreya's heaven for his. Such exemplary "journeys" were emulated by innumerable later Buddhists, Indian and non-Indian. Furthermore, Aris explicitly repudiates all theory even while attempting a study that demands considerable theoretical sophistication.

His book's central undertaking is to explain what happens when Tibetans believe they are witnessing miracles: yet, failing to recognize this as an anthropological question, he instead envisages it in quasi-parapsychological terms, and ends up falling between several stools, since anthropology and parapsychology alike are better done with lamas living than dead. The end result is a return to the theoretical naïveté of such Victorians as L. A. Waddell, whom Aris partially resembles in perceiving Tibetan Buddhism predominantly in terms of deliberate fraud preying upon superstition. (187)

A review by Per Kvaerne (1990) is less critical. It hails the historical detail provided by Aris and also his attempt to "divest the figure of Pemalingpa of all supernatural traits." Yet Kvaerne condemns the use of expressions like "fraud" which are "not particularly helpful in understanding Pemalingpa, or the entire tradition of 'treasure-revelations', a tradition which is still, in our day, very much alive in Tibet" (304).

54 Janet Gyatso discusses the importance of visions to tertön autobiographies in *Apparitions of the Self* (1998). She states: "Tibetans widely consider their dreams and other experiences to be personally significant, even if they do not result in a treasure revelation. Visions and dreams are a major focus of religious practice, and techniques to facilitate and master them are described at length in Tibetan literature. This interest, coupled with the fact that esteem and support reward the virtuoso who can report brilliant visions and prescient dreams, accounts for the prominence of such experiences in the autobiographies of Tibetan religious figures" (104–5). Gyatso also emphasizes that Tibetans, and tertöns in particular, were prolific writers of autobiography and views this as "striking evidence of the popularity of the charismatic individual in Tibetan society" (102).

55 Portrayals of both the visionary propensities and human foibles of a tertön's career are characteristic in autobiographies. According to Janet Gyatso (1993), this interplay between the human and visionary creates a dramatic juxtaposition. She states: "The personal nature of the revelation account, in which the frustrations and doubts of the human condition are not glossed over, contrasts strikingly with the mythic tone of the origin accounts" (116). Elsewhere Gyatso discusses the function of this type of self-representation as follows: "The discoverer's show of his own personal imperfection gives an aura of honesty to his rendering of his vision quest. Importantly, it suggests to his audience that his report of visions is not fabricated; rather, his humility engenders confidence that the revelatory visions he finally did have were indeed 'really' experienced by him" (118).

56 According to Tulku Thondup, "Most of the tertöns, before discovering any Ter

[treasures], seem to be ordinary people. They do not necessarily appear as scholars, meditators or Tulkus [reincarnate lamas]. However, due to their inner spiritual attainments and the transmissions they have received in their past lives, at the appropriate time, they suddenly start discovering mystical Ters [treasures] without the need for any apparent training." (1990: 154).

57 Gyatso 1998 makes this point: "The treasure traditions served as a vehicle for religious figures to distinguish themselves outside of the conventional monastic and academic avenues for self-advancement" (145).

58 Gyatso remarks: "Claims to memories of past lives were common among the treasure discoverers and became one of the grounds upon which Nyingmapas could achieve prestige on par with that of the Gelukpa and other hierarchs in the increasingly monastic establishment" (1998: 127).

59 According to Padma Tshewang, "[Pema Lingpa's] activity as a spiritual figure began when he was in his mid-twenties. It came upon him suddenly and unexpectedly, according to the records, in the form of dreams and messages leading to him to his first Terma discoveries" (1995: 45).

60 From "Flowers of Faith: A Short Clarification of the Story of the Incarnations of Pema Lingpa." See Chapter 1.

61 Janet Gyatso discusses the phenomenon of prophetic guides at length in "The Relic Text as Prophecy: The Semantic Drift of *Byang-bu* and Its Appropriation in the Treasure Tradition" (unpublished paper).

62 For a detailed account of the treasure discovery process, especially its prescribed ritual context, see Tulku Thondup's *Hidden Teachings of Tibet* (1986). Some features include the tertön's proper dealings with the treasure's guardian (*gter bdag*), placated through preparatory practices and the replacement of the treasure with a substitute object. Failing to execute the proper protocol regarding such prescribed ritual activity or instructions given by the certificate was thought to incur the guardian deity's wrath and result in sickness, hailstorms, or other catastrophes.

63 Tshewang 1995: 48.

64 From "Flowers of Faith: A Short Clarification of the Story of the Incarnations of Pema Lingpa." See Chapter 1. Pema Lingpa's own account of this episode is found in *Pad gling gter chos*, vol.14: 60.

65 Tshewang 1995: 47.

66 Tshewang 1995: 52: *Pad gling gter chos*, vol. 14: 245-248.

67 Pema Lingpa's dreams and visions were recorded by him in a journal which appears in his collected writings in a separate text, *Mnal lam dag snang gi skor rnams phyogs gcig tu sdebs pa* (*Pad gling gter chos*, vol. 13: 3–57). These visionary sequences were interpolated into his autobiography by his disciple, Gyalwa Döndrup. Concerning this interpolation, see Aris 1988b: 18, 53. For an account of Pema Lingpa's dreams and visions, some involving direct encounters with Padmasambhava, see Aris 1988b: 53–63.

68 Tshewang 1995: 48.

69 The existence of unseen beings was part of the cosmology of Tibetan and

Himalayan regions, and the treasure tradition utilizes both Buddhist and pre-Buddhist elements of this cosmology. The treasure guardians (*gter bdag*), who ensure that the treasure is accessible only to the destined revealer, were regarded as local spirits converted to Buddhism by Padmasambhava. The tertön is also seen to command the unseen forces of a region, part of the charismatic powers attributed to a Buddhist saint.

70 Aris 1988b: 68.

71 Aris 1988b: 70–71.

72. *Pad gling gter chos,* vol. 14: 293.

73 Tshewang 1995: 67.

74 For studies on the founding of Tamshing Monastery, see Yoshiro Imaeda and Francoise Pommaret, "Le monastére de gTam zhing (Tamshing) au Bhoutan central," *Arts Asiatiques* 42 (1987): 19–30. See also, Michael Aris, "The Temple-Palace of gTam-gzhing as Described by its Founder," *Arts Asiatiques* 43 (1988): 33–34.

75 Most recently, a nunnery is undergoing construction at the center of the Tang Valley. Towering above, on the hillside, stand the private shrine commemorating Pema Lingpa's birthplace and the dramatic cliffside retreat of Kunzangdrak.

76 Aris 1988b: 91.

77 The Tulku system originated with the Karmapa line in Tibet as a way to perpetuate the religious tradition of a saint within monastic institutions. In Weberian terms, this is called the "charisma of office," a ritual means to transfer the sacred power of a saint from generation to generation (Weber 1978: 248). Reginald Ray summarizes the process as follows: "Central to the Tulku tradition is the idea of 'lineal succession,' the notion that a Tulku is a previous Bodhisattva who a) has reincarnated, b) is discovered, and c) is reinstalled in the religio-political place or seat of his predecessor" (Ray 1986: 44). In Pema Lingpa's case, family and reincarnation lines often overlapped in the course of succession. For example, Aris cites that at least five of the Peling Sungtrul incarnations have been born into Pema Lingpa's family line, the Nyö clan (Aris 1994: 20). Gangteng Tulku clarified for me that the speech representation (*gsung sprul*) is considered to be a direct incarnation line (*sprul sku*), whereas the mind and body representations are considered emanations (*sprul pa*).

78 From "Flowers of Faith: A Short Clarification of the Story of the Incarnations of Pema Lingpa." See Chapter 1.

79 Personal interview, Bumthang, 30 May 2001. Translated by Sarah Harding.

80 ohn Ardussi suggests that "Tibetan officials were more solicitous of the eastern Bhutanese Nyingmapas, in part as a countermeasure against Ngawang Namgyal's government in the west" (personal correspondence). Indeed, the Fifth Dalai Lama became personally interested in Pema Lingpa's treasures and received a number of its initiations. It is possible that a further attempt to entice the nobility descending from Pema Lingpa into sympathizing with Lhasa was made, namely, by recognizing the Sixth Dalai Lama, Tsangyang Gyatso (1683–1706), from among the Nyö clan.

81 Aris 1988b: 105.

82 Aris 1979: 165.

83 See Aris 1988a, "New Light on an Old Clan of Bhutan: The *sMyos-rabs* of Bla-ma gSang-nags."

84 See Aris 1988a for details concerning the rapid rise of the Nyö (*Smyos*) clan in the period after the unification of Bhutan by Shabdrung Ngawang Namgyal.

85 Rose 1977: 32.

86 The Paro pönlop, who supported the Tibetan government against the British, was quickly replaced by a supporter of Ugyen Wangchuck, and the Trongsa pönlop, Ugyen Wangchuck, was rewarded with a British title. In the interests of a stable buffer state, the British supported Sir Ugyen Wangchuck in his bid to once again unify Bhutan (Rose 1977: 34).

87 With the exception of "Flowers of Faith: A Short Clarification of the Story of the Incarnations of Pema Lingpa" by the Eighth Peling Sungtrul (*Pad gling 'khrungs rabs kyi rtogs brjod nyung gsal dad pa'i me tog, Pad gling gter chos*, vol. 14: 511–600), the other five translations are of texts found in *Lama Jewel Ocean*. They are: *Lha lcam padma gsal gyi zhus lan gser gyi yang zhun* (*Pad gling gter chos*, vol. 1: 289–352), *Lha lcam khrom pa rgyan gyi zhus lan* (1: 353–70), *Slob dpon nam mkha'i snying po dang lha lcam rdo rje mtsho'i zhus lan* (1: 371–94), *Gu ru'i dmar khrid don gyi snying po* (1: 637–48), and *Lo rgyus stong thun dang bcas pa nor bu'i phreng ba* (1: 395–429).

88 *Rig 'dzin padma gling pa yi zab gter chos mdzod rin po che.* (See Appendix B.) This collection was reproduced from a set of manuscripts preserved at Gangteng Monastery, sponsored by Her Majesty the Royal Grandmother and edited by the great Nyingma master Dudjom Rinpoche. It was published in Thimphu by Kunsang Tobgay in 1975. There is also a two volume edition of *Lama Jewel Ocean*, published in Thimphu by Druk Sherig Press in 1984 from a manuscript preserved at Urgyen Chöling Monastery in Bumthang. A smaller collection of Pema Lingpa's treasures was published based on a rare manuscript collection from Manang in Nepal by Ngawang Tobgay (Delhi: Mujib Offset Press, 1977). This set includes three cycles: *Vajrapani, Suppression of Fierce Ones (Phyag rdor dreg pa kun 'dul), The Quintessence of the Mysteries of Luminous Space (Klong gsal gsang ba snying bcud),* and *Lama Jewel Ocean (Bla ma nor bu rgya mtsho).* Pema Lingpa's treasure corpus is available as digital scans at www.tbrc.org due to the efforts of Gene Smith and the generous contribution of Chris Tomlinson. It is also in the process of being digitally inputted in a project initiated by Gangteng Tulku.

89 Jamgön Kongtrul lists fourteen major treasure cycles in his short hagiography of Pema Lingpa found in his *Gter ston brgya rtsa'i rnam thar* as follows: (1) *Rdzogs chen klong gsal gyi skor*, (2) *Rdzogs chen kun bzang dgongs 'dus*, (3) *Rdzogs chen gnyis med rgyud bu chung gi skor*, (4) *Bla ma nor bu rgya mtsho*, (5) *Thugs rje chen po mun sel sgron me*, (6) *Bka' brgyad thugs kyi me long*, (7) *Phur pa spu gri*, (8) *Bdud rtsi sman grub kyi skor*, [*Bka' phur sman gsum* summarizes the previous three], (9) *Phyag rdor dregs 'dul dang gtum chung*, (10) *Drag po che 'bring chung gsum*, (11) *Tshe khrid rdo rje phreng ba*, (12) *Tshe sgrub nor bu lam khyer*, (13) *Nag po skor gsum*, and (14) *Las phran gyi skor*. This list can also be found in Dudjom Rinpoche 1991.

90 A collection of treasure teachings (*gter chos*) is an anthology of texts revealed by a particular tertön which may also include works written by the tertön, that are not strictly-speaking considered treasures, as well as supplementary material by other masters associated with the tradition. Considered to be teachings by Padmasambhava, the treasures are placed first in the collection, indicating their exalted status. Pema Lingpa's ordinary works follow and constitute three volumes: (1) a collection of Pema Lingpa's ordinary compositions, *Bka' 'bum yid bzhin gter mdzod*, in vol. 13; (2) Pema Lingpa's autobiography, *'Od zer kun mdzes nor bu'i phreng ba*, in vol. 14; and (3) an appendix to *Lama Jewel Ocean* in vol. 20, predominantly by Pema Lingpa. Ritual arrangements, composed by his subsequent incarnations, are placed in a single volume toward the end of the collection, *Kha skong min byed dbang gi mtshams sbyor* (Vol. 19). The texts in this volume were predominantly written by the Sixth Peling Sungtrul, Kunzang Tenpai Gyaltsen, and the Eighth Peling, Sungtrul Kunzang Dechen Dorje. Also near the end is a volume of liturgical materials, *'Don cha'i skor bdud 'jom sogs gsung* (Vol. 18) by Dudjom Rinpoche, the editor of the present collection. These serve as ritual elaborations for a number of Pema Lingpa's treasures. A hagiography of Padmasambhava, *O rgyan padma 'byung gnas kyi 'khrung rabs sangs rgyas bstan pa'i chos byung* (Vol. 21) is curiously found at the end of the collection. It may have circulated independently, only later to be added to the collection.

91 There are two important studies on genre in the treasure tradition by Janet Gyatso: "Genre, Authorship, and Transmission in Visionary Buddhism: The Literary Traditions of Thang-stong rGyal-po" (1992) and "Drawn from the Tibetan Treasury: The *gTer ma* Literature" (1996).

92 The root text for *Lama Jewel Ocean* is an Atiyoga or Dzogchen empowerment, *Rtsa ba'i dbang mchog rdzogs chen dbang gi phreng ba* (*Pad gling gter chos*, vol. 1: 41–45). Kongtrul includes another important text from this cycle, *Bla ma sprul sku'i sgrub pa 'od zer phreng ba* (*Pad gling gter chos*, vol. 2: 301–12), in his *Rinchen Terdzö* under the section of nirmanakaya guru sadhanas.

93 The final text on this list is included in Jamgön Kongtrul's *Rinchen Terdzö* under the category of "increasing crops" (*lo tog 'bras bu rgyas byed*). The name of this text is "The Chinese Waterwheel: Instructions for Rain-Making," abbreviated from the Tibetan: *Char 'bebs pa'i gdams ngag Rgya nag chu 'khor rdo rje'i chu 'bebs* (*Pad gling gter chos*, vol. 2: 857–75).

94 The role of women in Buddhist tantra has drawn a range of reactions among Western scholars. For differing views, see Anne Klein, *Meeting the Great Bliss Queen* (1995); Judith Simmer-Brown, *Dakini's Warm Breath* (2001); Miranda Shaw, *Passionate Enlightenment* (1994); and June Campbell, *Traveller in Space* (1996), among others.

95 For discussions on the role of the dakini in the treasure tradition, see "The Dakini Talks: On Gender, Language and the Secret Autobiographer" in Gyatso 1998 and "Protectors of the Tantric Teachings" in Simmer-Brown 2001.

96 For differing perspectives on the women's role in sexual yoga practices, see Shaw 1994 and Campbell 1996.

97 Buddhism in its long history and wide geographic spread has displayed a variety of attitudes toward women, including multiple views (both positive and nega-

tive) inherited from early Indian Buddhist literature. Alan Sponberg has summarized these into four categories: (1) soteriological inclusiveness, (2) androcentric institutionalism, (3) ascetic misogyny, and (4) soteriological androgyny. See Sponberg, "Attitudes towards Women in Early Buddhism" in Cabezón 1992. Other important studies include: Nancy Falk, "The Case of the Vanishing Nuns: The Fruits of Ambivalence in Ancient Indian Buddhism" in *Unspoken Worlds: Women's Religious Lives*, edited by Nancy Falk and Rita Gross (Toronto: Wadsworth, 2001); Rita Gross, *Buddhism after Patriarchy: A Feminist History, Analysis, and Reconstruction of Buddhism* (Albany: State University of New York Press, 1993); Liz Wilson, *Charming Cadavers* (Chicago: University of Chicago Press, 1996); Diana Y. Paul, *Women in Buddhism: Images of the Feminine in the Mahayana Tradition* (Berkeley: University of California Press, 1979).

98 For example, Subha in the *Therigatha* is pursued by an "admirer" until she gives him a formidable lesson on the impermanence of beauty by plucking out her eye. Translations of the *Therigatha* include: Andrew Schelling and Anne Waldman, *Songs of the Sons and Daughters of Buddha* (Boston: Shambhala Publications, 1996); Kathryn Blackstone, *Women in the Footsteps of the Buddha: Struggle for Liberation in the Therigatha* (Richmond: Curzon Press, 1998); C. A. F. Rhys-Davids, *Psalms of the Early Buddhists I: Psalms of the Sisters* (London: Pali Text Society and Oxford University Press, 1948). The seminal study on early nuns in Buddhism is by Horner 1930. See also "Saints of the Theragatha and Therigatha" in Ray 1994.

99 Each treasure cycle consists of a set of texts, arranged as a single cache from a particular site. The smallest cycle is a single text and the largest, *Lama Jewel Ocean,* includes more than one hundred. Some of Pema Lingpa's treasure cycles are focused on a narrow set of genres. For example, *The Small Child Tantra of the Innermost Essence,* one of three Atiyoga cycles in Pema Lingpa's collection, consists of tantras and commentaries. More often treasure cycles include a variety of genres focused on a central ritual or consolidated around a broad unifying theme. For example, *The Great Compassionate One, the Lamp That Illuminates the Darkness* consists of diverse genres focused on a single deity, Avalokiteshvara. However, most of Pema Lingpa's treasure cycles share the same basic features as found in *Lama Jewel Ocean*: narrative genres and instructional texts at the outset, initiations and practice manuals at the center, and a miscellany of mundane rites at the end.

100 Most of the treasure cycles in Pema Lingpa's collection contain empowerment and practice manuals associated with Mahayoga Tantra, arranged according to Eight Sadhana Teachings (*bka' brgyad*). This emphasis on Mahayoga reflects a general trend within the treasure tradition. As Janet Gyatso has pointed out, Jamgön Kongtrul's *Rinchen Terdzö* consists predominantly of texts classified as Mahayoga Tantra (see Gyatso 1996).

101 Each Ati cycle has a different emphasis and the three together function as a unit to a certain extent. In their internal catalogues, each is depicted as emphasizing a single genre: instructions (*khri*), empowerments (*dbang*), and tantras (*rgyud*) respectively. *The Union of Samantabhadra's Intentions* emphasizes instructions and also contains empowerments of peaceful and wrathful deities (*zhi khro*) and esoteric instructions (*sman ngag*) on advanced yogic topics. The first volume of *The Quintessence of the Mysteries of Luminous Space* is almost wholly taken up with empowerments. The second volume, which is buried at the back of the col-

lection, includes an interesting array of scattered texts (*kha 'thor*) including advice on the yogic art of swift walking (*rkang mgyogs*), protection against demons (*sri srung*), and guidebooks (*gnas yig*) to hidden lands (*sbas yul*). The entire volume of *The Small Child Tantra* consists of tantras and commentaries, related to an important section of *The Collection of Nyingma Tantras* on the "Seventeen Unsurpassed Secret Tantras of Dzogchen" (*Yang gsang bla na med pa rdzogs pa chen po'i rgyud bcu bdun gyi skor rnams*, volumes 9 and 10 of the *Nyingma Gyubum*). This cycle is considered a "rediscovered" treasure (*yang gter*), originally revealed by the tertön Sherab Membar.

102 The collection as a whole represents an amalgamation of narratives, instructions, and rituals. Some treasure cycles have a preponderance of instructions, while other cycles are dedicated primarily to ritual. Moreover, there are two full volumes dedicated to narrative accounts: one contains an extensive hagiography of Padmasambhava and the other contains Pema Lingpa's autobiography, followed by brief hagiographies of his successive incarnations. At the back of the collection are supplementary materials, ritual elaborations and liturgical arrangements.

NOTES TO CHAPTER 1

1 *Pad gling 'khrungs rabs kyi rtogs brjod nyung gsal dad pa'i me tog*, from *Pad gling gter chos* (Treasure teachings of Pema Lingpa), vol. Pha (511-58), written by the Eighth Peling Sungtrul incarnation. See Appendix B.

2 *spangs rtogs yon tan*. The two great qualities of a buddha: relinquishing all emotional and conceptual obscurations, and realizing all that there is to know, both in its nature and in its extent, or the understanding of both noumena and phenomena.

3 This poem incorporates some of the names of the incarnations that preceeded Pema Lingpa. The Lake-Arisen One (*Mtsho byung ma*) here is the goddess Sarasvati (*Dbyangs can ma*), the principal or basis of the emanations. Princess Lotus Light is Pemasal (*Lha lcam padma gsal*), Karmic Connection (*las 'brel*) together with Expression (*rtsal*) is the incarnation of Pema Lendreltsal. Stainless Expanse (*dri med [chos sku'i] klong*) and Light Rays (*'od zer*) refer to Longchen Rabjam Drimé Özer, and Lotus Land is a literal rendering of Pema Lingpa (*Padma gling pa*). The stories of these incarnations follow.

4 Poetics (*tshig rgyan*) includes poetic metaphor (*snyan gnag*) and composition (*sdeb sbyor*); linguistics (*brda*) is terminology and grammar (*sgra*); and synonymics or nomenclature (*mngon brjod*) is the third category mentioned here, all comprising lesser sciences.

5 These are all epithets for Padmasambhava, who came to the Himalayan region in the eighth century and is the source of all the treasure teachings of Pema Lingpa. He is also referred to as Padma, Padmakara, Guru Rinpoche, or simply as the Guru. Oddiyana is the land from which he came. The Tibetan word for it, Orgyen (*o rgyan*) is often used as his name as well. I have kept the Tibetan in those cases and used Oddiyana when referring to the place.

6 *khyad chos drug ldan* or *khyad par drug ldan*, endowed with the six qualities. According to the *Klong chen snying thig; ye shes bla ma*, fol. 69a, they are as follows: (1) Insight is elevated above the basis of confusion from the beginning. (2) Its *dharmata* shines. (3) It discriminates the particulars of individual, personal insight. (4) It liberates into the sphere of wisdom. (5) Its fruition is not dependent on other conditions. (6) It resolves as the nature of the inconceivable dharmata of directness. All these six qualities are known as the great stage of primordial liberation.

7 *Kun tu bzang po*; All Good or Ever Good, a name for the primordial principle of awakening, the original buddha. *Kun tu bzang mo*, Skt. *Samantabhadri*, is the feminine form.

8 *mdo sde sangs rgyas phal po che*, Skt. *Buddhavatamsakasutra*. Trans. T. Cleary, *The Flower Ornament Scripture*. 3 vols. (Boulder: Shambhala Publications, 1984–1987).

9 *byang chub kyi sems* or *sems bskyed*; Skt. *bodhichitta*.

10 *bde bar gshegs pa*; Skt. *sugata*, those who have gone or come to bliss, the buddhas.

11 That is to say that Pema Lingpa, really Sarasvati, is the basis of emanation (*sprul gzhi*) of all buddhas and bodhisattvas. (Oral commentary by Gangteng Tulku Rinpoche).

12 *Spur rgyal*, an ancient name for Tibet. According to Chandra Das, it was believed by some to mean the Kingdom (*rgyal*) of the Dead (*spur*), because the bardo was located somewhere below the Himalayas. The Tibetan story of the term is that the king Drigum Tsenpo (*Gri gum btsan po*) had made the town of Puo Drak (*Spu'o brag*) his capital, and he was known as the King of Pu (*Spur rgyal*), which evolved into the contempory name for Tibet: *Bod*.

13 *Bya rung kha shor*, the Great Stupa at Boudanath in Kathmandu, Nepal. The story goes that a poultry woman and her four sons undertook to sponsor and build the stupa for the benefit of all. Though she died before its completion, the four sons fulfilled her wish of finishing it and dedicated the merit accrued from this work, each making aspiration prayers to be born in Tibet for the sake of the Buddhadharma. At this time, the youngest son swiped at a mosquito that had stung him and inadvertently killed it. But he made profound aspiration prayers for its sake, that it would be born as a Buddhist prince in Tibet. The four sons were later reborn as King Trisong Detsen, Shantarakshita, Padmasambhava, and the Yarlung king. The mosquito was reborn as Princess Pemasal. From Keith Dowman's *The Legend of the Great Stupa* (Berkeley: Dharma Publishing, 1973).

14 *Mnga' bdag tsang pa lha'i me tog*, "Brahma Flower of Gods," the secret name for the great Tibetan Dharma king Trisong Detsen (755–97), received during the empowerment of the *Eight Transmitted Precepts* when his flower fell in the area of Chemchok, indicating also that in the future he would be the buddha Lhai Metok.

15 *bla rdzogs thugs gsum*, refers to the three general categories to which the three previously mentioned teachings belong: *Lama Jewel Ocean* (*bla ma nor bu rgya mtsho*) is a guru yoga of Padmasambhava; *The Union of Samantabhadra's Intentions* (*kun bzang dgongs 'dus*) is on the Great Completion; and *The Great Compassionate One, the Lamp That Illuminates the Darkness* (*thugs rje chen po mun sel sgron me*) concerns Mahakaruna (Avalokiteshvara).

16 *las kyi phyag rgya* (Skt. *karmamudra*), literally "gesture of activity," generally refers to tantric sexual practice. I am told that, since Pemasal passed away at the age of eight, this can be understood to mean that she rendered general service to the guru.

17 Mind treasures (*thugs gter*) in this case indicates *thugs sgrub kyi gter ma*, revealed treasures for mind practices, not the mind treasures that are revealed directly in the mind.

18 Lord Nyang (Ral) Nyima Özer, (*Mnga' bdag nyang [ral pa can] nyi ma 'od zer*), 1137–1204, or 1124–1192, the first of the five Tertön Kings.

19 *la yag*, the name of a place in Lhodrak (*Lho brag*) in south Tibet, bordering Bhutan.

20 Guru Chökyi Wangchuk (1212–1273), the second of the five Tertön Kings. With Nyang Nyima Özer (see note 18) these two were known as the sun and the moon, and the treasures they discovered were known as Upper and Lower Treasures (*gter kha gong 'og*).

21 *g.yo ru*, an area in Central Tibet, south of Lhasa.

22 Orgyen Lingpa (*O rgyan gling pa*) (c.1323–1360) of Yarje, also born in Yoru, was a revealer of many treasures.

23 *Iron Hair Hayagriva* (*rta mgrin lcags ral can*) and *The Great Completion, Padma Innermost Essence* (*rdzogs chen padma snying tig*).

24 Pagangpa Rinchen Tsuldor (*Pa sgang pa rin chen tshul rdor*, aka *Spang sgang pa rin chen rdo rje*) and Pema Lendreltsal (*Padma las 'brel rtsal*) are sometimes considered the same person, and sometimes Lendreltsal is the incarnation (*tulku*) of Pagangpa. According to Gangteng Rinpoche, they are two incarnations who are counted as one because the work of finding the predicted number of treasures was only completed by the two of them. See also Dudjom Rinpoche 1991 (1:582).

25 The female Iron Hare year was 1231 or 1291, the latter more likely as he was said to have been a contemporary of Karmapa Rangjung Dorje (1284–1339). However, 1248 is the birthdate given for Pema Lendreltsal in both *The Big Tibetan-Chinese Dictionary* 1985 (henceforth BD, 2:3230), and in Dudjom Rinpoche 1991 (2:427), which fits in well with other dates in his life.

26 *mkha' 'gro snying tig.*

27 *The Wheel of the Union of Lamas* (*bla ma spyi 'dus 'khor lo*), *Vajrapani Suppressing All Fierce Ones* (*phyag rdor dregs 'dul*), *Three Gods of Hayagriva Practice* (*rta mgrin gnyen po lha gsum*), and *Sealing the Mouth of Yama* (*gshin rje kha la rgyas 'debs*).

28 *gza' rgod dug gi spu gri*

29 *The Maroon-Faced Planet (Rahula)* (*gza' gdong dmar nag*) and *Red-Eyed Butcher* (*shan pa mig dmar*).

30 *drag sngags seng phur ma*

31 *kun thub chen mo*

32 This is from a classification of the treasures into east, south, west, north, and cen-

tral. Eastern treasures include those of Pema Lendreltsal and Sangye Lingpa (1340–1396). See Thondup 1986: 115 and 245, n.166.

33 *thal 'gyur rtsa ba'i rgyud*

34 This is the prophecy of the coming of Drimé Özer, Longchen Rabjam (1308–1363). The name here is Lodrö (*Blo gros*), meaning "good intellect" or "intelligence" (basically, smart). Among his given names were Lodrö Chok (*Blo gros mchog*) and Tsultrim Lodrö (*Tshul khrims blo gros*).

35 *Rgyal ba mchog dbyangs*, one of the twenty-five disciples of Padmasambhava and one of the first seven ordained monks in Tibet, known as the "seven probationers."

36 Namdru (*Nam gru*) is the twenty-sixth of twenty-eight constellations in Buddhist astrology, Andromeda. Other names for it are Sowai Lhamo (*Gso ba'i lha mo*, "Healing Goddess") or Rewati (*Re ba ti*). Remati (*Re ma ti*), however, is another name for the protector goddess Palden Lhamo (*Dpal ldan lha mo*) or Mahakali, who may be associated with this constellation.

37 *Drwa phyi tshong 'dus*. The Drachi Valley is several miles east of Dratang in Dranang County of southern Tibet. The Sakya monastery of Tsongdu Tsokpa still stands (Dorje 1999: 168-69).

38 *Gsang phu neu thog*, the great academy for the study of logic founded in 1073 by Ngok Lekpai Sherab and where he first took ordination from Atisha. Situated on the south bank of the Kyichu River, south of Nyetang and north of Onchangdo. (See Dorje 1999: 155).

39 Loppön Tsengönpa (*Slob dpon btsan dgon pa*), the fifteenth to hold the seat of Longtö at Sangphu. Ladrangpa (*Bla brang pa chos dpal rgyal mtshan*), who is mentioned next, was the sixteenth.

40 *mun mtshams*; a cloistered retreat where all sources of light are eliminated (a kind of sensory deprivation) and certain visionary practices are cultivated.

41 *Yar stod skyam kyi phu*: mountains dividing the Kyichu from the Tsangpo River.

42 *rdzogs pa chen po rang snang ris med kyi dgongs pa*. That is, that there is no bias or leaning in the direction of either form or emptiness, no dualistic conception whatsoever.

43 Palchen Heruka, "Great Glorious Heruka" (*Dpal chen po he ru ka*; Skt. *Sriheruka*), also *Yang dag he ru ka*.

44 *Ma cig lab kyi sgron ma*, or Single Mother Labdrön, the great eleventh/twelfth-century Tibetan yogini who is the primary source of the Chöd (*gcod*) tradition. For her life story and teachings, see Harding 2003.

45 *Srog sgrub ma*

46 *'od drwa*, Longchenpa's *mthong snang rin po che 'od kyi drwa ba*

47 *mkha' 'gro yang tig yid bzhin nor bu*. This seems to combine two text names. According to Dudjom Rinpoche 1991, Longchenpa developed the *Dakini Innermost Essence* into his own mind treasure, the *Dakini Further Essence* (*mkha' 'gro yang tig*), which was later condensed along with *The Guru Further Essence* (*bla ma yang tig*) and *The Profound Further Essence* (*zab mo yang tig*), making *The Fur-*

*ther Essence Trilogy. The Further Essence, Wish-Fulfilling Jewel (*yang tig yid bzhin nor bu*) or Guru Further Essence was developed by Longchenpa from The Innermost Essence of Vimalamitra.* (1:580–88 and 2:51)

48 *Further Essence Trilogy (*yang tig skor gsum*), Natural Freedom Trilogy (*rang grol skor gsum*), Trilogy of Rest and Recovery (*ngal gso skor gsum*), Seven Great Treasures (*mdzod chen bdun*).*

49 *Sgom pa kun rin* or *kun dga'.* This man of the Drikungpa was seen as an opponent by Tai Situ Jangchub Gyaltsen of the Pakmodrupa, who was then in power. Longchenpa's association with him thus led to his exile to Bhutan for some ten years, during which time he established many great temples and Dharma instructions. However, Longchenpa kept his connection with Jangchub Gyaltsen, as is mentioned below.

50 *brtan ma*, earth goddess protectors, usually twelve in number.

51 Dorlek, or Damchen Dorje Lekpa (*Dam can rdo rje legs pa*; Skt. *Vajrasadhu*), a worldly protector who had been converted into service by Guru Rinpoche, rides an oath-bound lion.

52 s *a phag*, refers to the conflicts of the Sakya and Pakmodrupa sects/families, as well as the Drikung and Karma Kagyu, who all vied for power during this time of disunity in Tibet, with Longchenpa inadvertently involved. The army of Yarlung would be that of the Pakmodrupa.

53 *gsang ba snying tig*

54 *Padma gling*, sometimes Rinchenling (*Rin chen gling*).

55 *snying tig zhu len gser 'phreng*, a text from the *Dakini Innermost Essence* cycle.

56 *ta' si* (or *ta'i si tu*) *byang chub rgyal mtshan*, (1302–1373) the founder of the political power of the Pakmodrupa family/sect who ruled for some time. See note 49.

57 *Sa skya pa dpal ldan bla ma*, Sönam Gyaltsen. Longchenpa's reply is called "A Petition: The Lamp of Gold" (*zhu yig gser gyi mchod sdong*).

58 *Ra mo che*, one of the earliest temples in Lhasa, built by Songtsen Gampo's Chinese queen.

59 *Si tu sha' kya bzang po*, the myriarch (*khri dpon*) of upper Uru, the area of Central Tibet north of Lhasa.

60 *'od gsal rdo rje snying po*, *Clear Light Vajra Essence*. A synonym for the Great Completion, Dzogchen, in general and the Esoteric Instruction Section (*man ngag sde*) of Dzogchen in particular.

61 *Flawless Light (*dri med 'od*)* and *Mirror of Key Points (*gnad kyi me long*).*

62 *nying mtshams sbyor ba*, an expression that means specifically entering the consciousness into the connecting of the parent's fluids, causing conception.

63 *rgyal*, Skt. *Pusya*, Delta Cancri.

64 *'od gsal myos kyi nang rus.* The Nyö (*myos*) clan was one of the most important clans of ancient Bhutan, believed to be descended from the gods, hence the appellation "radiant."

65 *'brog ma*, a female of the yak-herding or nomadic tribes. Dudjom Rinpoche 1991 (1:796) has her name as Trongma Palsaom, and Tshewang (1995: 40) as Pema Dronma.

66 *Ma ni dgon pa*, the ruins of which are in the forest below Kunzangdrak in Chel, Bumthang area, according to Padma Tshewang et al. 1995.

67 *Rdor gling thugs sras chos dbyings*, aka Tertön Dorje Lingpa (1346–1406).

68 *Stang gi brag ri mo can*, striped or criss-crossed cliff of Tang Valley, also sometimes spelled *Tag ri mo can*, "tiger-striped"; it is now a monastery built up against the rock face a few hours walk from Bumthang. It was the site of several discoveries for Pema Lingpa.

69 *nga la dro zhig byon* (mistake for *byin*). In the longer biography, the instruction is specifically to cook the mushrooms and prepare some roasted barley flour.

70 *ston pa*, the Buddha Shakyamuni.

71 *kun tu bzang mo klong gsal gsang ba snying bcud*.

72 *Ratna gling pa*, a great treasure-revealer, contemporary of Pema Lingpa. Dudjom Rinpoche (1991, 2:429) has 1403–1479 for Ratna Lingpa's dates. The years 1476 and 1478 are also given for his death in BD (3244).

73 *dgongs pa bla med*

74 This would be south of Bumthang, where the Tang, Kujé and Lower Rivers (*chu smad*) meet.

75 *skyu ru ra*, emblic myrobalan; kind of medicament.

76 *klong gsal gyi zab khrid*, instruction on his first treasure, *The Quintessence of the Mysteries of the Luminous Space of Samantabhadri* (*kun tu bzang mo klong gsal gsang ba snying bcud*).

77 *Sku rjes*, "Body Print," a cave in a cliff at Bumthang with the body print of Guru Rinpoche in the rock, now the name of the temple complex built on the site. The treasure discovered there is *tshe sgrub nor bu lam khyer*.

78 *Bu le*, now called Keng.

79 *drag dmar me rlung 'khyil pa*. Of Pema Lingpa's treasure texts concerning practices of Guru Rinpoche, this is the lesser of the three (*che bring chung*; greater, middling, and lesser) on the wrathful aspect (*gu ru drag po*). The one on the peaceful aspect (*gu ru zhi ba*) is *Lama Jewel Ocean* (*bla ma nor bu rgya mtsho*).

80 *Chos 'khor*, one of the four major valleys of Bumthang. The others are Chumé, Tang, and Ura. The Chökor Temple is the same as the present-day Jampal Lhakhang of Bumthang. The statue of Vairochana remains at Könchoksum Lhakhang, also called Tselung Lhakhang.

81 *bla ma drag po dpa' bo gcig pa*

82 *ma ni*, that is, like the sound of the recitation of the *mani* mantra: *om mani padme hung*.

83 *t sha tsha* or *sa' tstsha*, a small representation of a stupa or image, usually clay.

84 *bka' brgyad yang gsang thugs kyi me long*

85 *bla ma yang gsang bka' 'dus*. Mutik Tsenpo (*Mu tig btsan po*) was the son of King Trisong Detsen, also known as Mutik Tsepo and Senalek Jingyön. See Chapter 6, notes 23 and 25.

86 Here the alternate name is used: (*Ma dros [mtsho]*), Anavatapta, "The Ever Cool Lake." However Manasarovar (*Mtsho ma pham*), "Undefeated Lake," is the better-known name for this sacred lake situated near Mount Kailash, the site of many legends.

87 *Shel ging dkar po* (White Crystal Ging), a treasure protector often mentioned in association with Pema Lingpa. Possibly associated with Pehar. See Aris 1979: 50-51 and 297-98. Also see Padma Tshewang et al. 1995: 49.

88 *gur drag dmar chen me lce'i 'phreng*, the greater of the three Wrathful Guru treasures. See note 79 above. Here he is in the form of three faces, six arms, and in union.

89 *'kha byang*, the address or prophetic guide to the hiding places of treasure, usually a prerequisite to revealing it.

90 This would seem to be a mistake, since the closest Earth Hare years are 1459 and 1519. The female Fire Hare year is given as the discovery date in the history of *Lama Jewel Ocean, Strand of Jewels*, making it 1507, the beginning of the ninth cycle.

91 *rta mgrin lcags ral can gyi sgrub skor*

92 *phyag rdor gtum po'i skor*

93 *mkha' 'gro nye lam rgya mtsho*. Genyen Khari (*Dge bsnyen mkha' ri*), or Genyen Kulakangri, is the protecting deity of the mountain, on the northern border of Bhutan, and one of the main treasure protectors.

94 *la bse'i ga'u*; apparently, this is a box of which one side is made of rhinoceros hide (*bse*) and the other from a kind of resin that is also used for seals, which is actually the leftover dregs of the process of making dye from insect dung (Ganteng Tulku, oral communication).

95 *dgongs pa kun 'dus*

96 *La 'og yul gsum*; literally "the pass, below, the country, these three," a place name in the east of Bhutan in Mön, contemporary Arunachal Pradesh (Aris 1979: 80).

97 Spirit turquoise (*la g.yu*) is the main turquoise stone that many people wear close around their neck; it represents their supportive life force or spirit. The name mentioned here as the princess's stone, "red house snow peak" (*gung ri kha dmar*), is given in Dudjom Rinpoche 1991 (1:798) as that of her father, Trisong Detsen.

98 For a translation of a more detailed narrative of this incident, from the longer autobiography of Pema Lingpa, as well as some analysis of the Khenpalung legend, see Aris 1979: 61-62.

99 *rdzogs chen rgyud bu chung* or *rdzogs chen gnyis med rgyud bu chung gi skor* or, as in the table of contents of the collected works, *snying tig yang gsang rgyud bu chung ba*. This is the third, or "child," text of the three Great Completion cycles dis-

covered by Pema Lingpa. The "mother" is *The Quintessence of the Mysteries of the Luminous Space of Samantabhadri*, and the "father" is *The Union of Samantabhadra's Intentions*.

100 *Shes rab me 'bar* (1267–1326), born in Kham in Tibet and said to have come to Bhutan late in life after making many discoveries. Some of his discoveries were reburied after he lost them due to inauspicious circumstances (Aris 1979: 158). In particular, his problems arose because his patron forced him under threat of cruel punishment to reveal treasures that it was not actually his destiny to reveal.

101 *drag po mthing ka'i sgrub skor*

102 *Bdud rtsi 'khyil pa*, one of the "wrathful kings" (*khro rgyal; khro bo'i rgyal po*), the main wrathful deities.

103 *khrom gter*, treasures discovered in the presence of an audience, as opposed to secret treasures (*gsang gter*).

104 *snang bzhi zad sa*; the four visions are stages of experience in the practice of Tögal in the Great Completion. The stage of "exhaustion" is the final experience.

105 Chamara (*Rnga yab gling*), the island abode of Guru Ripoche, location of the Copper-Colored Mountain; Five Peak Mountain (*Ri bo tse lnga*) in Tibet, sacred to Manjushri; Changlochen (*Lcang lo can*), pure land of Vajrapani, and also the realm of Vajradhara, etc.; Potala (*Po ta la*), the pure realm of Avalokiteshvara; and Ghanavyuha (*Stug po bkod pa*), Dense Array Pure Land.

106 *dge bsnyen lcham srings gsang 'dus*

107 *Dung rang le chung*, in eastern Bhutan or Mön, Arunachal Pradesh.

108 An interlinear note was inserted in the text here by a later, unknown author. It reads, "In the biography of Gyalwa Döndrup it says that he went there fourteen times, which is found to be inconsistent with the extensive biography." Gyalwa Döndrup (*Rgyal ba don grub*) was Pema Lingpa's son, who completed his autobiography entitled *Bum thang gter ston padma gling pa'i rnam thar 'od zer kun mdzes nor bu'i phreng ba zhes bya ba skal ldan spro ba skye ba'i tshul du bris pa*, in *Pad ling gter chos*, vol. Pha. See Appendix B.

109 Avalokiteshvara, Manjushri, and Vajrapani.

Notes to Chapter 2: Refined Gold

1 *Bla ma nor bu rgya mtsho las: lha lcam padma gsal gyi zhus lan gser gyi yang zhun*, in *Pad gling gter chos*, vol. 1 (Ka): 289–352. See Appendix B.

2 *Bu tshab gser khang gling* (here, *Bu tshal gser khang gling*), Golden Orphan Temple, at Samye.

3 *bar do gsum*, three intermediate stages or states: the intermediate state of the moment of death (*'chi kha'i bar do*), the intermediate state of reality (*chos nyid bar do*), and the intermediate state of rebirth (*srid pa'i bar do*).

4 *s hes rab gsum ldan*, the wisdom or transcendent intelligence of listening, contemplating, and meditating.

5 c *hos sku dag pa gnyis ldan*, essence primordially pure and nature radiantly pure (*ngo bo ye dag dang rang bzhin gsal dag*).

6 *nges pa lnga*, five certainties: (1) the certain place is the Densely Arrayed Akanishta (*'og min stug po bkod*); (2) the certain teacher is Vairochana Gangchentso (*rnam snang gangs chen mtsho*); (3) the certain retinue are bodhisattvas of the tenth level (*sa bcu'i byang sems*); (4) the certain teaching is the Great Vehicle (*theg pa chen po*); and (5) the certain time is the "continuous wheel of eternity" (*rtag pa rgyun gyi bskor ba*).

7 *tshad med bzhi*: love (*byams pa*), compassion (*snying rje*), joy (*dga' ba*), and equanimity (*btang snyoms*).

8 *tshul khrims gsum*, the three kinds of discipline according to the bodhisattva vehicle are: gathering the virtuous doctrine (*dge ba chos sdud*), benefiting sentient beings (*sems can don byed*), and controlling malpractices (*nyes spyod sdom pa'i tshul khrims*). Another set is: the discipline of renunciation (*nges 'byung gi tshul khrims*), the discipline of protecting from fear (*'jigs skyob kyi tshul khrims*), and the discipline of well-wishing (*legs smon gyi tshul khrims*).

9 *brtson 'grus dag*, diligence (or enthusiastic perseverance) being in plural here may indicate one of the enumerated sets, such as the five kinds of diligence that cause good qualities to arise: the diligence of armor (*go cha'i*), of application (*sbyor ba'i*), of not shirking (*zhum med pa'i*), of not turning back (*mi ldog pa'i*), and of not being satisfied (*chog par mi 'dzin pa'i*).

10 *kusulu*, in Sanskrit, is translated in Tibetan as beggar (*sprang po*), but refers to a yogin.

11 *Om svabhawa shuddha sarwa dharma svabhawa shuddho 'ham.*

12 *mtshams med lnga*, the five acts so severe that they propel one to the lower realms without any intermediate existence: matricide, patricide, killing an arhat, creating a schism in the sangha, and intentionally wounding a bodhisattva.

13 This is a rough phonetic transliteration according to popular pronunciation. The reversal of the two lines *anu rakto mebhawa* and *supo kayo mebhawa* from the more common version is not a mistake, according to Gangteng Tulku Rinpoche. Roughly translated, the mantra means "*Om* Vajrasattva, keep (your) pledge. Vajrasattva, reside (in me). Make me firm. Make me satisfied. Fulfill me. Make me compassionate. Grant me all siddhis. Also, make my mind virtuous in all actions. *Hum ha ha ha ha hoh* all the blessed Tathagatas, do not abandon me, make me indivisible. Great Pledge Being, *ah hum.*" (From Khetsun Sangpo Rinbochay 1982: 146).

14 *bla med* (*rgyud*), or anuttara tantra, the supreme tantra, with three aspects of outer, inner, and secret.

15 There are two phases to the meditation on a deity in Vajrayana, the creation or generation phase (*bskyed rim*), during which the visualization is developed and the mantra recited, and the completion or perfection phase (*rdzogs rim*), in which the visualization is dissolved.

16 *dam tshig sems dpa'*; Skt. *samayasattva*, the visualized or created form of the deity.

The wisdom being (*ye shes sems dpa'*; Skt. *jnanasattva*) is the actual presence of the deity that is evoked and enters the sacred pledge being.

17 See note 16 above.

18 *bsnyen sgrub*

19 Repetition of the fifty vowels and consonants of the Sanskrit alphabet (*a k'a lnga bcu* or *a' li k'a li*) and the *ye dharma* mantra are said to purify mispronunciations and other flaws. It is: *a a, i i, u u, ri ri, li li, e ai, o au, am ah, ka kha ga gha nga, cha chha ja jha ña, ta tha da dha na, ta tha da dha na, pa pha ba bha ma, ya ra la va, sha sha sa ha kshah. Om ye dharma-hetu-prabhava hetum tesham tathagato hyavadat tesham cha yo nirodha evam vadi mahashramanah svaha.*

20 Ati or Atiyoga is the ninth vehicle in the Nyingma system of classification of nine Buddhist approaches. It is said to be the pinnacle of all spiritual practice and realization, and its viewpoint is considered distinct from the others. In Ati are found the teachings of the Great Completion (*rdzogs chen*).

21 *rnam snang chos bdun*, sevenfold posture of Vairochana. This position is described as having the legs in full lotus, the spine straight, the shoulders broadened, the neck slightly bent, the hands in the gesture of equanimity, the tip of tongue touching the palate, and the gaze placed in the direction of the nose.

22 These are all terms used in Ati or Great Completion practice. Cutting Through Resistance (*khregs chod*) and Direct Crossing (*thod rgal*) are the two broad phases of the practice. The four lamps (*sgron ma bzhi*), or often six lamps, refer to psychosomatic constituents employed in the Direct Crossing practice, and the four visions (*snang ba bzhi*) to the stages of visionary experience that result. The place of extinction (*zad sa*) is the final experience, the cessation of clinging to reality (*chos nyid du 'dzin pa zad pa*).

23 This passage is replete with repeated words that suggest different meanings in each usage. In order to ensure integrity in the English, the word *spyod pa* is variously translated as "conduct," "to act," "activity," "act out of" (for *spyod pa bya*), "the act" (for *spyod bya*), and "performing the action" (for *spyod byed*). The word *don* is translated as "meaning" or "purpose." It can also mean "the absolute" when used with words such as *chos nyid* ("reality itself"), though this possibility could not be included without totally losing the connection with "purpose" or "for the sake of."

24 *ye thog dang po'i (sa)*

25 The usual descriptions of the fruition according to the bodhisattva vehicle are in terms of the ten levels (*sa bcu*; Skt. *dasabhumi*). Other levels going up to fifteen are also employed to describe buddhahood. Here the "levels," or more appropriately, "states," are not the usual ones at all but employ the language of the Ati vehicle.

26 Lord Nyang Ral Nyima Özer (*Mnga' bdag nyang ral nyi ma 'od zer*), 1137–1204, the first of the five Tertön Kings.

27 *Bde chen gnas* or *Bde ba can*, Skt. *Sukhavati*, the pure land of Amitabha.

28 *Tshul rdor*, a short form for Tsultrim Dorje Lodrö (*Tshul khrim rdo rje blo gros*), one of the names for Longchen Rabjam (aka Longchenpa, aka Drimé Özer).

29 *skye mtha'*, final birth, or farthest birth, might seem confusing since emanations of Pema Lingpa continue to this day. Gangteng Tulku explains this as the difference between emanation (*sprul pa*) and incarnation (*sprul sku*). After this series of incarnations described here, Pema Lingpa attains the highest state and exists in the pure land of Chamara, whence emanations continue to appear.

30 According to the biographies, Pema Lingpa was actually born in the Iron Horse year (1450). The Earth Snake year was 1449, and the prophecy here may be providing a margin of variation due to mitigating karmic circumstances in giving either the Horse or the Snake year.

31 *gsang ba'i yang bcud dam pa*, the longer name being *kun tu bzang mo klong gsal gsang ba snying bcud*, *The Quintessence of the Mysteries of the Luminous Space of Samantabhadri*, discovered in 1476.

32 *dgongs pa kun 'dus; dgongs pa bla med; nor bu rgya mtsho; sems phyogs chos sde; mun sel sgron me* (or *thugs rje chen po mun sel sgron me*); *'khor ba kun skyob; yang gsang snying po; bla med don rdzogs; mkha' 'gro snying tig; rdor sems 'od gsal rgyud; rgyud chen bcu bdun; nyi ma'i gsang rgyud; rgyud bu chung* (or *rdzogs chen gnyis med rgyud bu chung gi skor*); *yang gsang skor dgu; rdzogs rim khrid kyi skor.*

33 *bsnyen sgrub yi dam skor dgu* (or *yang gsang skor dgu*): *gshin rje; rta mgrin; phyag rdor* (or *phyag rdor gtum po'i skor*); *phur ba; tshe dpag; thugs kyi me long* (or *bka' brgyad yang gsang thugs kyi me long*); *lcag ral can* (*rta mgrin nag po*); *bla ma zhi; bla ma drag.*

34 *mkha' 'gro'i chos bka' lnga*: (*mkha' 'gro*) *nye lam rgya mtsho; khro nag; phag dmar; rdo rje rnal 'byor ma; dbyangs can ma.*

35 *chos skyong skor: gnam lcags rdo rje 'bar ba'i rgyud las: ma ning; ae ka tsa ti; srog bdud nag mo* (could either be referring to *srog bdud nag po* [Black Vitality Devil, masculine] or *srog sgrub nag mo* [Black Vitality Accomplishing Goddess, feminine], both treasures of Pema Lingpa which sound nearly alike); *gza' mchog; phung byed dmar nag; rdo rje legs pa; bdud mgon seng gdong; (dpal ldan) lha mo; dpe kar.*

36 *dge gshes gdugs thog* means literally "parasol-holding professors," referring to the custom of holding a parasol over the heads of very important religious persons.

37 *chags sdang ngan lto*; "bad food" indicates jealousy.

38 *rig 'dzin rnam bzhi*. The state of awareness-holder is the fruition of the tantric path. The four kinds are: maturation awareness-holder (*rnam par smin pa'i rig 'dzin*), power of life awareness-holder (*tshe dbang rig 'dzin*), great seal awareness-holder (*phyag chen rig 'dzin*), and spontaneous presence awareness-holder (*lhun grub rig 'dzin*).

39 Refers to the two rebirths as Longchen Rabjam and Pema Lingpa, who shared some of the treasures. Some of the "addresses" for treasure locations came to Longchen Rabjam, but they weren't actually revealed until the time of Pema Lingpa. Some were revealed and then rehidden by Longchen Rabjam, to be rediscovered later by Pema Lingpa.

40 *rdzogs chen bla med chos skor; klong gsal snying tig skor gsum; kun bzang dgongs pa kun 'dus; nor bu rgya mtsho; bla med don rdzogs.*

41 These are all titles of respect and rank still in common use, so the Tibetan, or sometimes the Sanskrit, has been used. Literally they could be translated as: Dharma Lord (*chos rje*), Precious One (*rin po che*), Realized One (*rtogs ldan*), Accomplished One or Siddha (*grub thob*), Master of Training (*slob dpon*), Preceptor or Abbot (*mkhan po*), Great Meditator (*sgom chen*), Ascetic Practitioner or Yogin (*zhig po*), Virtue Upholder or Monk (*dge slong*), Virtuous Friend or Theologian (*dge bshes*), and Virtue Striver or Sangha (*dge 'dun*).

42 *mi 'gul ba gsum*: (1) without moving from the posture of the body, the energy channels and currents are relaxed of their own accord; (2) without moving from the gaze of the eyes, appearances are enhanced; and (3) without moving from the state of the unfabricating mind, the expanse and awareness are integrated. From Jigme Lingpa, *khrid yig ye shes bla ma*, p. 49a, cited in Dudjom Rinpoche 1991 (2:122).

43 *'gong po*, a type of evil spirit symbolizing ego-clinging, sometimes counted among the eight classes of gods and demons. They are also described as enchanters, sorcerers, bewitching demons, craving spirits, evil spirits, and demons who cause disease.

44 The Hor were variously associated with Uighurs of Turkestan, Mongols, nomads of the northern plains of Tibet, or just fierce hordes of the north. The idea here is of very fierce, unidentified invaders.

45 This apparently refers to a belief that someone who poisons an intruder or outsider will acquire the dead person's merit and vitality.

46 That is, nuns will have illegitimate children and have to raise them.

47 *rin chen lnga*: gold, silver, turquoise, coral, and pearl. Alternatively, gold, silver, copper, iron, and lead.

48 *dkar gsum mngar gsum*, the three whites and three sweets: curd, milk, butter, sugar, molasses, honey.

49 *man mo*, female spirits associated with lakes.

50 *btsan*, one of the eight kinds of gods and spirits (*lha srin sde brgyad*).

Notes to Chapter 3: The Dialogue of Trompa Gyen

1 *Bla ma nor bu rgya mtsho las, lha lcam khrom pa rgyan gyi zhus lan* in *Pad gling gter chos*, vol.1 (Ka): 353–70. See Appendix B.

2 *tshangs rigs spyod pa* or *tshangs spyod*, brahminlike conduct, monastic discipline, pure conduct.

3 See Chapter 2, note 13. Again, the slight variations from the usual rendition have not been altered here, on the advice of Gangteng Tulku Rinpoche.

NOTES TO CHAPTER 4: DORJE TSO

1 *Bla ma nor bu rgya mtsho las, slob dpon nam mkha'i snying po dang lha lcam rdo rje mtsho'i zhus lan* in *Pad gling gter chos*, vol.1 (Ka): 371–94. Dorje Tso is also called Dorje Tsogyal (*Rdo rje mtsho rgyal*) at one point in this text, and Shelkar Dorje Tso (*Shel dkar rdo rje mtsho*) by Jamgön Kongtrul (*Gter ston brgya rtsa'i rnam thar*, fol. 20b). In Kongtrul's account, Namkha'i Nyingpo is a fully ordained monk (*dge slong*), which is certainly not indicated here, where he is referred to as a yogin.

2 *Lho brag mkhar chu dung gi gzhal yas khang*; Lhodrak is a district in south central Tibet. Kharchu is a town in the south of the district, almost on the border of present-day Bhutan. It is known as the retreat place of Padmasambhava's mind, a pilgrimage site of buddha mind.

3 *Shangs rta nag gi skyang bu tsha thog*; Shang and Tanak are areas of south central Tibet, quite some distance northeast of Lhodrak. Kyangbu Tsatok is evidently a town in that area.

4 *ru lu snying po*; the essential mantra of Palchen Heruka: *om rulu rulu hung jo hung*.

5 *Dpal chen po* or *Dpal chen he ru ka*; Skt. *Shriheruka*, "Great Glorious," also called Pal Yangdag (*Dpal yang dag*).

6 This translates *mi nga rang gar dga' gar skyid yin*. If it should be read as _ming_ rang *gar dga' gar skyid yin,* then it should be "my name is whatever you like, whatever makes you happy."

7 That is, the smoke that is normally used to cure the bows.

8 The breath or energy movement (*lung*; Skt. *prana*) of the body is often likened to a horse, and the mind that is so interdependent with it is likened to the rider of that horse, hence this poetic analogy.

9 *Brag phug dpal gyi lcags phur*; presumably the same cave referred to above as Palgyi Phukring (*dpal gyi phug ring* or *rings*), the "Glorious Long Cave" that is "like the mandala of Iron Kilaya" (*Lcags phur*).

10 *bkrag med*, "lusterless," one who drains the vital essence.

11 *ma mo*, wrathful female spirits or dakinis that can cause trouble if disturbed.

12 A partial and variant list of the "nine dramatic airs" or modes of expression (*gar gyi nyams dgu*) for a wrathful deity. They are: seductive (*sgeg pa*); heroic (*dpa' ba*); ugly (*mi sdug pa*); fierce (*drag shul*) (here "abusive" [*gshe*]); humorous (*gad*) (here "wild" [*rgod*]); terrifying (*'jigs su rung ba*); compassionate (*snying rje*); awesome (*rngoms*) (here "voracious" [*rngams*]); and tranquil (*zhi ba*).

NOTES TO CHAPTER 5: THE GURU'S RED INSTRUCTIONS

1 *Gu ru dmar khri don gyi snying po* in *Pad gling gter chos*, vol. 1 (Ka): 637–48. See Appendix B. "Red instructions" are a type of teaching that is especially pithy. It means "exposed" or "naked." Gangteng Tulku Rinpoche (GTR) describes it as "stripped of skin." Gangteng Tulku gave a thorough commentary on these teach-

ings in Santa Fe, New Mexico, in the spring of 1999, and I have closely followed his interpretation, with references in the notes.

2 Mutik Tsenpo (*Mu tig btsan po*) was the youngest son of the great Dharma king Trisong Detsen (742–c. 797); he had already ascended to the throne by the time of these teachings. Thus he is sometimes referred to as "prince" (*rgyal sras*) and sometimes as "king" (*rgyal po*). Also see Chapter 6, note 23.

3 "Appearance" (*snang ba*) refers to experiences that occur to any of the senses, including the mind, not just to visually appearing forms.

4 Recognition of yourself and others refers to the functioning of the two kinds of knowing or pristine wisdom: knowing (things) as they truly are (*ji lta ba mkhyen pa*) and as they manifest (*ji snyed pa mkhyen pa*). That is, a buddha's self-awareness is absolute, but there is also awareness of how beings experience things in a deluded way. [Oral commentary by GTR]

5 The realization that just as oneself has buddha nature or buddha mind, so do all beings have it in the same way. [GTR]

6 The following correction to the text was made by GTR: *sangs rgyas dang sems can gnyis kyi mtshang rig ma rig gnyis las med.*

7 *rtse gcig*, literally, "one-pointed" or undivided attention, the first of the four levels or yogas of meditation described in the Mahamudra tradition. The others, which follow, are free of embellishment or concept (*spros bral*), one taste (*ro gcig*), and no-meditation (*sgom med*).

8 That is, the radiance of the lamp is not different from its source, the lamp itself. So since there is freedom from all embellishment (*spros bral*), it cannot be said that the form or physical aspects arise out of the formless dharmakaya as something different from it. [GTR]

Notes to Chapter 6: A Strand of Jewels

1 *Bla ma nor bu rgya mtsho las, lo rgyus stong thun dang bcas pa nor bu'i phreng ba* in *Pad gling gter chos*, vol.1 (Ka): 395–429. See Appendix B.

2 *sku lnga* are the body of reality (*chos sku*; Skt. *dharmakaya*), the body of perfect rapture (*longs spyod rdzogs pa'i sku*; Skt. *sambhogakaya*), the emanation body (*sprul sku*; Skt. *nirmanakaya*), the body of awakening (*mngon byang gi sku*; Skt. *abhisambodhikaya*), and the vajra body (*rdo rje sku*; Skt. *vajrakaya*).

3 *(gu ru) mtshan brgyad*, eight manifestations or emanations of Padmasambhava (I prefer "identities" for *mtshan*, which normally means "name" or "sign"). They are: Padmakara, Padmasambhava, Loden Chokse, Shakya Senge, Senge Dradrok, Padma Gyalpo, Dorje Trolö, and Nyima Özer.

4 *Thod phreng rtsal*, "Skull-Garland Power," a wrathful manifestation of Padmasambhava.

5 *tsheg drag*, the final aspiration or Sanskrit symbol called *visarga*, consisting of two small circles lined up vertically.

6 *Chos blon tri na 'dzin* (sometimes *Trig na 'dzin*); Skt. *Trigunadhara*, seems to be called Krishnadhara in some sources.

7 *dung dkar*; it is believed that a conch thrown into the mouth of a sea-monster could protect against it. Also, the conch with its eternal swirl indicates emptiness, the best defense against any monster. See Dowman 1984: 198, n. 52.

8 *Dur khrod bsil ba'i tshal*; Skt. *Sitavana*.

9 *Rgyal po'i dza*, King Dza (or Ja) of Zahor, sometimes associated with King Indra-bhuti. But the name Indrabhuti is applied to two or three persons, of which King Dza may be identified as the intermediate Indrabhuti.

10 *rgyal thabs spyi blugs*

11 *Rtsub 'gyur tshal*; Skt. *Parusakavana* (a charnel ground).

12 *grub pa bka' brgyad* or *sgrub sde brgyad*. Eight Sadhana Teachings. Eight chief yidam deities of Mahayoga and their corresponding tantras and sadhanas: Manjushri Body, Lotus Speech, Vishuddha Mind, Nectar Quality, Kilaya Activity, Liberating Sorcery of Mamos, Maledictory Fierce Mantra, and Mundane Worship.

13 *Padma 'byung gnas*, Pema Jungne, is the name usually rendered in translations as Padmasambhava, although the Sanskrit Padmakara also translates it. The second identity is traditionally kept in the Sanskrit, that is, Padmasambhava, which has become the one used by Western scholars.

14 Here *Khri rje btsad po*, but usually *Khri lde btsad po*, also called *Khri lde gtsug brtsan*.

15 *mdo za ma tog rgyas 'bring rnam gsum* or *za ma tog bkod pa'i mdo*, Sutra Designed As a Jewel Chest, Skt. *Ratnakaranda Sutra*. A sutra on Avalokiteshvara's life, belonging to Kriya Yoga.

16 This would weigh down the arrow, making the measurements for the temple much shorter, the aim of those frugal ministers.

17 *dbu rtse rigs gsum* or *dbu rtse rim gsum*, the three-storied, triple-styled central temple, the central structure at the temple complex of Samye.

18 Some sources have the place of Mangyul near the Nepal border as the place where Padmasambhava waited for the envoys, who are sometimes also said to be five in number.

19 *rgyal chen bzhi*, Skt. *caturmaharajika*, the guardians of the four directions.

20 In many accounts, these three shrines or temples were sponsored by the three queens: Queen Gyalmo Tsun of Phogyong built the Golden Orphan Shrine (*bu tshal gser khang gling*); Queen Margyen of Tsepang built the Triple-Realm Copper Shrine (*khams gsum zangs khang gling*); and Queen Jangchub Men of Tro built the Flourishing Virtue Sand Shrine (*dge rgyas bye ma gling*).

21 There is much speculation on the dates of Samye's construction, not to be explored here. In many descriptions of the temples at Samye, the central temple represents Mount Meru, four direction temples represent the four continents, and each of those four has two satellite shrines for the two islands, making a total of

thirteen shrines and copying the layout of the world system according to ancient cosmology. Usually it seems that the stupas, the iron mountains, and the queens' temples are not counted in those thirteen, although here they are.

22 *Dmar rgyan,* or *Tshe spang bza' dmar rgyan;* Lady Margyen of Tsepang, the primary queen of King Trisong Detsen.

23 *Mu rum btsan po* (also *Mu rug* or *Mu rub*) in some accounts is the second son of Trisong Detsen and Margyen, exiled for killing a minister. Not mentioned at this point is the supposed first son, Muné Tsenpo (*Mu ne btsan po*), who ascended the throne after his father's death and married his younger queen. In most accounts, he ruled for less than two years before his mother, Margyen, murdered him and his queen. In this account, that incident occurs to one Mutri Tsenpo (*Mu khri*), who must be the same as Muné, although in other places Mutri seems to be confused with Mutik (*Mu tig*), the younger son. However, the so-called Lhasa Chronicles give the succession: Mutri, Muné, Muruk, Tridé Songtsen.

24 See note 23 above.

25 *Mu tig btsad po,* or, more often, *Mu tig btsan po,* even more confusing than the other Tsenpos, was by some accounts the third son of the king and Margyen, although here he is the son of another queen (as is Mutri, which makes his murder only slightly less horrible than if it was by his own mother). The year 823 is sometimes given as his date of birth. This would seem to be the same person as Tridé Songtsen (*Khri lde srong btsan*), aka Senalek (*Sad na legs*), who continued Trisong Detsen's Dharma work, and who is most important in this history. Many accounts also have the age for his ascension to the throne as very young (four or seven), necessitating regents, although this account may be unique in having Padmasambhava himself as regent.

26 (*bla ma*) *yang gsang bka' 'dus* (*chos kyi rgya mtsho*); same as *The Compendium of the Lama's Most Secret Precepts, Ocean of Dharma* (Chapter 1, note 85).

27 *srin po*; Skt. *raksha* or *rakshasa.* One of the eight classes of gods and demons. Also the cannibal savages inhabiting the southwestern continent of Chamara.

Notes to Appendix A

1 An alternate series for the Thugs-sras Rinpoche line is contained in the work *Bod dang / bar khams / rgya sog bcas kyi bla sprul rnams kyi skye phreng deb gzhung,* dated *Wood Dog* (1814) (but revised up to 1820), contained in *Bod kyi gal che'i lo rgyus yig cha bdams bsgrigs* (*Gangs can rig mdzod,* vol. 16, 327-8. Lhasa: Bod ljongs bod yig dpe rnying dpe skrun khang, 1991). This collection lists incarnations that were registered in the records of the Chinese ambans, but not officially submitted for approval by the Emperor (*Rgya tang rtser 'khod kyang gser snyan du mi 'gro gras*). Thus, these are records that would have been kept in Lhasa for use by the local authorities. The names and sequence of the Second and Third Thugs-sras agree with the account in Guru Bkra-shis (*Gu bkra'i chos 'byung:* 657f), but the traditional lists maintained in Bhutan are less clear about these two incarnations. Also, this is the only source giving their ages. The Fifth - Seventh incarnations in

the list are completely different names than those maintained in the Bhutanese sources. They lived during the time of the Dzungar invasion of Tibet and their persecutions that disrupted many Nyingmapa establishments.

1.	Zla ba rgyal mtshan.	Born in Mon Bumthang.	Died at age 96.
2.	Nyi zla rgyal mtshan.	Born at Mon Bang-steng lung-pa.	Died at age 20.

(The text is corrupt; he was born in Mang-sde lung (modern Trongsa), once considered a part of Bumthang.)

3.	Nyi zla klong yangs.	Born at Mon Bumthang.	Died at age 4.
4.	Bstan 'dzin 'gyur med rdo rje.	Born at Mon Bumthang.	Died at age 50.
5.	Blo bzang 'jigs med.	Born at Snye-mo Bya-sgo-ba	Died at age 52.
6.	Blo bzang phun tshogs rgya mtsho.	Born at Bumthang.	Died at age 50.
7.	Ngag dbang 'jigs med.	Born at Samye.	Aged 37 at time of writing.

2 Born in Mang-sde Lung (near modern Trongsa), central Bhutan, and founded Sga-sgar Monastery there.

3 Born in Bumthang Chos-'khor Sham-khar and installed at Sga-sgar, but died of childhood illness. Neither he nor his predecessor are counted in the abbatial lineages of Lha-lung or Guru Lha-khang, as they were never installed there (details in *Gu bkra'i chos 'byung:* 657f).

4 I owe the information on Thugs-sras X and the dates of Thugs-sras IX to Francoise Pommaret.

5 *Gu bkra'i chos 'byung* (p. 654) refers to him as the Chos-lung Mkhan-chen, which appears to have been a certain Chos-lung Monastery in Lho-brak. He was the seventh in his lineage and had distinct bodily marks which were recognized on the child Padma-'phrin-las.

Bibliography

WESTERN-LANGUAGE SOURCES

Aris, Michael. 1979. *Bhutan: The Early History of a Himalayan Kingdom*. Warminster, England: Aris & Phillips.

———. 1988a. "New Light on an Old Clan of Bhutan: The *sMyos-rabs* of Bla-ma gSang-nags." In *Tibetan Studies: Proceedings of the Fourth Seminar of the International Association for Tibetan Studies*. Edited by Helga Uebach and Jampa Panglung. Munich: Kommission für Zentralasiatische Studien, Bayerische Akademie der Wissenschaften.

———. 1988b. *Hidden Treasures and Secret Lives: A Study of Pemalingpa (1450–1521) and the Sixth Dalai Lama (1683–1706)*. Delhi: Motilal Banarsidass.

———. 1994. *The Raven Crown: The Origins of Buddhist Monarchy in Bhutan*. London: Serindia Publications.

Blondeau, Anne-Marie. 1971. "Le Lha-'dre Bka'-thang." In *Études tibétaines dédiées à la mémoire de Marcelle Lalou*. Edited by Ariane Macdonald. Paris: Adrien Maisonneuve.

———. 1980. "Analysis of the Biographies of Padmasambhava According to Tibetan Tradition." In *Tibetan Studies in Honour of Hugh Richardson*. Edited by Michael Aris and Aung San Suu Kyi. Warminster: Aris & Phillips.

———, ed. 1998. *Tibetan Mountain Deities, Their Cults and Representations: Papers Presented at a Panel of the Seventh Seminar of the International Association for Tibetan Studies*. Wien: Verlag der Österreichischen Akademie der Wissenschaften.

Bond, George. 1988. "The Arahant: Sainthood in Theravada Buddhism." *Sainthood: Its Manifestation in World Religions*. Edited by Richard Kieckhefer and George Bond. Berkeley: University of California Press.

Buffetrille, Katia and Hildegard Diemberger, eds. 2002. *Territory and Identity in Tibet and the Himalayas*. Leiden: Brill Academic Publishers.

Cabezón, José, ed. 1992. *Buddhism, Sexuality, and Gender*. Albany: State University of New York Press.

———. and Roger Jackson, eds. 1996. *Tibetan Literature: Studies in Genre*. Ithaca, N.Y.: Snow Lion Publications.

Campbell, June. 1996. *Traveller in Space*. New York: George Braziller.

Crossette, Barbara. 1995. *So Close to Heaven: The Vanishing Buddhist Kingdoms of the Himalayas.* New York: Random House.

Dargyay, Eva. 1977. *The Rise of Esoteric Buddhism in Tibet.* Delhi: Motilal Banarsidass.

Diemberger, H. 1997. "Beyul Khenbalung, the Hidden Valley of the Artemisia: On Himalayan Communities and their Sacred Landscape." In *Mandala and Landscape.* Edited by A.W. Macdonald. New Delhi: D.K. Printworld.

Dorje, Gyurme. 1999. *Tibet Handbook.* 2nd ed. Bath, England: Footprint Handbooks.

Dorji, C. T. 1994. *History of Bhutan Based on Buddhism.* Delhi: Prominent Publishers.

————. 1995. *A Political and Religious History of Bhutan.* Delhi: Prominent Publishers.

————. 1997. "Sources of Ancient History of Bhutan." In *The First Colloquium on "Dawn and Early History of Bhutan."* Paro: National Museum of Bhutan.

Douglas, Kenneth, and Gwendolyn Bays, trans. 1978. *The Life and Liberation of Padmasambhava.* 2 vols. Berkeley: Dharma Publishing.

Dowman, Keith, trans. 1973. *The Legend of the Great Stupa. The Life Story of the Lotus Born Guru.* Berkeley: Dharma Publishing.

————. 1984. *Sky Dancer.* London: Routledge and Kegan Paul.

Dudjom Rinpoche, Jikdrel Yeshe Dorje. 1991. *The Nyingma School of Tibetan Buddhism: Its Fundamentals and History.* Trans. Gyurme Dorje and Matthew Kapstein. 2 vols. Boston: Wisdom Publications.

Germano, David. 1998. "Re-membering the Dismembered Body of Tibet." In *Buddhism in Contemporary Tibet: Religious Revival and Cultural Identity.* Edited by Melvyn C. Goldstein and Matthew T. Kapstein. Berkeley: University of California Press.

Gyatso, Janet. 1986. "Signs, Memory and History: A Tantric Buddhist Theory of Scriptural Transmission." *Journal of the International Association of Buddhist Studies* 9 (2): 7–35.

————. 1987. "Down with the Demoness: Reflections on the Feminine Ground in Tibet." *Tibet Journal* 12 (4): 38–53.

————. 1992. "Genre, Authorship, and Transmission in Visionary Buddhism: The Literary Traditions of Thang-stong rGyal-po." In *Tibetan Buddhism: Reason and Revelation.* Edited by Ronald Davidson and Steven Goodman. Albany: State University of New York Press.

————. 1993. "The Logic of Legitimation in the Tibetan Treasure Tradition." *History of Religions* 33 (1): 97–134.

————. 1994. "Guru Chos-dbang's *Gter 'byung chen mo:* An Early Survey of the Treasure Tradition and Its Strategies in Discussing Bon Treasure." In *Tibetan Studies: Proceedings of the Sixth Seminar of the International Association for Tibetan Studies.* Edited by Per Kvaerne. Vol. 1. Oslo: Institute for Comparative Research in Human Culture.

————. 1996. "Drawn from the Tibetan Treasury: The *gTer ma* Literature." In *Tibetan*

Literature: Studies in Genre. Edited by José Cabezón and Roger Jackson. Ithaca, N.Y.: Snow Lion Publications.

————. 1998. *Apparitions of the Self: The Secret Autobiographies of a Tibetan Visionary.* Princeton: Princeton University Press.

————. n.d. "The Relic Text as Prophecy: The Semantic Drift of *Byang-bu* and Its Appropriation in the Treasure Tradition." Unpublished paper.

Harding, Sarah. 2003. *Machik's Complete Explanation: Clarifying the Meaning of Chöd.* Ithaca, N.Y.: Snow Lion Publications.

Hasrat, Bikrama Jit. 1980. *History of Bhutan: Land of the Peaceful Dragon.* Thimphu: Education Department of Bhutan.

Hawley, John, ed. 1987. *Saints and Virtues.* Berkeley: University of California Press.

Horner, I. B. 1930. *Women under Primitive Buddhism: Laywomen and Almswomen.* New York: E. P. Dutton.

Huber, Toni. 1994. "Putting the gnas Back into gnas-skor: Rethinking Tibetan Buddhist Pilgrimage Practice." *Tibet Journal* 19 (2): 23–60.

————, ed. 1999. *Sacred Spaces and Powerful Places in Tibetan Culture.* Dharamsala: Library of Tibetan Works and Archives.

Kapstein, Matthew. 1989. "The Purificatory Gem and Its Cleansing: A Late Tibetan Polemical Discussion of Apocryphal Texts." *History of Religions* 28 (3): 217–44.

————. 2000. *The Tibetan Assimilation of Buddhism: Conversion, Contestation, and Memory.* Oxford: Oxford University Press.

Karmay, Samten. 1996. "The Tibetan Cult of Mountain Deities and Its Political Significance." In *Reflections of the Mountain: Essays on the History and Social Meaning of the Mountain Cult in Tibet and the Himalaya.* Edited by Anne-Marie Blondeau and Ernst Steinkellner. Wien: Verlag der Österreichischen Akademie der Wissenschaften.

————. 2000. "Dorje Lingpa and His Rediscovery of the 'Golden Needle' in Bhutan." *Journal of Bhutan Studies* 2 (2): 1–37.

Kieckhefer, Richard and George Bond, eds. 1988. *Sainthood: Its Manifestation in World Religions.* Berkeley: University of California Press.

Klein, Anne. 1995. *Meeting the Great Bliss Queen.* Boston: Beacon Press.

Kvaerne, Per. 1990. Review of *Hidden Treasures and Secret Lives. Acta Orientalia* 51: 302–6.

Lopez, Donald. 1988. "Sanctification on the Bodhisattva Path." In *Sainthood: Its Manifestation in World Religions.* Edited by Richard Kieckhefer and George Bond. Berkeley: University of California Press.

Mayer, Robert. 1992. Review of *Hidden Treasures and Secret Lives. Religion* 22(2): 187.

————. 1994. "Scriptural Revelation in India and Tibet: Indian Precursors to the gTerma Tradition." In *Tibetan Studies: Proceedings of the Sixth Seminar of the International Association for Tibetan Studies.* Edited by Per Kvaerne. Vol. 2. Oslo: Institute for Comparative Research in Human Culture.

Namgyel, Dorji. 1997. "Monuments of Bhutan." In *The First Colloquium on "Dawn and .Early History of Bhutan."* Paro: National Museum of Bhutan.

Olschak, Blanche. 1979. *Ancient Bhutan: A Study on Early Buddhism in the Himalayas.* Zurich: Swiss Foundation for Alpine Research.

Orofino, G. 1991. "The Tibetan Myth of the Hidden Valley with References to the Visionary Geography of Nepal." *East and West* 41 (1): 239–72.

Padma Tshewang, Khenpo Phuntshok Tashi, Chris Butters, and Sigmund Saetreng. 1995. *The Treasure Revealer of Bhutan: Pemalingpa, the Terma Tradition and Its Critics.* Bibliotheca Himalayica, ser. 3, vol. 8. Kathmandu, Nepal: EMR Publishing House.

Pommaret, Françoise. 1994. "Entrance-Keepers of a Hidden Country: Preliminary Notes on the Monpa of South-Central Bhutan." *Tibet Journal* 19 (3): 46–62.

———. 1996. "On Local and Mountain Deities in Bhutan." In *Reflections of the Mountain: Essays on the History and Social Meaning of the Mountain Cult in Tibet and the Himalaya.* Edited by Anne-Marie Blondeau and Ernst Steinkellner. Wien: Verlag der Österreichischen Akademie der Wissenschaften.

———. 1997. *Bhoutan: Forteresse Bouddhique de l'Himalaya.* Genève: Editions Olizane.

———. 1999. "The Mon-pa Revisited: In Search of Mon." In *Sacred Spaces and Powerful Places in Tibetan Culture.* Edited by Toni Huber. Dharamsala: Library of Tibetan Works and Archives.

———. 2000. "Recent Bhutanese Scholarship in History and Anthropology." *Journal of Bhutan Studies* 2 (2): 139–63.

Ray, Reginald. 1986. "Some Aspects of the Tulku Tradition in Tibet." *Tibet Journal* 11(4): 35-69.

———. 1994. *Buddhist Saints in India: A Study in Buddhist Values and Orientations.* New York: Oxford University Press.

Ramble, Charles. 1995. "Gaining Ground: Representations of Territory in Bon and Tibetan Popular Tradition." *Tibet Journal* 20 (1): 83–124.

Reinhard, J. 1978. "Khembalung: the Hidden Valley." *Kailash* 6 (1): 5–35.

Rinbochay, Khetsun Sangpo. 1982. *Tantric Practice in Nying-ma.* Translated and edited by Jeffrey Hopkins. Ithaca, N.Y.: Snow Lion Publications.

Robinson, James. 1996. "The Lives of Indian Buddhist Saints: Biography, Hagiography and Myth." In *Tibetan Literature: Studies in Genre.* Edited by José Cabezón and Roger Jackson. Ithaca, N.Y.: Snow Lion Publications.

Rose, Leo. 1977. *The Politics of Bhutan.* Ithaca, N.Y.: Cornell University Press.

Samuel, Geoffrey. 1993. *Civilized Shamans: Buddhism in Tibetan Societies.* Washington, D.C.: Smithsonian Institution Press.

Shaw, Miranda. 1994. *Passionate Enlightenment: Women in Tantric Buddhism.* Princeton: Princeton University Press.

Shils, Edward. 1975. *Center and Periphery: Essays in Macrosociology.* Chicago: University of Chicago Press.

Simmer-Brown, Judith. 2001. *Dakini's Warm Breath: The Feminine Principle in Tibetan Buddhism.* Boston: Shambhala.

Singh, Nagendra. 1972. *Bhutan: A Kingdom in the Himalayas.* Delhi: Thomson Press.

Smith, E. Gene. 2001. *Among Tibetan Texts: History and Literature of the Himalayan Plateau.* Edited by Kurtis Schaeffer. Boston: Wisdom Publications.

Tambiah, Stanley. 1984. *The Buddhist Saints of the Forest and the Cult of Amulets.* Cambridge: Cambridge University Press.

———. 1987. "The Buddhist Arahant: Classical Paradigm and Modern Thai Manifestations." In *Saints and Virtues.* Edited by John Hawley. Berkeley: University of California Press.

———. n.d. "The Charisma of Saints and the Cult of Relics, Amulets and Shrines." Unpublished paper.

Thondup, Tulku. 1986. *Hidden Teachings of Tibet: An Explanation of the Terma Tradition of Tibetan Buddhism.* Boston: Wisdom Publications.

———. 1990. "The Terma Tradition of the Nyingmapa School." *Tibet Journal* 15 (4): 149–58.

———. 1996. *Masters of Meditation and Miracles: The Longchen Nyingthig Lineage of Tibetan Buddhism.* Boston: Shambhala.

Thurman, Robert. 1991. Review of *Hidden Treasures and Secret Lives.* *The Journal of Asian Studies* 50(2): 375–77.

Tshewang, Padma. 1995. "The Biography of Pemalingpa." In Padma Tshewang et al. 1995, 23–98.

Tucci, Giuseppe. 1949. *Tibetan Painted Scrolls.* 3 vols. Rome: Libreria dello Stato.

Wangchuk, Karma. 1998. *Buddhism: The Spiritual Lineage of Dzogchen Masters.* Delhi: Anmol Publishing.

Weber, Max. 1978 (1968). *Economy and Society.* 2 vols. Berkeley: University of California Press.

White, David Gordon, ed. 2000. *Tantra in Practice.* Princeton: Princeton University Press.

Wilson, Stephen, ed.. 1983. *Saints and their Cults: Studies in Religious Sociology, Folklore and History.* Cambridge: Cambridge University Press.

Zeppa, Jamie. 1999. *Beyond the Sky and the Earth: A Journey into Bhutan.* New York: Riverhead Books.

TIBETAN AND BHUTANESE SOURCES

Bod rgya tshig mdzod chen mo ("Tibetan-Chinese Dictionary"). 2 volumes. Beijing: Mi rigs dpe skrun khang, 1985.

Dalai Lama V, Ngawang Lozang Gyatso. *Zab pa dang rgya che ba'i dam pa'i chos kyi thob yig gang ga'i rgyun.* 4 volumes. Delhi: Nechung & Lhakhar, 1971.

Dudjom Rinpoche, Jikdrel Yeshe Dorje. *Bdud 'joms 'jigs bral ye shes rdo rje'i gsung 'bum dam chos rin chen nor bu'i bang mdzod.* Kalimpong: Dupjung Lama, 1979.

———. *Pad gling 'khrungs rabs rtogs brjod dad pa'i me tog gi kha skong mos pa'i ze'u 'bru.* In *Pad gling gter chos,* vol. 14: 601–629.

Jamgön Kongtrul Lodrö Thaye. *Gter ston brgya rtsa'i rnam thar.* Tezu, Arunachal Pradesh: Tibetan Nyingmapa Monastery, 1973.

———. *Rin chen gter mdzod chen mo.* Paro: Ngodrup & Sherap Drimay, 1976.

Lama Sang-ngak. *'Brug tu 'od gsal lha'i gdung rabs 'byung tshul brjod pa smyos rabs gsal ba'i me long.* Thimphu: Mani Dorji, 1983.

Longchen Rabjam. *Bum thang lha'i sbas yul gyi bkod pa me tog skyed tshal.* In *Kun mkhyen klong chen pa dri med 'od zer gyi gsung thor bu,* vol. 2. Gangtok: Pema Thinley, 199–?.

Padma Tshewang. *'Brug gi rgyal rabs slop dpon, Padma tshe dbang gi sbyar ba 'Brug gsal ba'i sgron me.* Thimphu: National Library of Bhutan, 1994.

———. *Pad gling lo rgyus drang gtam, Padma tshe dbang gyis brtsams pa.* Thimphu: National Library of Bhutan, 1991.

Peling Sungtrul VIII, Kunzang Tenpai Nyima. *Pad gling 'khrungs rabs kyi rtogs brjod nyung gsal dad pa'i me tog.* In *Pad gling gter chos,* vol. 14: 511–600.

Pema Lingpa, Tertön Gyalpo. *Rig 'dzin padma gling pa yi zab gter chos mdzod rin po che (Pad gling gter chos).* 21 volumes. Thimphu: Kunsang Tobgay, 1975.

———. *Bum thang gter ston padma gling pa'i rnam thar 'od zer kun mdzes nor bu'i phreng ba.* In *Pad gling gter chos,* vol. 14: 3–510.

———. *Bla ma nor bu rgya mtsho.* 2 volumes. Thimphu: Druk Shering Press, 1984.

———. *Rituals for the Propitiation of the Various Deities of the Lama Jewel Ocean.* Paro: Ngodrup and Sherab Demy, 1978.

———. *A Rare Manuscript Collection from Manang.* 7 volumes. Delhi: Ngawang Tobgay, 1977.

Sonam Thinlay Ladhingpa. *Gter ston padma gling pa dang bdud 'dul gling pa'i gsung 'bum gyi dkar chag* (The catalogue of the collected works of Padma Lingpa and Dudul Lingpa). In Catalogue Series 6: Nyingmapa Catalogue Series, volume 2. Gangtok: Sikkim Research Institute of Tibetology, 1996.

Terdak Lingpa. *Zab pa dang rgya che ba'i dam chos kyi gsan yig rin chen 'byung gnas.* New Delhi: Sanje Dorje, 1974.

Printed in the United States
by Baker & Taylor Publisher Services